SOUNDINGS

*Man hath but a shallow sound,
and a short reach, and dealeth
onely by probabilities and
likely-hoods.*

MILES SMITH
BISHOP OF GLOUCESTER
1612–24

SOUNDINGS

Essays Concerning Christian Understanding

EDITED BY

A. R. VIDLER

CAMBRIDGE

AT THE UNIVERSITY PRESS

1962

PUBLISHED BY
THE SYNDICS OF THE CAMBRIDGE UNIVERSITY PRESS

Bentley House, 200 Euston Road, London, N.W. 1
American Branch: 32 East 57th Street, New York 22, N.Y.
West African Office: P.O. Box 33, Ibadan, Nigeria

©

CAMBRIDGE UNIVERSITY PRESS

1962

Printed in Great Britain at the University Press, Cambridge
(Brooke Crutchley, University Printer)

QVAESTIONVM
INTER AMICOS IACTATARVM
HOS QVANTVLICVMQVE SVNT FRVCTVS
IN PIAM MEMORIAM

JOSEPHI SANDERS

COLLOQVIORVM PARTICIPIS
SEMPER ACVTI SEMPER IVCVNDI
COMITIS DESIDERATI COMITES
DEDICAVERVNT

CONTENTS

CONTENTS

INTRODUCTION

THE AUTHORS of this volume of essays cannot persuade themselves that the time is ripe for major works of theological construction or reconstruction. It is a time for ploughing, not reaping; or, to use the metaphor we have chosen for our title, it is a time for making soundings, not charts or maps. If this be so, we do not have to apologize for our inability to do what we hope will be possible in a future generation. We can best serve the cause of truth and of the Church by candidly confessing where our perplexities lie, and not by making claims which, so far as we can see, theologians are not at present in a position to justify.

Volumes of essays by different authors can vary widely in the nature of their origin and in the manner of their composition as well as in the value of their contents. There are those that owe their publication to the initiative of an enterprising editor or publisher who has conceived the idea that it would be profitable to assemble a collection of views on a subject of topical interest. He therefore invites a miscellaneous group of persons, who may be unknown to one another and might not wish to know one another, to produce essays on some aspect of the subject. The contributors do not collaborate, they need never meet, and they may not see any other essay than their own before the whole volume appears in print. The essays will be related in subject-matter, but the essayists themselves do not have to be connected in any other respect.

There is, however, another kind of volume which to the casual reader or browser in a bookshop may look much the same but in fact has a different origin and purpose. In this case, a group of friends or colleagues or associates decides that it wants to produce a concerted work, maybe to serve some cause or to bear some testimony or to promote a shared interest. Either they will have met, perhaps often and at length, to plan and discuss their project, or they will be already known to one another and have adequate reasons for appearing, as it were, on the same platform. Not indeed that the contributors to a volume of this kind need see eye to eye. They may of course have arrived together at a common mind, but on the other hand their kinship may move them to desire that incongruous approaches to, or opinions about, one general subject shall be published within the covers of one book. In other words, they may desire to stir thought rather than to enforce a party line or a rule of orthodoxy.

Anglican theologians appear to have developed a penchant for this kind of enterprise. Quite a long list of such volumes could be made. It will suffice to mention four that acquired some fame: *Essays and Reviews* (1860), *Lux Mundi* (1889), *Foundations* (1912), and *Essays Catholic and Critical* (1926). These volumes were not all prepared in the same way. *Lux Mundi* was the achievement of a group of friends who for many years had been discussing the matters concerning which at length they felt they had a common mind to express. The collaboration behind *Essays and Reviews* was nothing like so close, but the contributors were kindred spirits who wanted to bear a conjoint testimony at a time when they considered that a dangerous theological complacency was prevalent. *Foundations* was the work of a more compact group of young divines at Oxford, who were however less intimately associated with one another than the members of the *Lux Mundi* group. The contributors to *Essays Catholic and Critical* were more heterogeneous, but they were all imbued with an ethos that was signified by the two epithets in the title of their volume.

We do not claim that the present volume is worthy to be placed in that high succession, but it has a similar character. The contributors, or most of them, started meeting regularly several years ago with a view to learning from one another. Only gradually and after much hesitation did we decide to collaborate in producing these essays. Our hesitation arose not only from diffidence, but from doubt whether we ought not to wait until we could be as positive, coherent and constructive as we should naturally like to be. But we came to the conclusion that it is not only obtuseness or incompetence that prevents us from adumbrating a re-interpretation of the Christian faith comparable with that so courageously and confidently essayed by the authors of *Lux Mundi*. We consider our situation to be more analogous to that which prompted the publication of *Essays and Reviews*.

That is to say, we believe that there are very important questions which theologians are now being called upon to face, and which are not yet being faced with the necessary seriousness and determination. We do not profess yet to see our way through them: and we do not want to have to reproach ourselves with looking for a way round them. Our task is to try to see what the questions are that we ought to be facing in the nineteen-sixties. It goes without saying that they are different from what they were in the eighteen-sixties, even if there is an analogy between the two periods. At an early stage in the Roman Catholic modernist movement, Maurice Blondel told Alfred Loisy that his work would surely not be in vain but that it might not be possible to reach a sound judgment about its value till towards the twenty-fifth century![1] We do not wish to evade the assessment of our work by our contemporaries—we shall welcome it; but we believe we are handling questions that are not likely to receive definitive answers for a long time to come.

We share this appraisal of the present state of Christian theology but beyond that, as will be evident, we are not altogether of one mind. Upon some of us one range of questions presses hardest, upon others another range of questions. Some of us are moved to pursue novel investigations, others to re-examine old themes. The subjects handled in the essays have been determined with regard to the special interests of the writers, not by an attempt to cover the whole area of theological inquiry. There are plenty of other subjects

[1] René Marlé, *Au cœur de la crise moderniste* (1960), p. 87.

that might have been included and that another group of essayists might have taken up.

It will appear that, in so far as we point to a way ahead for Christian theology, we do not all point in the same direction. We are all sure that there is a way ahead, else we should not have taken up our pens. We have been less disconcerted by our differences than surprised by our concurrences. We have found that there is exhilaration as well as severe testing and a need for much patience in the conditions in which we are set to do our work.

Metaphors can be treacherous if they are pressed too hard, but we can say in the terms of our title that we are thankful all to be in the same ship; whatever we do not know, we know that the ship is afloat; and the fact that we make these soundings is evidence of our conviction that there is a bottom to the sea. 'O depth of wealth, wisdom, and knowledge in God! How unsearchable his judgements, how untraceable his ways! Who knows the mind of the Lord? Who has been his counsellor? Who has ever made a gift to him, to receive a gift in return? Source, Guide, and Goal of all that is— to him be glory for ever! Amen' (Rom. xi. 33–6, *N.E.B.*).

A. R. V.

SYNOPSIS

The present *malaise* of natural theology. The ambiguities of the attempt to combine philosophical integrity and apologetic utility. Criticisms of natural theology from the standpoints of philosophy and dogmatic theology.

The health of theology and of faith as dependent upon the health of natural theology. Natural theology and the secularized mind.

Traditional models of natural theology—Descartes and scholasticism. The oddity of the received models. The powers and limitations of recent philosophical criticism. The construction of new models and the necessity of experiment and risk. Metaphysics and religion. The inevitability of metaphysics and the implicit irrationalism of anti-metaphysical philosophy and theology.

The mistake of identifying natural theology with particular philosophical forms. The disengagement of natural theology from non-theological thought, feeling, and creative imagination. Theological misunderstanding of this disengagement and the theologian's isolation.

The malnutrition of a natural theology cut off from wider ranges of life and experience. Nourishment to be found in that world, often depicted by artists, which rejects the conventional ways in theology and religion.

BEGINNING ALL OVER AGAIN

IN A VOLUME of untraditional essays, soundings, dealing with theological subjects, there is both logic and propriety in beginning where the traditional theological text-books begin. The subject of this essay is natural theology or, if you prefer, philosophical or metaphysical theology. In the following pages these three terms will be used interchangeably, and readers will remember that natural theology is commonly defined as 'that body of knowledge which may be obtained by human reason alone without the aid of revelation'.[1] Most people who think about these things at all agree that natural theology is in a poor state. Ninian Smart has aptly called it 'the sick man of Europe'.[2] Everyone has his own ideas about the reasons for this *malaise*. Not everyone agrees that it is unfortunate. There are theologians who would be glad to let the sick man die. Natural theology, outside Catholic traditions, has generally been regarded as the poor relation if not the black sheep of the family. Theologians have never been convinced that he had a proper job of work to do. If he did do any work the result usually embarrassed the rest of the family. On the other side, philosophers have seldom been happy to acknowledge the philosophical theologian as one of their family. For some time philosophers have been rather sensitive about family relations and have been very quick to exclude any whose credentials and pedigrees were not flawless. At one time Professor Ayer drew the line so sharply that the family seemed to have almost no members at all.[3]

There has been point in the philosopher's suspicion of philosophical theology. From its beginnings in Christian history it has had its feet in two different camps. On the one hand it has attempted to

---

[1] Cf. *Oxford Dictionary of the Christian Church* (1957), p. 940.
[2] *Prospect for Metaphysics*, ed. I. T. Ramsey (1961), p. 80.
[3] *Language, Truth and Logic*[2] (1946), *passim*.

deal with traditional and fundamental metaphysical questions, the stock-in-trade of everyone who was not ashamed to be known as a metaphysician: the existence of God, evil, free will, immortality, the nature of man, the meaning of history. But it has treated these questions within a special kind of theistic framework which to the independent metaphysician has seemed parochial. Not always, of course. Professor Broad's respect for the work of F. R. Tennant was that of one philosopher for another, despite the theism. On the other hand (the other foot in the other camp) philosophical theology has been engaged in Christian apologetic. It has adjusted its sights to a narrower target, the defence of Christian theism. Assuming the ultimate truth of Christian theism it has worked away at providing metaphysical arguments for the first article of faith, the existence of God. Even today, when natural theology is so widely discounted by theologians, introductory text-books on Christian belief still often begin with something like cosmological or teleological arguments for the existence of God. To the philosopher, this apologetic tendency or interest has seemed incompatible with a claim to philosophical independence. The philosopher's job is to inquire. The philosophical theologian has only pretended to inquire. His conclusions were prescribed from the outset.

There are grounds for these different suspicions voiced by theologians and philosophers. From the standpoint of dogmatic theology, natural theology will always look a dangerous enterprise. Speculative metaphysics has a way of colouring or distorting everything it tries to accommodate within its own systems. Christian theologians can never forget bygone struggles, with gnosticism, platonism, aristotelianism, and idealism. The metaphysician's motive may be of the best. He might say that he is only trying to give rational coherence to certain Christian beliefs which in their raw state lack consistency and philosophical polish. But for the theologian this process of rationalizing and polishing rubs away features of Christian faith which are essential to it and in fact make it what it is, a faith

4

and not a metaphysical construction. Even when the philosophical theologian is himself a Christian believer, he cannot avoid the pitfalls of metaphysical speculation. He may feel that what he does is in the interest of faith, but the terms of his labours commit him to an exaltation of human reason, a usurpation of divine prerogative. His questions are about what is or is not rational in Christian belief, not about what God has chosen to reveal of himself. The most characteristic elements in Christian faith (so the charge would continue) will always resist metaphysical categories. Philosophical theology will always remain a contradiction in terms.

For his part, the philosopher is right to expose that defensive or apologetic aspect of philosophical theology which sets it apart from the independent philosophical investigation. It is somehow a degradation of philosophical intelligence to employ it simply for means of persuasion. Whatever the end, this is more like sophistry than philosophy. When the philosophical theologian does claim an independence or philosophical wholeness for his work, the philosopher has every right to scrutinize that work with the greatest care. If he finds rhetoric masquerading as argument, or argument vitiated by inconsistency, he has a professional duty to point it out.

Any discussion of the purpose or the health of natural theology has to take into account the uneasiness of its relationship with both theology and philosophy. In our own time we cannot expect to find much encouragement for it from either side. The fashionable biblical theology, which never sees need to go beyond the words and concepts of Scripture, has no place for a philosophical examination of fundamental theological concepts, even those peculiar to Christianity. The fashionable analytic philosophy, which sees no need to open Scripture at all, has yet to be convinced that philosophical theology is a logical possibility. In such circumstances it is not surprising that philosophical theology should suffer from poor health. Would it not be simplest to let it die? The mourners would be few, and amongst them even fewer could say exactly who it was

5

whose death they mourned. Yet to accept this situation would, to some of us, be the acceptance of a betrayal and the beginning of the end of faith.

For the sake of bringing the issues into the boldest relief, let us put them as strongly as possible. It could be argued that the attrition and death of natural theology could not but be a prelude to the death of all theology, and even of faith, in so far as faith has any conceptual content and is not simply a matter of feelings and postures. It could further be argued that the health of Christian belief, in any period, can be measured by the health of that natural theology on which it not always visibly depends. (Parallel arguments could be made about the connexion between philosophical theology —or metaphysics—and the whole of philosophy. These, however, are not the immediate concern of this essay.) Lest this sounds the exaggeration of an academic specialist with professional interest in the survival of his subject-matter, we can add a further observation. It would be wildly disproportionate to claim that the rescue of natural theology was in itself the most important task confronting Christianity and the Church in the twentieth century. It would be almost as wild to claim that recent philosophical criticism of traditional arguments in natural theology was in our time the only formidable intellectual challenge to faith.[*] The great problem of the Church (and therefore of its theologians) is to establish or re-establish some kind of vital contact with that enormous majority of human beings for whom Christian faith is not so much unlikely as irrelevant and uninteresting. The greatest intellectual challenge to faith is simply that thoroughly secularized intelligence which is now the rule rather than the exception, whether it expresses itself in science or philosophy or politics or the arts. It is by no means clear that anything like Christian faith in the form we know it will ever again be able to come alive for people of our own time or of such future time as we can imagine. It is just as uncertain that Christian ideas and ways of thought, as we know them, will be able to reengage an intelligence and imagination now so far separated from them. In comparison with these issues, the momentary fate of natural theology is of little concern. If the health of natural theology matters, it matters only because it is bound up with more important things. The burden of this essay is that it is so connected.

The connexion can be brought out only if we look more carefully and then think again about the role which natural theology does or ✶ might play. Our usual conception and our dictionary definitions of natural theology derive from the philosophical practice of the last two or three hundred years. At the beginning of the *Meditations*, Descartes wrote: 'I have always been of opinion that the two questions respecting God and the soul were the chief of those that ought to be determined by help of philosophy rather than theology, for although to us, the faithful, it is sufficient to hold as matters of faith, that the human soul does not perish with the body, and that God exists, it yet assuredly seems impossible ever to persuade infidels of the reality of any religion, or almost even any moral virtue, unless, first of all, those two things be proved to them by natural reason.'[1] The whole problem of natural theology might be written as a gloss on that revealing sentence. There was nothing startling or revolutionary about Descartes' opinion that the existence of God and the immortality of the soul might be proved by natural reason. St Thomas was clear enough about the former even if he found subtleties in the latter. And yet one suspects that in Descartes' formulation there is an important shift of emphasis from scholastic notions of natural theology and natural reason. Not only has the word reason a new set of connotations for Descartes and his age, but the relationship between philosophy and theology is seen in a different focus. We know what the scholastic manuals say about the subordination of philosophy to theology, but in the hands of philosophical and theological genius—a St Thomas—one is impressed more by the unity than the division. There is much grand (and

[1] *A Discourse on Method*, etc., Everyman's Library (1949), p. 65.

7

often empty) talk about the Medieval Synthesis, but that talk, even when exaggerated, points to a reality, an atmosphere and background in which it was possible to think theologically without cutting oneself off from those other ranges of thought and imagination which, in our day, have no contact with theology whatever. Perhaps this is no more than to say that while St Thomas might have understood Descartes' sentence, he would have found it puzzling that a philosopher should write it, or write it in quite that way. Did St Thomas really believe that the existence of God could be proved in the sense that Descartes believed it?

Descartes' sentence, for good or ill, is a typical model for the conventional understanding of natural theology. It could be expanded like this. There is something called natural reason which is native to all men, part of the endowment bequeathed to finite creatures by a benevolent creator. Its powers are limited, or at least in the light of Christian revelation they are called limited. That revelation is the proper subject-matter of theology. It is for the theologian to expound it to the faithful. Despite its limitations natural reason had plenty to keep it occupied. Drawing upon arguments at least as old as Aristotle it could work its way from contemplation of the natural order to certainty about the existence of a creator. The fulfilment of natural reason was metaphysics. This model is exposed to awkward questions. If such items as the existence of God could be more immediately known by revelation, why bother to cultivate natural reason? Or why not somehow make natural reason a limb of revelation, or revelation an end-product of natural reason? Others were to do both of these things, to the astonishment and horror (as we have noticed) of both theologians and philosophers. But Descartes had learned his lessons from the Jesuits well. As between natural reason and revelation, or theology and philosophy, there was a great gulf fixed. Still, he had his own kind of boldness. Even though certainty about God's existence could be gained from revelation and expounded by theology, he

8

perceived that this certainty was of a very special kind. It failed to impress anyone who was not already, by some means or other, a faithful believer. This suggests that there are two ways to knowledge (or kinds of knowledge) of God's existence. For the believer it was given. (Descartes' boldness had its limits. He did not ask, How?) For the unbeliever, it could be gained by rational argument. Of course, rational argument could take the unbeliever only as far as the bare belief that God exists. To learn more he would have to humble himself before revelation. But to do that much, so Descartes and others thought, was in itself a thoroughly worthy achievement.

We are so used to this model that we usually fail to notice its oddity. At one time or other people are inclined to say 'Reason can only take you so far'. Reason is thereby likened to a railway line which takes one to a frontier station. There the line ends. We all have to get off the train. There are people about who tell us what the country is like on the other side of the frontier, and it sounds very unlike what we know on this side. But this is where public conveyance ends. It is not even clear how we can get to the other side. From the railway terminus we cannot see across the frontier. Do we go on foot? Some have tried this and never came back. Others have come back and reported that there was nothing on the other side at all. Still others have come back and made detailed reports. Yet how diverse and contradictory those reports seem. But what is the matter with the railway line? Why not extend it beyond the frontier? If it can take us thus far, why not a mile or so further? How do we know that trains will not run over there, until we have tried?

This analogy must not be pressed too hard, but the kind of questions we might naturally ask about railway lines have their parallel in questions we ought to ask about natural theology and the conventional model which shapes our understanding of it. What the railway-line analogy brings out is that one conventional model will not do at all. If this is in fact what natural theology does it should

9

come as no surprise that both theologians and philosophers would well like to be rid of it. It simply does not work. In their different ways, philosophers and theologians have shown this clearly enough. Philosophers, from at least the time of Hume and Kant, have exposed the weakness of traditional arguments for the existence of God. They have pin-pointed logical inconsistencies, and they have put a question-mark beside the whole process of moving by a chain of causal arguments from the contents of the world (or its bare exist-ence) to something outside the world. Theologians have worried less about logical propriety and have been chiefly dissatisfied with the premises and conclusion of the arguments. They are pessimistic about the powers of natural reason to encompass reality, and they find little or no contact between the God allegedly proved by argument and the God who, they say, can never be known except through that revelation they are charged to expound and safeguard. But as is so often the case, these criticisms from both sides, however telling in detail, have not rid us of the model itself. Our thinking is still confined to the familiar grooves: natural and revealed; reason and faith. It may seem paradoxical, but there would be point in saying that a restoration of natural theology will finally depend upon the abandonment of our present understanding of what it is.

Criticisms of specific features of the traditional model, whether from philosophers or theologians, can help in the work of revision, if only by showing us what natural theology is not. But such criticisms can just as easily mislead, for they may distract us from the main problem, the construction of some new model or models for the whole enterprise. In the last decade or so there has been a good deal of philosophical discussion which illustrates this useful but distracting kind of work. A selection of papers was recently edited by A. G. N. Flew and A. C. MacIntyre.[1] The editors claimed that these essays were new not only because recently written but because they displayed something new in the way of an approach to philo-

[1] *New Essays in Philosophical Theology* (1955).

sophical theology. The novelty was not striking, for on the critical side it consisted in little more than a series of illustrations showing that the empirical grounds for belief in God are not obvious and that traditional ways of speaking about God have serious limitations. Recent philosophical fashions have given this kind of discussion a keener edge than it has had for a long time, but it would be hard to say exactly what was new about it—what, for example, would surprise Hume or Kant. Nevertheless, this kind of work has its own excitements. The philosophical theologian—and I now mean the one who is a Christian believer—finds himself led by it into a succession of discussions about the logic of religious language, as exemplified, say, in such sentences as 'God loves us' or 'God created the world'. He is put through his paces on verification, meaning, and the status of metaphysical thinking. There is no doubt that this kind of discussion can sharpen logical discernment and put one on guard against that inflation of language which so often mars theological discourse. The danger is that one comes to think of philosophical or natural theology as the formulation of a position which one has a duty to defend and justify. In some cases one sees the crudity of philosophical arguments which claim to dissolve but in fact never reach the substance of many theological utterances. It is often as easy to show the crudity as it was to perpetrate it in the first place. No one can say that this work is without value, but so far it has produced very little by way of positive statement or construction. The sceptical philosopher becomes understandably impatient: 'All right, I see what you don't mean, but what *do* you mean?' And here, if only from exhaustion, the discussion is likely to fall back into the old clichés about reason and faith and the railway-line model for natural theology.

How are we to get ourselves out of these well-worn grooves? There is little to comfort the philosophical theologian in the fashions set by his theological colleagues. Too often genuine philosophical difficulties are put on one side. Revelation is more talked about than defined. There is a great deal of talk about biblical categories, as though to claim their existence made it unnecessary to ask whether they were adequate for whatever it is they are supposed to express. The philosophical theologian is condescendingly reminded that Christianity is a matter of history, not of metaphysics, as though this somehow conferred greater dignity and settled questions of truth and falsity. Theologians speak at length about eschatology but find it difficult to say anything at all about the rational grounds for belief in a divine providence of any kind. In this atmosphere of discussion the philosophical theologian wants to press upon his theological colleagues the kind of questions which philosophers press upon him. The result is yet another impasse or breakdown in communication. The dogmatic theologian is confirmed in his suspicion of logic and metaphysics, and his philosophical friend wonders again whether there can be any point in pursuing inquiries which philosophers suspect and theologians prefer to ignore.

In the light of these gloomy reflections, some of the remarks made earlier in this essay may seem strange. It was suggested that the health and vitality of theology and Christian faith depended upon the health of natural theology. It was suggested too that the fate of natural theology in our time was crucial because if it failed to survive we should have to admit the complete triumph of the secularized or post-religious temper over the whole range of human thought and imagination. (By post-religious temper I mean something like this: a state of mind and feeling in which questions about God, the meaning of life, the nature of reality and human destiny no longer engage living attention. Religious questions are no longer treated seriously, whether in belief or unbelief, because they have ceased to be matters of what Tillich calls ultimate concern.) Is it possible to take the fate of natural theology so seriously as this? If it is, what kind of natural theology? How is it done?

At this point and in an essay of this kind it is not possible to do more than suggest a few possible lines for further investigation. The one thing we can be sure of is that answers to the fundamental questions, even presuming we know which questions should be asked, will not come easily or quickly. We shall not be able to recognize the right answers until we know more clearly what we are looking for. That will come only with lengthy trial and error, risk, and intellectual experiment.

First then a few remarks about the underlying assumptions which make the task at least conceivable. Christian theology without metaphysics (that is, for our purposes, natural theology) is an illusion. However much some theologians may wish to avoid the issue by speaking of revelation there comes a point when the question can no longer be evaded: Why believe in God at all? If the only grounds for belief in the Christian revelation are part of that alleged revelation, the theologian has cut himself off from profitable communication with people who wish to think about their beliefs. If there are no grounds for believing that a Christian scheme is preferable to some non-Christian one, the choice between Christianity and some other religion (or none) becomes arbitrary, irrational, even trivial. I take it here that the function of metaphysics is to work at the construction of an ordered and consistent picture of the world. The special task of a Christian metaphysic, natural theology, is to show the grounds for that total picture of the world which we indicate when we speak of the Christian faith. It is a picture of the world in so far as it is articulated in theologies, doctrines, creeds. It is more than a picture in that it commends and inculcates attitudes and feelings which are more than descriptive. Religious practices, prayer, worship, are certainly connected with beliefs about the world, but they engage other ranges of human personality and are not patient of exhaustive metaphysical description. It is one thing to write a love-poem. It is another thing to be in love. (If the analogy is not too far-fetched, it might be said that believers are in love, theologians write love-poems, and metaphysicians—natural theologians—write criticisms of poetry. But of course poets and critics are at least sometimes in love themselves.) Whenever theologians use the word God they are doing metaphysics. The only question is whether they are doing it well or badly.

This leads to a second assumption, broader, but of the same kind. Metaphysical construction, crude or polished, is natural to human beings. The impulse can be explained in any number of ways: at two extremes, theologically or psychologically. It can also manifest itself in any number of forms. Whenever and wherever men reflect seriously upon their own concerns, they find themselves pushing beyond the limits of what is certified as known by those who trade in scientifically or historically verifiable descriptions of human life. This much is commonplace. The far more difficult matter is to say which metaphysical constructions, if any, are worthy of attention or development. We are not agreed upon the criteria. Philosophically, metaphysics is not yet quite in fashion. Philosophers are still largely engaged with the analysis of the tools of their own trade. Few theologians indulge in metaphysical exercises. The present pre-occupations of philosophers and of theologians may have their intrinsic importance, but they do nothing to fortify men's minds against all the shallow metaphysical speculations which multiply and spread in the absence of serious criticism or attention. In this regard the anti-metaphysical temper of much recent philosophy has played into the hands of irrationalism. If Professor Ayer was right to hold that all metaphysical utterances are meaningless (according to the strictures of the Verification Principle)[1] then academic philosophy is obliged to abandon men to the crudest imaginings. It leaves nothing to choose, rationally, between Rosenberg and Bonhoeffer, Buchman and Barth, Mosley and Niebuhr. The theologians have an equal responsibility. If natural theology is out of court and there is no appeal to metaphysical reasoning, what rational basis can there be for opposing, say, the most illiterate varieties of fundamentalism? There is something ironic in the pronouncements of many biblical

[1] *Language, Truth and Logic*[2] (1946).

14

theologians on fundamentalism and other religious authoritarianisms. By enclosing themselves within the circle of revelation (which rational argument cannot reach) they invite all those terrors which they, of all men, have most reason to fear. In abandoning natural theology they have lost the only weapon which could ward off their adversaries. Once again, the question is not whether men can or will do metaphysics but only whether they will do it well or badly.

None the less, neither the scepticism of the philosopher nor the dogmatism of the theologian is likely to stifle the metaphysical impulse. But is it any longer possible that this impulse should be directed in the channels of natural theology and Christianity? How does it happen that the impulse takes one direction rather than another? That second question might be answered on the basis of extensive historical investigation. It also invites us to consider again what we understand by natural theology. It is an example, certainly, of constructive metaphysics, but a metaphysics already predisposed towards theism. How does this happen?

One of the faults of the received picture of natural theology is that it describes so poorly the processes of mind and imagination which contribute to metaphysical construction. It may be that for the scholastics certain logical operations were the most powerful instruments available to men in their search for metaphysical order. Arguments for the existence of God began with premises universally accepted. For the most part, a St Thomas could count upon a universality of response to his procedures. More than this, there was an atmosphere of excitement about the use of these logical tools, comparable perhaps to the excitement a generation ago over the logical discoveries of Russell and Whitehead. There was genuine engagement between the theological and philosophical imagination. The mistake came later when it was assumed that natural theology was tied to certain forms of logical argument. It was a mistake because it confused a particular mode of natural theology with the enterprise itself. Is there now any reason why natural theology should be identified with the Five Ways of St Thomas? (Any more reason, for instance, than for its identification with the neoplatonic gnosticism of Clement and Origen?) The identification may have seemed plausible to the rationalistic philosophers of the seventeenth century (Descartes, again) because with the emergence of natural sciences, the importance of proofs, of mathematically demonstrable conclusions, became a major preoccupation of thinking men. Metaphysical thinking, including natural theology, had to be a matter of logical arguments leading to indisputable results. If one could have final proofs in mathematics and mathematical physics, then one must also have proofs in metaphysics and natural theology. Otherwise these would seem less securely grounded in reason. Natural theology might then become disengaged from those activities of mind and imagination which were refashioning human sensibility.

The irony is that disengagement came because of the effort to maintain intellectual respectability. For a Descartes it was possible to do both physics and metaphysics as though one method, one mode of reasoning, were fully appropriate to both. Any plausibility this programme may have had was finally shattered by Kant. In our own time the analytical philosophers, the logical empiricists, have further underlined Kant's critical work. Whatever metaphysics may be, it is not a kind of super-science, using the mathematical tools of natural science and in some mysterious way reaching conclusions about the world which scientific inquiry can never reach. Yet this idea manages to survive. Professor Alan Richardson has spoken confidently of theology (not just natural theology) as a science, and has maintained that the only real difference between theology and physics is that they study different objects and make use of different categories.[1] (It is not so often noticed that on these criteria astrology could be called a science.) The errors of Descartes, understandable enough in the seventeenth century, are thus perpetuated; but in our time they are without excuse. They only serve to confirm the wide-

[1] *Christian Apologetics* (1947), p. 50 *et passim*.

spread conviction that metaphysics and theology no longer have any job at all. The surest way to kill natural theology is to cling to the idea that its job is as straightforward as Descartes thought it was.

The history of metaphysics and natural theology since the seventeenth century is of course a far more complicated story than these remarks suggest. It was not only the desire for respectability which petrified natural theology as a series of exercises in causal argument. But however that history be told, we can be in no doubt that what we have to face today is a divorce of natural theology from the mind and imagination of the most sensitive segment of our society. The disengagement of theology from imagination is all but complete. To point out that disengagement is the whole theme of this essay. When we consider the future or the very possibility of natural theology, we are on the threshold of the most serious problem which Christian faith faces in our time: the existence of a secularized (or post-religious) imagination for which natural or metaphysical theology is no longer alive. Theologians and ecclesiastics who realize the problem at all have a way of stating it which obscures half of its significance. They speak as though the loss were wholly on the side of the secular world and mind. They talk about the debility of much modern philosophy, the poverty of modern art and literature. They attribute these things to the fact that the modern mind is cut off from its roots in religion and faith. There is point in these observations. (They are made most forcibly by many modern thinkers and artists who remain sceptical about the relevance of theology, as they understand it, to their predicament.) What the apologists and theologians less often notice is the debility and poverty of our modern theology, which results from its disengagement from the deepest sources of intellectual and artistic creativity. The loss is sustained on both sides. On the side of theology we see it less clearly. Our conception of natural theology, tied to obsolete models, allows us to forget that the inspiration for natural theology must reach men at the deepest levels of thought and imagination. The dilemma is this:

It is now weakened by malnutrition. For decades, if not generations, Christian faith has lived in a state of imaginative impoverishment. How should it not? The Church has lived in almost total isolation from the arts. Academic theology has lived on its own fat. The supply of fat is running out. There is, of course, an escape. The theologian can turn himself entirely into an historian or bibliographer or textual critic. That way lies a kind of security. What lies in the other way is not at all certain or secure. It will take decades or generations before we know whether natural theology still has enough life in it to seek new kinds of nourishment. Manna lay thick on the ground, but the Israelites were very dubious about it. To try new food always means taking a chance. Some of those who try it may be poisoned. That is the risk. Natural theology can no longer survive on the food of its fathers; the supply is exhausted. It has several choices; no one quite knows the nutritional or toxic properties of any of them. There is only one way to find out.

In the end, any plea for the restoration of natural theology must be an appeal to boldness. We shall have to contemplate and absorb the disturbing visions of human nature which find expression in serious modern literature. We shall have to come to terms with a world in which old patterns of morality no longer direct or inspire because they no longer have life. We shall have to admit that we have no ready answers to the questions people ask because for so long we have insulated ourselves against their questions. Christian faith has been an ark of retreat. We could shut ourselves inside it when the pressure upon our lives and imagination seemed to lead to nameless perils. We have relied upon the several establishments, religious, political, and moral, to protect us from the barbarians. Our first lesson will be to learn that our greatest ally is not the dying establishments but the hungry and destitute world which is still alive enough to feel its own hunger. The starting-point for natural theology is not argument but sharpened awareness. For the moment it is better for us that the arguments have fallen to pieces.

2

THE UNEASY TRUCE BETWEEN SCIENCE AND THEOLOGY

BY

J. S. HABGOOD

SYNOPSIS

I. The prevailing complacency about the relation between science and theology.

(*a*) Some causes:
    1. The complexity of the notion of 'fact'.
    2. The desire by both sides to stress their independence.

(*b*) Some dangers for theology in the present situation:
    1. Breakdown in communication.
    2. The unconscious psychological impact of science.

(*c*) The value of works of synthesis.

II. An attempt to be constructive.

(*a*) Some dangers for science in the present situation:
    1. Loss of concern for truth.
    2. Preoccupation with mathematico-physical types of explanation.

(*b*) Illustration of the many-levelled structure of science from:
    1. Biology.
    2. Sociology.

(*c*) Conclusion. The relation between science and theology is more complex than is often recognized.

THE UNEASY TRUCE BETWEEN
SCIENCE AND THEOLOGY

I

AMONG THE MANY fronts on which theology has been attacked or questioned there now seems to be at least one on which a truce has been declared. Almost every book on the relation between science and theology bears witness to it.[1] There are many who assure us that there are now no grounds for conflict between the two disciplines, and that they should never have been fighting in the first place. Among Christian writers it is rare to find any who seem to be aware that all is not well.[2] The terms of the truce are variously described. Science is concerned with empirical truth, theology with symbolic truth.[3] Science deals with the objective world, theology with the existential world.[4] Science tells us about efficient causes, theology about final causes.[5] Science is a matter of preliminary concern, theology of ultimate concern.[6] These distinctions are designed, laudably enough, to ensure that the mistaken claims of the past are never repeated. Whereas the advances of science were once thought to raise difficulties for theology, the impression is now given that these difficulties were illusory and that theology would be compatible with virtually any scientific discovery. On the factual level this may possibly be true. The thesis of this essay is that on the psychological level it is certainly not true; and this may be the reason why the innumerable books on the subject have, on the whole, so little impact.

[1] E.g. C. A. Coulson, *Science and Christian Belief* (1954).

[2] David Lack's *Evolutionary Theory and Christian Belief* (1957), and the various writings of John Wren-Lewis, are notable exceptions.

[3] T. R. Miles, *Religion and the Scientific Outlook* (1959).

[4] Karl Heim, *Christian Faith and Natural Science* (1953).

[5] E. L. Mascall, *Christian Theology and Natural Science* (1956).

[6] Paul Tillich, *passim*. I am much more sympathetic towards this distinction than towards the others. But so far as I am aware Tillich nowhere looks at science long enough to make his remarks about it really acceptable to scientists.

First let us consider the factual level. The truce has been made possible by a softening of the scientific world view and a reduction in the factual claims made by theology. Science claims to reign exclusively in the realm of facts, but scientists have not always been aware of what a complex notion a 'fact' is. There is a primary scientific use of the word, namely, what a scientist can observe directly; but whereas there have been times when theoretical concepts like 'atoms' and 'electrons' were regarded as having much the same objectivity and concreteness as these primary facts of experience, now such an assumption seems intolerably naïve. We see that it is impossible to give a straight answer to the question, 'Do atoms and electrons really exist?' Indeed this is the kind of question which most working physicists have learnt to ignore as being of no particular scientific interest. It is sufficient to say that as theoretical concepts they are useful, and to refuse to probe any further. To introduce the notion of 'facts' or 'reality' plunges one into a philosophical discussion of the kind which scientists, *qua* scientists, are generally most anxious to avoid. The result is that while on the practical experimental level science is as firmly entrenched as ever, on the philosophical level final statements about the nature of reality are rarely made; and this gives theologians their chance. A typical example of the changed situation is the claim that modern physics cannot support an old-style determinism.[1] The point to note about this is that it is not a positive philosophical assertion about whether determinism is true or not; it is a refusal to give an answer to what is not a scientific question, but which in the past has been treated as if it was. This is what I mean by a softening of the scientific world view.

The role of factual assertions in theology has been changing too in an equally complex way. On the one hand it is clear that theology ought never to be a competitor with science in the empirical realm. Theological systems are not alternative cosmological hypotheses set

[1] Mascall, *op. cit.* p. 190.

up in opposition to scientific cosmology. The proper way, for example, to find out about the early history of the universe is by the study of astronomy and not by theological speculation. A great deal of unnecessary confusion has been caused by the different senses in which the words 'origin' and 'creation' can be used by both scientists and theologians. So much would be generally agreed; and it is the recognition of this by both sides that has made a great deal of the *rapprochement* possible. But on the other hand where the theologian should draw the line and say, 'Here I must make factual claims', is not clear at all. Some factual claims, at least, must be made about the life of Jesus; but these need not disturb this particular truce too badly because, unfortunately or otherwise, historical facts, especially those in the remote past, are relatively immune to experimental investigation.

However, there remains an awkward set of borderline cases in which it still seems as if theology is making pseudo-scientific statements about what actually goes on in the world. The answer to the question, 'What does intercessory prayer do?' is almost always of this kind, though generally couched in language which aims to put it beyond the reach of science. Thus Farmer summarizes a long argument on the subject by writing: 'God so uses his all-inclusive *rapport* with the ultimate entities which constitute the inner, creative, present reality of the natural order, that their various routine activities are not overridden, but used by redirecting them in relation to one another.'[1] An unsympathetic scientist might ask, 'What is the scientific status of a remark like that?' This is not the place to discuss the problem further, though it is worth noting that it arises whenever theologians use language about 'the acts of God'. The reason for mentioning it now is simply to illustrate the nature of the truce between science and theology, and to recall that there are points of strain.

Nevertheless, despite the strain, there are strong forces working

[1] *The World and God* (1935), p. 178.

to keep the truce in being. Theologians want to find a position which is secure against any possible advances in scientific knowledge. This can be done by accepting science as the final arbiter in the realm of facts, and by removing theology as far as possible from dependence on such facts. Likewise scientists, if they care about theology at all, are generally anxious to keep it quite separate from science, because as soon as theological notions are introduced into science, research comes to a full stop. Some sort of language about purpose and design, for example, is indispensable to biology; but every biologist knows that if he uses these words too loosely, and especially if he tries to read theological implications into them, then he will soon stop asking the sort of question which produces scientific results. It is no accident, therefore, that the tendency nowadays is to emphasize the complete distinctness of science and theology. We are going through a necessary phase of sterilization in which, it is to be hoped, the old causes of confusion will be destroyed. Yet we cannot be content to remain in this phase; it is dangerous in two obvious senses for theology; and, as I hope to show later, in a less obvious sense for science.

The first obvious danger is of a breakdown in communication. This is already happening, and it is common knowledge how difficult it is for scientists and theologians to talk to one another with mutual understanding. In part this difficulty is just a symptom of the general fragmentation of knowledge; but whereas within science such fragmentation can be recognized for what it is, and can be deliberately countered because scientists know that they belong to the same community of thought, the separation between science and theology goes much deeper. It is not between different kinds of specialization, but between different kinds of world. The metaphysical difficulties confronting theologians reveal the breakdown at a different level, and in this connexion it is worth recalling that linguistic analysis is in some sense the heir of science. Problems about the meaning of theological terms arise not only for professional philosophers whose job it is to be puzzled about what seems perfectly clear to everyone else. They are met also among those who have grown up in a scientific culture; and it is this whole new culture, with its own criteria of what is meaningful, which Christians may find themselves more and more incapable of addressing.

The second danger lies in the psychological impact of science. We cannot confine our discussion of the relation between science and theology to the factual level, because science affects the way we feel about the world just as much as it affects the way we think about it. No logical distinctions can suffice to keep the peace as long as there is this psychological overlap. What seems on the surface to be a workable truce may be slowly undermined until the whole structure collapses because theology, while remaining logically unassailable, has ceased to matter.[1] Even if theology adopts an extreme position, makes no factual claims whatever and concerns itself solely with the evocation of certain feelings and attitudes, it cannot escape the influence of science in the shrunken territories left to it. It may be the neglect of this factor which makes so much that is said about science and theology seem so irrelevant. Thus a man who has been trained in science, whose mind has first been awakened by a vision of the grandeur and beauty of classical physics, which he then saw as the perfect archetype of all explanation; who subsequently learnt the power of higher mathematics as an explanatory tool; who knows something of the history of science and has seen how mystery after mystery has been dissolved; who through all his training has been conditioned to think of metaphysics as empty speculation unconcerned with experimental evidence; such a man is not likely to be impressed by philosophical arguments about the limitations of science. Nor will he feel the need of a different and unrelated set of symbols to give his world a sense of significance. As far as he cares to pursue the quest, science seems to give him the emotional

---

[1] Compare the remark quoted in George Macleod's *Only One Way Left* (1957): 'You have proved your case up to the hilt, and it doesn't mean a thing' (p. 42).

satisfaction which he needs.[1] And what is true in an extreme case, is true to a lesser degree for those who have grown up in a scientific culture without themselves being scientists. The solidity and success of science cannot be ignored. It is one of the great powers in the modern world. It has built up a stable and, for the most part, universally accepted body of knowledge by its slow, cautious, piece-meal approach to practical problems which can actually be solved. No matter how much it may be agreed in theory that other types of approach to reality are legitimate or even necessary, emotionally those who have grown up in a scientific culture tend to find themselves unmoved. At best theology seems to be a private affair. There may be some place for personal mysticism, but theological dogma-tism has had its day. Theology's claim to say significant things about the world seems unable to bear comparison with that of science. And the theologian's protest that it should never be asked to bear comparison because it is trying to do a different kind of thing, is largely unheard, or is accepted merely as evidence of the subjective, and hence private, character of religion.

A further reason for the emotional rejection of theology, in ad-dition to the impressiveness of scientific achievements, may be the doubts in the minds of many about the wideness of theological vision. If one of the functions of theology is to help us to break through our usual man-centred finite circles of thought to an en-counter with God, then the symbols which help us to do this must be at least as evocative as those thrown up by science. In an age when the perspectives of space and time have been bewilderingly enlarged, when man has been shown new depths in himself by psychology, and has radically revised his estimate of his place in nature by seeing himself in his evolutionary context, there is a danger of ordinary religious symbolism appearing trivial. This feel-ing is constantly being expressed in such questions as, 'How can we

[1] See the section on the religion of scientists in G. W. Allport, *The Individual and his Religion* (1960 ed.), pp. 110-17.

believe in a God who really cares about man now that we are beginning to discover the vastness of the universe?' or, 'How can we
make unique claims for the tiny fragment of time called human
history?'. Logically the difficulties behind such questions are not too
formidable, and they are constantly being tackled by religious
apologists; but emotionally many people continue to be worried.
Perhaps one of the reasons for the attention given to Teilhard de
Chardin is that in his presentation of man's place and significance
in evolution[1] he provided a new set of symbols, claiming to have
their origin in science, yet able to convey a sense of the wholeness
and purposiveness and religiousness of the world in a way which is
the very opposite of trivial. As a purely scientific work his book has
already run into criticism. In a slashing review in *Mind*,[2] Medawar
has dismissed it as bogus and unintelligible. It is perhaps note-
worthy, however, that a large part of the attack is devoted to Teilhard
de Chardin's style and what Medawar calls his wilful misuse of
scientific terms. Undoubtedly the book needs a great deal of clean-
ing up. But when the obvious criticisms have been made, there
remains a difference of temper and aim between the two men which
shows itself in the complete lack of sympathy of the one for the
other. Teilhard de Chardin was using words in a deliberately
evocative way; as many critics have said, he was writing science in
a consciously poetic style. His motive was that he conceived himself
as engaged in a great work of synthesis; he believed he had seen
something of the wholeness of the creative process, and he wanted
to convey this vision. To do so he had to devise a new language, in
common with most other metaphysicians. His language can be
criticized as vague, imprecise and concealing a large element of
evaluation; but at least it is a corrective to that other style of
scientific writing which, though precise, well-defined, and the proper
medium for all ordinary scientific discourse, equally conceals an

---

[1] *The Phenomenon of Man* (1959). A best-seller in both France and Great Britain.
[2] January 1961, pp. 99–106.

element of evaluation. Phrases like 'random mutation' and 'chance variation', when used outside their strict genetical context, are not evaluatively neutral; and if it is claimed that they should never be used outside their strict context, this is tantamount to denying science any part in determining how we are to feel about the world as a whole.

Be that as it may, the fact remains that people are influenced in their value judgments one way or another by the discoveries of science, and it seems reasonable to account for the popularity of *The Phenomenon of Man* in terms of the liberation of the imagination it was able to effect. After reading it people could feel, even if they did not understand, a new significance in the whole evolutionary process. As a work of metaphysical construction the book will probably be of only passing interest. But at least it encourages us to think that there is still some point in trying to construct large-scale syntheses, even though these can never be regarded as 'definitive maps of reality' in the way the old metaphysical systems were thought to be. Perhaps Waismann's words about metaphysicians in general can be applied to Teilhard de Chardin. 'Metaphysicians, like artists, are the antennae of their time; they have a flair for feeling which way the spirit is moving.'[1] As long as there are those[2] who are prepared to risk such works of synthesis, basing them on the scientific knowledge of their time, science and theology will not simply exist in separate compartments, and some of the dangers inherent in the present uneasy truce may be avoided.

II

In the second half of this essay, therefore, we must try to sketch the outlines of a more positive relationship between the two, showing why the attempt is important for science as well as for theology.

The danger for science in ignoring theology is that it may forget

---

[1] *Contemporary British Philosophy*, 3rd series (1956), ed. H. D. Lewis, p. 489.

[2] Like M. Polanyi, *Personal Knowledge* (1958). A far more important book than *The Phenomenon of Man*.

that its ultimate concern is the question of truth. Theologians, unless they lose their nerve, go on posing this question in spite of all its difficulty. They insist that we must go on fumbling about with such concepts as 'ultimate reality' or 'final truth', and that the question, 'What is true?' cannot be whittled down to 'What is useful?' or 'What works?'. In an age which dislikes metaphysics it may be that the theologian can do no more than insist that the question be heard. But even the mere repetition of the question is important and constitutes a reminder which science needs. Apologists for science often claim that the one sufficient criterion of a good hypothesis is its ability to make successful predictions. But this is not so. In the last resort it is only strictly true of technology. The criterion of a good technological achievement is that the thing works, and this is a perfectly adequate criterion so long as the attainment of a particular practical end is all that is required. Engineers are constantly making use of rules of thumb without referring back to, and sometimes without even understanding, fundamental theory. There is a sense, however, in which those engaged in so-called pure science have always been more interested in theories than in results. They have seen the aim of science as not simply to increase man's control over his environment, but to make that environment intelligible; and to this end other criteria than practical success are employed, even though their use may be unrecognized. Thus there is a growing awareness among scientists of the role of aesthetic appreciation in deciding between hypotheses.[1] There is a famous illustration of this in the early history of chemistry.[2] Prout asserted for basically aesthetic (and perhaps also theological) reasons that the atomic weights of the elements were whole numbers, and he stuck to this belief in spite of conflicting experimental evidence. His theory was eventually rejected, and was only vindicated years later in a far

[1] E.g. Sir Cyril Hinshelwood's Presidential Address to the Royal Society, November 1959.
[2] The story is well told in R. E. D. Clark's *Christian Belief and Science* (1960), pp. 101 ff.

more subtle way than he could have anticipated. Prout's willingness to give weight to the elegance of his hypothesis, and our own feeling of satisfaction that he was at least partly right after all, are ways of expressing the belief that scientists are doing more than learn successful techniques of manipulation. Somehow they expect their theories to make aesthetic sense and to conform to an intelligible pattern because, despite the lack of support from some philosophers of science, one of the driving forces behind scientific research has been the assumption that science discloses the nature of reality. In the end this kind of concern finds its most complete expression in asking those ultimate questions which are the business of theology. This is not to say that the results of science in any way depend on theology. It is simply to point out that where no religious concern is felt, in the long run pure science will be one of the losers. Science regarded as a quest for power ultimately stops asking fundamental scientific questions; it becomes technology. Conversely, science regarded as a quest for truth cannot ultimately ignore the values which support it or the metaphysical problems which open up in front of it.

There are indications that some scientists are already becoming alive to this situation. Efforts are being made to humanize science, to destroy the popular image of the scientist as an infallible, inhuman calculating machine obtaining his results by the simple application of certain rules of procedure. Stress is laid on the practice of science as an art, on the fact that the process of scientific discovery is not essentially different from that of any other discovery; the actual leap of the mind which suddenly enables the facts to be seen in a new perspective is a highly personal affair and not by any means automatic. Science should involve many levels of the personality. Men do not become scientists by learning a few techniques; they have to be initiated into a whole culture. The growing emphasis on the educational value of science witnesses implicitly to the same belief.[1]

[1] E.g. H. P. Ramage, *School Biology as an Educational Model* in *Models and Analogues in Biology* (1960).

To become a scientist should entail a training in values as comprehensive as that gained by studying the humanities. A scientific training may or may not fulfil this ideal at the moment; but the belief that it could do so presupposes that science ultimately leads to the great questions about existence.

If it is correct to think of science in this way, as a quest for truth and as involving many levels of the personality, values and all, then we have already made some progress in trying to establish a positive relationship with theology. But before we can go any further there is an enormous obstacle to be removed, namely the psychological hold of mathematical ideals of scientific explanation; it is these ideals which, rightly or wrongly, give the impression that science is preoccupied with reduced descriptions of nature, and is thus in some sense anti-religious. In popular language, 'science shows us that life is nothing but a complex physico-chemical process; the brain is nothing but a very elaborate computer...' and so on. Wherever the words 'nothing but' appear, there we have a reduced description. But note that my concern in this essay is with the psychological effects of this kind of talk; I do not wish to deny the value of reduced descriptions or the importance of the mathematical ideal.

There are good reasons why theoretical physics should enjoy a privileged place within science. To lay bare the mathematical structure of a phenomenon is to have achieved some kind of finality; it is to have reached the point beyond which one cannot go on asking meaningful scientific questions. Within such a structure the answer to the question 'Why?' about any particular part of it, is simply to demonstrate the correct mathematical interrelationships. The ideal of a strictly objective, accurate and logically transparent explanation is thereby fulfilled. For this reason, when the various branches of science are arranged in a hierarchy, it is natural for theoretical physics to take its place at the top, and for physics and chemistry to be regarded as fundamental in a way that, say, biology is not.

Indeed in some school curricula 'Science' means physics and chemistry, whereas biology is relegated to the position of an inferior subject suitable only for study by girls. Scientists themselves sometimes argue about whether particular subjects deserve the name 'science'. Thus within psychology there is a school of thought represented by Eysenck[1] which would dismiss, as completely unscientific, the whole theoretical basis of psychotherapy because it does not make use of experiments yielding mathematical results. It seems that a distinction is being made here between 'real science' which makes use of mathematics and 'pseudo-science' which does not. This, in turn, can be taken as an illustration of the way in which the hierarchy of sciences can be subtly transformed into a hierarchy of approximations to truth. An analysis of the logical relationships between the various sciences may be held to exhibit the fundamental role of physics and mathematics. What is not so clear, however, is whether their logical importance within the scientific hierarchy necessarily carries with it a corresponding importance in the quest for truth. Talk about 'real science' and 'pseudo-science' assumes that it does. Real, that is, logically fundamental, science somehow gets one nearer to certainty and hence to 'reality'; the world of physics is somehow more 'real' than the world of biology or psychology. It is the train of associations following from such ideas as these which needs to be broken, and which has been referred to above as 'the psychological hold of mathematical ideals'.

To loosen this hold we need to look again at the notion of a hierarchy of sciences, this time asking questions, not about its internal logic (if there is one), but about its relationship to facts in the basic scientific sense of that word. At once the hierarchy assumes a different shape. The most intimately known facts, the ordinary basic data of experience, are furthest removed from the highly abstract laws of physics. This is obvious enough, though it is worth recalling it, especially as a reminder of how small is the

[1] *The Uses and Abuses of Psychology* (1956).

34

number of actual situations to which the fundamental laws of physics can be strictly applied. The uncertainties of science often derive, not from inaccuracies in the laws, but from doubts about their closeness of fit to actual as opposed to ideal situations. As Heisenberg has put it: 'When we represent a group of connections by a closed and coherent set of concepts, axioms, definitions and laws which in turn is represented by a mathematical scheme we have in fact isolated and idealized this group of connections with the purpose of clarification. But even if complete clarity has been achieved in this way, it is not known how accurately the set of concepts describes reality.'[1] What is true of physics, already dealing with fairly abstract phenomena, is even more true of other subjects. In fact with increasing attention to actual experience in all its complexity we note how mathematical language must more and more give way to personal language.

Biology is an interesting borderline case. We can explore the borderline by trying to find the distinctive characteristics which make biology a separate branch of science, and which determine its place in the hierarchy. Following Braithwaite[2] we might attempt a definition in terms of the plasticity of response of a biological system, its ability to pursue a certain goal in a variety of different ways. But supposing this were agreed, we should then have to face the question whether or not such a definition should be framed so as to exclude the more versatile types of calculating machine, which can demonstrate a similar plasticity. Some biologists would want to stress the resemblance, but most people feel that too comprehensive a definition would betray something vital. It would fail to reflect the peculiar status given to what we call 'life' by the fact that we ourselves are alive. An element of evaluation enters in when we call something 'living', and this element is even more pronounced when we use the word 'human'. To call a machine 'human' would be to

---

[1] *Physics and Philosophy* (1959), p. 96.
[2] *Scientific Explanation* (1953), p. 329.

3-2

admit that it not only behaved like a human being, but was also in some obscure sense 'one of us'.[1] In the same way, to call something alive is to admit a sense of kinship with it,[2] despite the fact that with some creatures we are happy to add that the kinship is pretty remote. This sense of kinship expresses itself scientifically in the use of teleological descriptions which would be ridiculous and unhelpful if applied to non-living things. Biologists freely use words like 'adaptation', 'regulation', 'coordination', which in the first instance derive their meaning from our own experience as personal beings. To escape from the apparent subjectivity implied in this, the words can be given a secondary meaning derived from the behaviour of machines, and capable of precise mathematical formulation.[3] But the escape is only apparent, because although the physical characteristics of a machine may be completely specified and although it may demonstrate adaptive behaviour (as in a rocket homing on a moving target), all the time our physical description of it surreptitiously includes our personal experience of purposive action and of our intentions in constructing machines.[4]

One way or another, to some extent we read our own experiences into the behaviour of animals, and this is a part of what we mean by understanding them. Sometimes the language of personal experience is essential; at other times it is a barrier to scientific progress. It might be possible, therefore, to construct a hierarchy within biology itself in which could be expressed the different degrees of usefulness of such concepts. Thus biochemistry is perfectly content with ordinary chemical concepts; the study of the circulation makes use of the ordinary principles of hydraulics; the central nervous system can be studied in terms of communication theory; but without intolerable artificiality it would be impossible to describe the behaviour of an animal as a whole without using words like 'aim',

[1] R. Abelson in *Dimensions of Mind* (1960), ed. S. Hook, p. 268.
[2] C. F. von Weizsäcker, *The World View of Physics* (1952), p. 24.
[3] G. Sommerhoff, *Analytical Biology* (1950), pp. 68 and 144.
[4] Polanyi, *op. cit.* pp. 369 ff.

'purpose', 'intention', etc., derived from our experience as personal beings. If this is thought to be intruding a mystical or subjective element into biology, and even if the extreme definition of biology is accepted which allows no theoretical distinction between living things and calculating machines, it is still not practicable to dispense with this kind of language. As has been said already, it is not even practicable to describe a machine without talking about its purpose or the operational principles underlying its structure. These are not extra factors added to the physico-chemical components of the machine. They are our way of understanding it as a machine rather than as a collection of parts. Simply to have a physico-chemical description would not be to understand it at all. And what is true of simple machines is even more true of animals, whether we like to call them complex machines or not.

Incidentally, we must not be misled by the word 'complex' into thinking that it can bridge every gulf. It is simply not good enough to say, as many do,[1] that the main difference between biology and physics lies in the incredible complexity of the former. Different *types* of explanation are involved in the two, not least because biology is always concerned with individual organisms, with structures and patterns, in a way that physics is not.[2] There is a hierarchy of explanation within biology, and whatever may be the logical relationship between its various levels, the whole hierarchy is necessary for what we call 'full understanding'. The fear, mentioned earlier, that overmuch use of teleological language in biology puts a stop to research, can now be seen in its proper perspective. The notion of a hierarchy should ensure that questions answered on one level do not beg questions on a different level. It should at the same time make plain the inadequacy of explanations confined to the fundamental mathematical level.

---

[1] Niels Bohr, in *Models and Analogues in Biology*, p. 5.
[2] M. Grene, 'The Logic of Biology', in *The Logic of Personal Knowledge* (1961), pp. 194 ff.

The point can be made even more clearly by a reference to sociology. There are those who would claim that there is no fundamental difference between natural and social science, and that the one is ultimately reducible to the other. It is asserted, as in the case of biology, that the distinguishing characteristic of social science is the complexity of its subject-matter. But as Peter Winch[1] has argued, this is to misunderstand what a society is and to ignore the importance of 'concepts' in the making of its life. Social science presupposes an understanding of human activities according to their own rules, because only in the light of these rules are they intelligible; and knowledge of the rules is impossible without some degree of participation in the society to which they belong. A purely external description of social groupings and observable behaviour would have very little point without some understanding of what the behaviour signified. Thus social science must have its own criteria of intelligibility, and these almost certainly will not be reducible to those of physics and chemistry. It makes its claim to be a science, not because it can demonstrate its continuity with the physical sciences, not even because it satisfies the oft quoted and very misleading definition 'science is measurement', but because of the methods it employs. Science is fundamentally an attitude of mind, a way of approaching problems. The fact that sociologists are studying human behaviour in human terms makes their task more difficult than that of the physicists, but only on a very narrow definition of science could their claim to be called scientists be disallowed.

What is true of biology and sociology is true also of science as a whole. Mathematico-physical types of explanation, though they may be logically fundamental, can never allow us to dispense with other types of explanation, or even with ordinary descriptions; in fact they depend upon the latter to provide their point of reference. We need a whole series of levels of explanation, including those levels where we use words derived from our own experience of personal being.

[1] *The Idea of a Social Science* (1958).

In a particular case this may amount to no more than affirming that, say, psychology needs concepts derived both from biology and from introspection, and that these are complementary, not mutually exclusive. Nevertheless the point is an important one to establish, not only because it has been denied directly, but also because only by appreciating the many levels on which we actually understand things can we avoid the imaginary horror of finding the world reduced to a conglomeration of physical particles. The aim of this discussion has been to show that while in one sense the scientific ideal of complete objectivity and logical transparency, the ideal which finds its most complete expression in theoretical physics, is rightly regarded as fundamental, yet in another sense this ideal only directs us to one part, and that an extreme part, of the whole complex structure we call knowledge. At the other extreme, and having just as important a place in the whole, is knowledge by participation, the knowledge of sociology, for example, which can only be ours because we are ourselves members of a society and can to some extent participate in the social structures we study, and thus understand them in their own terms.

If this very brief analysis of the sort of relationship between the different branches of science is on the right lines, it ought to have some bearing on the relationship between science and theology. It might seem easy to go on from here to construct a hierarchy of levels of knowledge with theology fitted in at one end. In fact it is common to find theological systems which admit some degree of explanatory value in science, but then overarch the whole structure with the notion of 'ultimate explanation' which only theology can provide. Many scientists and philosophers are understandably suspicious of such a procedure, and resent the implication that scientific explanations are not complete, while at the same time wondering what explanatory value an 'ultimate explanation' might be supposed to have.[1]

[1] E.g. K. E. M. Baier, *The Meaning of Life* (1957). Contrast this with a defence of the notion of ultimate explanation in G. F. Woods, *Theological Explanation* (1958).

Both sides perhaps are right. Scientific explanations are complete in relation to what they set out to do. And theology, if it seeks to raise ultimate questions, must at least search for some kind of ultimate explanation. The danger lies in upsetting the balance between these; either in ignoring the real element of discontinuity between the different levels of knowledge; or in acquiescing in too facile and radical a distinction. My main theological criticism of Teilhard de Chardin is that he blurs the discontinuity; my uneasiness about the writings of many others on science and theology is that they seem to imagine prematurely that by stating a distinction they have solved all the problems.

The actual situation is far more complex, and requires far deeper digging than has yet been done. Within science itself there are different levels of explanation, and these must relate to theology in different ways. Nor can we assume that these different levels necessarily merge into one another. Thus within physics different and complementary explanations may be needed, making use of different conceptual frameworks not directly related to one another. For example, it is often said that the relationship between classical and quantum physics is that one is a limiting case of the other. But this is not so. As Hanson has argued,[1] their completely different languages show that there is a discontinuity between them. They are related analogically, not by the merging of one into the other. If this sort of discontinuity exists even within physical explanations, we ought not to be afraid to find it within the broad structure of science as a whole; and we ought to be even more on our guard against any attempt to slide from scientific explanations into theological ones. The conceptual framework implied in theology, and the sort of questions which theologians try to ask, are quite different from those of the scientists.

But this does not mean that the one has nothing to say to the other. It has been the contention of this essay that theology is still

[1] N. R. Hanson, *Patterns of Discovery* (1958), p. 154.

suffering from a great many criticisms implied by science, even if these are no longer stated as openly as they were. There needs to be a clearing of the ground, not in order to make way for a synthesis of science and theology into some all-inclusive system, but in order to remove the philosophical and psychological objections against hearing the great questions about existence which theologians want to ask, or believing that any answers to them are possible. To see science as a complex whole, in the way I have tried to indicate, makes no difference to actual scientific results, though it could have an important liberating effect on scientific aims and methods. It is the perennial temptation of scientists to become immersed in some tiny fraction of the whole field of knowledge, and then to derive all their criteria of judgment from this one fraction. To stress the many-levelled nature of science enables us to fit it into its proper context as part of the quest for truth, involving us in differing degrees at different levels as persons who participate in what they study. This emphasis also deliberately challenges the narrowing down of the quest to one particular kind of truth, the abstract, impersonal, mathematical kind of truth found at one end of the scientific spectrum. To do this is not to open science to floods of theological speculation. Theological answers must not be given to scientific questions. Yet there is not a totally unbridgeable gulf between the two disciplines; nor are scientists and theologians totally different kinds of people with no subject-matter or methods in common. We must keep the conversation going in the belief that in the long run those who care about science will make better theologians, and those who care about theology, better scientists.

3

THE IDEA OF THE TRANSCENDENT

BY

G. F. WOODS

SYNOPSIS

I. *The Transcendent*

1. It is now widely assumed that the transcendent is beyond the limits of our possible experience.
2. The discouraging consequences of this view for traditional Christian theology.
3. Two unsatisfactory replies to this challenge:
   - (*a*) A theology of pure revelation;
   - (*b*) A theology of pure symbolism.
4. Ideas of the transcendent which are meaningless or preclude any unprejudiced inquiry whether in fact we are able to experience that which transcends us.

II. *Analogical Thinking*

5. Analogical thinking does not depend upon any exact likeness but upon an analogical likeness between what is explained and what is used to explain.
6. It follows that no analogy is perfect but each must be judged upon its merits.

III. *The Analogies of Transcendence*

7. The original use and the analogical use of words.
8. The analogy of transcending.

IV. *Our Experience of the Transcendent*

9. Our experience of self-transcendence and of transcending and of being transcended.
10. The problems of transcendence are the problems of being.
11. Our experience of God, analogically described, as pure, necessary, absolute or transcendent being.
12. The idea of God as transcendent is less inadequately explained in personal than in impersonal analogies.

THE IDEA OF THE TRANSCENDENT

'THE LANGUAGE of "transcendence", the thought of God as a personal being, wholly other to man, dwelling apart in majesty—this talk may well collapse into meaninglessness, in the last analysis. And yet to sacrifice it seems at once to take one quite outside Christianity.'[1] I think Professor Hepburn in his penetrating critique of some recent theological writing states the issue concisely and accurately. We are living in an age when the transcendent is either widely denied or not confidently affirmed. In this essay I want to examine the effort of man to think about what transcends him.

I

It is now widely assumed that the transcendent is beyond the limits of our possible experience. It is supposed that we are imprisoned for life within the confines of human experience and that this experience can never include an experience of the transcendent. This general disbelief in our capacity to apprehend what transcends us includes a series of more particular assertions concerning the limitations upon our ability to experience the transcendent. It is said that we can never understand the idea of the transcendent because it lies beyond the forms of thought or categories in which alone we are able to understand what is capable of being understood. We can have no idea of it. In fact, as we can have no idea of the transcendent, it is a meaningless word for us. It is not an idea which we may hope to understand more clearly later. It is not a meaningful idea at all. And even if we could form an idea of the transcendent, we cannot prove that it exists because it lies outside the realm in which we can devise proofs and organize tests. We cannot know *what* it is and we cannot prove *that* it is. The idea is withering like a leaf in autumn and it will fall and decay when winter comes.

[1] R. W. Hepburn, *Christianity and Paradox* (1958), pp. 193 f.

45

This outlook and temper have consequences which are discouraging for traditional Christian theology, both natural and revealed. Natural theology, understood as the knowledge of God which may be derived from a study of nature by the natural reason, loses its persuasiveness. It does so because no way seems to be available of passing from the natural order to what may lie outside that order as its cause or ground. The various forms of explanation which are appropriate and adequate in explaining for example the working of a television set lose their ordinary meaning when they are used to describe how the natural world came into being. Revealed theology is also virtually precluded. In the absence of a confident natural theology, there is no reasonable belief in a God who may choose to reveal himself. There is no preparation of the mind to receive or expect a divine revelation. And, if it is thought that a revelation has been made, it is impossible to see how men could have understood it, if they are incapable of understanding anything which rises above their limited modes of apprehension. Moreover, the traditional evidence for the truth of divine revelation is weakened. The external evidence for the truth of revelation appealed to wonders and signs done by those who claimed to be speaking on behalf of God. The fact that they could do works which man could never do by his own power showed that they possessed divine power and authority. Their miracles and prophecies were their credentials. But when there is no confidence in our capacity to apprehend the transcendent, it becomes impossible to identify a genuinely supernatural event. It may always be a natural event of such complexity that for the time being no adequate natural explanation is available. And those who approach the canonical scriptures with the presupposition that the transcendent is unknowable or meaningless are unlikely to find the narratives acceptable. A restricted place may be left for mystical theology on the ground that exceptional people may enjoy an experience of the transcendent which is not shared by the majority of mankind. But the contemporary critic is likely to doubt whether such experiences are genuine experiences of the transcendent and will probably add that, in any case, those who may have such experiences cannot communicate to others what they have experienced. The mystic should remain mute. All these serious misgivings about natural, revealed and mystical theology derive from a fundamental doubt concerning the capacity of man to apprehend the transcendent.

There are two responses to this challenge which do not seem to me to be satisfactory. It may be said that God is the wholly other. He is not disclosed but hidden in the natural order. He makes himself known in revelatory acts which can never be discerned or understood by those who study the course of nature and the course of human history with merely natural modes of understanding. They will never see what lies outside the narrow field of their vision. Divine revelation is not open to natural verification; it is unique and can be received only in faith. It may also be said that doctrinal statements about the being and activity of God are merely symbolic. They do not represent what God is like in himself; they do not correspond, as it were, point for point with what might be called the structure and operations of God; they simply indicate in a symbolic manner what is incapable of direct representation. Their proper function may be to evoke the right attitude towards God and the right kind of conduct towards men. When doctrinal statements are understood in this way, they are not true or false in the ordinary sense of corresponding or failing to correspond with the facts but they are useful or useless in arousing the right kind of religious feeling and moral resolution. Each of these types of theology is conveniently compatible with the view that the transcendent exceeds our natural powers of apprehension. The extreme theology of revelation substitutes faith for natural reason; and symbolic theology makes no claim that natural reason can represent God as he is in himself. Neither type of theology seems to me to preserve the balance of natural and revealed theology which is characteristic of

47

the classic Christian doctrinal tradition. Both the theology of pure revelation and the theology of pure symbolism emphasize points which are true, but I do not think that we need be so dispirited about the capacity of man to experience the transcendent. Is there a more excellent way of replying to the twentieth-century form of Naturalism and Agnosticism, that is, to the belief that the natural order is the only reality and that we can know nothing for certain about what may lie beyond the limits of the natural?

If we are to make any progress towards a more satisfactory response, we must examine more carefully the form of the challenge and the words in which it is being expressed. The main charges are that we cannot know what the transcendent is and that we cannot prove that it is. It cannot be known or proved. Let us consider these two assertions.

In order to assert that we cannot know the transcendent, it is necessary to have some idea of what it is which we cannot know. If, in speaking or thinking of the transcendent, we are thinking of no idea at all or of some idea which is so vague as to be almost meaningless, we cannot make an assertion, or the assertion which we make is very vague. It is, therefore, legitimate to ask what notion of the transcendent the critic has in mind. No one can fairly criticize any important philosophical word on the ground that it is not immediately quite clear and distinct. The transcendent is such a word. But it is quite possible to think of the transcendent in ways which make it impossible to think that we can ever know it. If, for example, the transcendent is defined as what lies outside the limits of all human experience, we are bound to say that no one can ever experience it. If it is conceived as what is unknowable, we can never hope to know it. Failure is not only invited, it is ensured. It is like asking whether we can ever make a successful expedition to an inaccessible country. Our inability to understand what is defined as incapable of being understood is a logical inability. We cannot overcome this incapacity by asking our question on another occasion in more favourable circumstances. We cannot by dint of linguistic ingenuity pick the logical lock. But we may escape from this logical prison by realizing that it is a question of fact, not of definition, whether we are imprisoned. If in fact we are not in this prison, the question of making our escape does not arise. I see no need or justification for asserting that the transcendent must be taken to mean what we cannot understand. And it is by no means plain that we know what we mean when we describe the transcendent as what we cannot understand. It may mean simply what we cannot yet understand. It may mean what we can never understand. What does this mean? It may mean the empty concept of what is incapable of being understood by us. But, when we begin to use this empty concept as a description of some thing which we can never understand, we run into difficulties. We are saying that this thing has the character of never being understood by us. What, then, is this character? It seems impossible to say. We are in danger of slipping from an act of logical negation to an attempt to understand the characteristics of something which we can never hope to understand. This is a vain endeavour. It is as though we said that on arrival at the frontier we should continue our journey in a not-bus. This may be a curious way of saying that we shall take some form of transport other than a bus, but it does not describe any kind of actual vehicle. And, if I abandon the attempt to describe the characteristics of this transcendent which cannot be understood, I may begin to think of the transcendent as what lies wholly beyond all that is in being. I am then vainly trying to conceive of something in being which I have said to be outside all that is in being. This seems to be a self-contradictory conception which is indistinguishable from nothing. In these strange mental enterprises, I seem to be about to launch into logical outer space but I doubt whether I ever leave the ground. That I have no hope of ever experiencing these curiously conceived transcendents need cause me no distress. Invincible ignorance of what is not there to be known is not a reasonable ground for depres-

whether I can say that the two offices are really alike. I begin to see that they are not really alike either in general or in a number of particular points of exact likeness. The whole comparison, in general and in particular, is not an exact likeness but an analogous likeness. There is analogy between the two offices but never precise similarity. At some points the analogy is closer than at others but at no point is exact similarity to be found. In fact, if this were found we should not need to use analogy at all to explain such a point. It would be a mere replica or repetition of what the American already knew. Analogies cease to be when they attain perfect similarity with what is being explained by them. Wholly successful analogies like good teachers render themselves dispensable.

When analogical explanation is taken to be the discovery of exact likenesses between what is being explained and what it is being used to explain, analogical thinking becomes an act of classification. It is like grading eggs or compiling a catalogue or an index. As the form of classification has been devised to be reasonably appropriate to what is being classified, it usually happens that most of the material is fairly easily classified. But there is often an unclassified residue, a miscellaneous surplus. These melancholy rejects can be called un-classifiable in relation to the scheme of classification but they do not cease to be, simply because they have not been classified. This understanding of analogical explanation leaves no place for the apprehension of the unique, the novel, the unfamiliar, the uncon-ventional. It is the bureaucratic notion of analogy. On such a view it is bound to be useless as a means of explaining the transcendent when this is understood as what is quite unlike anything in our experience. An instrument which depends for its utility upon the presence of exact similarities is useless in their absence. The view that analogical explanation is then futile in regard to the transcendent is not a conclusion which is improperly drawn, but a conclusion which is untrue because it is based upon presumptions about the nature of analogical explanation which are false.

The curious and fascinating point about genuine analogies is that they are not at any point exactly like what they are supposed to explain. And yet they do work. They do help to explain what is obscure. How can this happen? No theory can be adequate which concludes that what happens cannot take place. What is the central characteristic of what analogies do? Somehow, they express sameness in difference and difference in sameness. There is a sudden and exciting recognition of an analogical likeness between entities or situations which are strictly speaking not alike. This is a mysterious capacity. It resists clear and distinct understanding. There is no logical room for an analogical likeness which is somewhere between strict likeness and unlikeness. It is like the strict line between partiality and impartiality which an Irish chairman is said to have pursued. Formal reasoning has a proper abhorrence of such notions. To the mathematical mind, they are detestable. Our capacity to explain analogically is more than an ability to exploit the mobility of our mental standpoint in order to gain more advantageous standpoints from which we can discern exact similarities. A blind man does not improve his view of a royal procession by gaining permission to stand on a balcony. Nor is our use of analogies just a matter of making an ingenious employment of the limited number at our disposal. It is more than a skilful use of the limited number of tools provided with our mental car. We are somehow able to apprehend what is novel and unusual, and in this act of expanding apprehension we perpetually make use of explanatory analogies. We invent them. We modify them. We discard them. We use them. Our power to invent, modify, discard and use them is not identical with the analogies which we invent, modify, discard and use. It is this creative power which is the secret of analogical explanation. It seems to be endless. It can notice analogical likenesses which have hitherto been overlooked. It can express these mysterious likenesses between things which are strictly unlike in all kinds of analogical models, frameworks, structures, and constructions. Analogical thinking may be the source of the universals, such as 'man' and 'stone' which we use in our thought and speech. It is by no means obvious that all legitimate understandings of the transcendent must fall outside the range of all analogical explanation.

We may hazard a guess about the reasons which have led to this failure to recognize the mysterious essence of analogy. Historically, the study of analogy has often begun from the study of mathematical ratios between geometrical shapes or between numbers. When these analogies are used to explain the use of analogy, I suspect that certain unfortunate consequences follow. The entities between which the ratios are discerned are of different quantities but each is composed of some kind of plurality of agreed quantitative units. These units are formal. Between these formal units, the ratios are measurable and formal. The perspicuity of the situations in ratio to one another depends upon the absence of the imperfections and obscurities which are introduced when we are discerning analogical likeness between actual situations in the actual world. And the study of formal quantitative ratios directs our attention away from analogical explanation and towards analogical proof, which is a different though related matter. The examination of ratios was congenial to rational inquiry but the mysterious essence of analogical explanation is not open to rational investigation in any narrow sense. Lastly, the study of the working of analogy in terms of the not very happy analogy of ratios has introduced a confusing vocabulary. As quantities or portions were taken as the material of analogical comparisons, efforts were made to express the mysterious nature of analogy in terms of proportion and proportionality. These two traditional terms are never easily distinguished because they are being used analogically in a situation which is far more complex than that of the artificially simple situations of mathematics.

But even the genuine use of analogical explanation has certain limitations which are not defects. This is true of any kind of instrument which through the very fact of being utilizable in certain circumstances is incapable of being useful in other circumstances. For example, a good spoon is not good as a thermometer. The most obvious limitation of analogical explanation has already been mentioned. It can never, so long as it remains an analogy, become exactly similar to what is being explained. Even the best analogy is not as good as the genuine article. Like an understudy, it is never quite the same as the principal. It follows that no analogy is perfect. There is a ceaseless oscillation between confidence and diffidence about the usefulness of analogical explanation. The debate about the utility of analogy becomes more fruitful when it becomes less abstract. The value of particular analogies can be very usefully discussed. Each one can be examined on its merits. Some are better than others. It is not unlike the situation in which, having been told that there is no substitute for *The Times* newspaper, we may still have legitimate preferences between the newspapers which are in fact available. Some may still give accounts of the events of the day which are better than others. But the possibility that we may be able to give an analogical explanation of what the transcendent is like does not show that we can experience it or prove that it exists.

In assessing the utility of any analogy, it is essential to study its origin as well as its later development. We need an historical approach to the meaning of words, particularly to the use of analogies. This approach is not in itself enough to display the whole potentialities of a word, but it is a mistake to think that we can dispense with the historical study. We need to study the derivations of analogies because each one is composed of a basic word and its analogical application. The basic word is the primary use of the word in its original site. This is its direct, unanalogical use. These plain, commonplace words are the foundation of innumerable analogical explanations. It is not surprising that many of these are based upon the well-known verbs which describe quite common human experiences. They are useful bases just because they are so commonplace and provide so easily instruments for the analogical communication of meaning. Everybody knows what they mean. Many of these basic verbs describe our common experience of intentionally moving from place to place or intentionally refusing to move. By the use of appropriate prepositions, the utility of these basic verbs is greatly increased. The verb 'to come' is made more useful by speaking of 'come in', 'come out', 'come across', 'come over', etc. These modified uses of the original verb may lead to a number of substantives such as 'income' or 'outcome', though there are always curious gaps in the possible series. It is obvious that words have many uses and that their analogical use is particularly wide. But the distinction remains between their original use and their analogical use. The value of looking carefully at the use of the word in its original situation is that we are thereby enabled to see more clearly the propriety or impropriety of transporting it for use in another situation. If we want to know a word well it is illuminating to study its behaviour at home as well as abroad. This may show that some verbal trips abroad are unfortunate. Some words cannot stand very violent climatical or social changes. The social mobility of words, at least of English words, is somewhat limited.

III

Analogies of transcendence are based upon the verb 'to transcend'. This originally meant to climb over or across some obstacle. Its direct use is to describe the act, for example, of climbing over a wall or clambering across a narrow ditch. The extensive vocabulary of transcendence is originally used by those who have experience of the act of transcending. Usually, the accounts of the experience are given by the climber or by some spectator. What is transcended is usually impersonal and incapable of thought and speech. Memoirs are written by mountaineers, not by mountains. There may be occasions at gymnastic displays when the human obstacle may be in a position to give reports which may not always be flattering about the performances of his colleagues. From these direct uses of the verb there is a progress towards its indirect or analogical use when it is employed to describe a situation which is comparable to those experienced when climbers overcome some kind of obstruction. For example, someone must sometime have felt that his experience of being overwhelmed or overpowered could be aptly and vividly described in terms taken from the experiences of climbing and clambering. The frequent occasions on which the analogy was found to be appropriate gradually established the use of the words. But the use of the particular word 'transcendent' has been somewhat curious. If it had become customary to use it as the word 'regent' is used, it might have come to mean the person who transcends as the regent is the person who reigns. How has it popularly come to mean what we cannot transcend? Possibly, in the ordinary experience of climbing or crossing, we meet an obstacle which we cannot climb or cross. A mountaineer, for instance, may arrive at an overhanging cliff which he cannot climb. The cliff is beyond the limits of his capacity to climb. It transcends his powers as a climber. It is transcendent. It is as if the cliff is a more powerful mountaineer than himself. He becomes the transcended obstacle. The cliff becomes the transcendent. The fact that the analogical use of the term 'the transcendent' still survives is proof that it remains useful. But its analogical use is not equally happy on all occasions. Like a builder's crane, it can collapse if it is used to carry an excessive weight of meaning. In short, the term 'the transcendent' is an analogy and shares the characteristic usefulness and limitations of all analogies.

The deepest use of the vocabulary of transcendence is to describe the fact of being in existence. To be is to transcend. To be transcended is to lose being. A personal being knows himself to be existing because he is outstanding above or transcending over what is not. The use of the word 'immanence' has a comparable reference to persistence in being. The original use of this word is to describe the state of remaining within some kind of limits or enclosure. But in order to be immanent within an environment, it is essential not to be identical with the environment. There must be some kind of a distinction between what is enclosed and what encloses. A floating ball in water can be immanent in the water only because it is not identical with the water. It transcends and is transcended by its fluid environment. It is exerting the power of remaining in being in spite of the engulfing pressure of the water. Both transcendence and immanence are rather curious analogies describing what is and what remains in being.

IV

If it be true that the transcendent is an analogical description of what is in being, the question whether we can experience the transcendent and prove that it exists becomes the question whether we can experience and prove the existence of what is in being. This is an odd question because if we have experience of something, we know that it is sufficiently in being for us to experience it. If I experience a dream, I am sure that the dream had sufficient being for it to be an object of experience. If I have experience of a table, I am sure that it has sufficient being to be an object of experience. How do I decide that the table is more established in being than the dream? By applying various tests of the unity and continuity of my experience. But how do I know that these tests are trustworthy? I believe that in the last resort all proofs of existence rely upon some experience of existence which is taken as not requiring any further proof. There would be an infinite regress of tests if no test was accepted as final. To put to the proof is to put to the test. An existential proof is to put to the test of experience. We do not trouble consciously to prove the existence of those things which are traditionally accepted by us as in existence. Any act of proving the existence of things which undoubtedly exist has an air of artificiality. We produce the proofs if we are challenged to justify our existential beliefs or if we are subjecting our existential beliefs to academic doubt. The function of the existential proofs is to put us in the position from which we can have experience of what we are seeking to prove. The form of the proof is to facilitate and purify the experience. No existential proof can ultimately work for us if we have no capacity to apprehend what is in being. Without this mysterious capability we can make no effective use of the various proofs which are designed to put us in a position to exercise this faculty. But can we experience the transcendent? This is not a logical question but a factual question. It can, therefore, be legitimately rephrased as the inquiry, 'Do we experience the transcendent?' If, in fact, we do, the questions whether we can do so and whether we can prove that we do so cannot be raised in isolation from the fact of our experience. They are questions which are raised within the experience.

But do we have experience of the transcendent, in the sense of having experience of beings which are other than our own? I believe we do. But we must try to look for it in the right way. We are not likely to be successful in a treasure hunt at a garden fête if we consciously or unconsciously decide to search only in the library of the house and insist upon envisaging the treasure in our own way. Without some freshness of approach and openness of mind we are foredoomed to an endless and unsuccessful peregrination round the library, occasionally raising our drooping spirits by bouts of mild indignation against the organizers of the fête for not arranging the treasure hunt according to our presumptions. We see nothing if we do not look, or if we do not look for the right thing. What do we expect an experience to be like? The word itself originally described the act of going or passing through something, as a person might go through a doorway. We can, therefore, say 'I would not like that experience again', or 'I would not like to go through that experience again', and intend to say the same thing on the two occasions. If, then, we speak of experiencing the transcendent, we are using two analogies. We are speaking of the odd manœuvre of going through what we cannot climb over or across. (Though if a train could speak, it might claim to experience the St Gothard tunnel beneath the Alps which it cannot transcend.) In speaking of an experience of the transcendent we are speaking in terms of the movement of embodied persons in some stable physical environment. But where in fact can I find any experience of the transcendent, in the sense of beings which are other than my own? Obviously, in everyday experience of life. I acknowledge the presence of personal and impersonal beings around me. How I come to this conviction I do not understand. No theory of knowledge in the last resort explains how we know, though it may throw some light on some of the machinery which is used in the act. When I acknowledge the presence of other people and things, I am admitting that, in a variety of ways, they are transcending me and I am transcending them. They are there, I am here. I am not the only thing in being. But what am I experiencing? The transcendent of which I am aware is not, for example, a visible feature of each visible being, as I might notice some characteristic coloured feather in the wings of a particular kind of bird. I cannot see the transcendence of other people and things by looking for some kind of sensible experience or for some kind of experience which might later be classified as a kind of sensible experience beyond the usual range of my senses. And my experience of the transcendent within my world is not of some kind of hidden thing behind each observed thing. If I pick up a pencil, I do not think that it encloses within itself the real transcendent pencil which is very much the same as the outer pencil, though presumably slightly smaller. To think of the transcendence of the pencil in this way is to start thinking of an infinite series of inner pencils, as children delight to find smaller boxes in larger boxes. I am not assisted in thinking of the transcendence of the pencil, if I assume that the real, transcendent pencil is something totally unlike the pencil. It is doubtful whether such a notion has any meaning but it is a useless notion in any case. I believe that when I experience the transcendence of the pencil, I simply acknowledge that it is there and that it is not part

59

of my being. It is transcendent in the sense that it is. My experience of transcendence is experience of being. It is very difficult to say whether I experience the experience of transcendence or whether I simply have the experience of transcending and of being transcended. These may not be alternative experiences but aspects or elements of human experience. We touch here the mysteries of self-transcendence. I act and I know that I act. I think and I know that I think. I speak and I know that I speak. Fortunately, in this limited essay, it is sufficient for my purpose to draw attention to the manifold experiences which we have in everyday life of transcending and being transcended by beings which are other than our own. These experiences are not of observable physical features of these beings nor of ghostly replicas behind them but quite simply of their sheer presence. If we admit this experience, we are admitting that somehow we are not confined to the limits of our private experience in the sense that we cannot transcend our own experience sufficiently to acknowledge that other people and things are in existence, as well as ourselves. We are able to experience transcendence in this sense. But this does not mean that we experience the transcendence of all things and of all persons in exactly the same way. We experience their presence in a wide variety of analogous ways. I readily admit that a person and a pebble both are but I do not really think that each is in precisely the same way. I find that in acknowledging that they are there I wish to say that each is in being in its own way, but not so diversely that one is and the other is not. Where the acknowledged beings are apparently impersonal, I can experience their presence only as from outside. But where the acknowledged beings are taken to be personal, I can by sympathetic imagination understand more intimately what it means for them to be and to act. The main point which is now being emphasized is that the manifest subtlety of our experience of the transcendent in our daily acquaintance with the ordinary world should warn us against being too dogmatic about the limits of our possible experience. It is not difficult to state a logical limit but it is hard to determine where the limits lie in fact. Originally a limit was the uncultivated strip of ground which marked the division between two cultivated strips of land in the ancient open field system of agriculture in which a common field was divided amongst all the cultivators. Even in that simpler situation, it must have been easier to talk about the limits than to keep them indubitably precise in fact. We ought not to expect simplicity in determining the exact landmarks of the boundaries around the area of our possible experience.

We may appear to be making very slow progress towards the main problem, namely, the transcendence of God, but it is always a mistake in philosophical theology to try to run before we can walk. I think a few preliminary points have been proposed, even if they have not been established. It is plain that we cannot simply use the word 'transcendent' and assume without more ado that it always has the same meaning. No one assumes that 'the adjacent' has only one meaning. The particular use to which it is being put always influences the answers which are given to questions about its utility. We can best discover the usefulness of the word by pondering our use of it in situations which we judge to be aptly described as transcendent situations. It is a fact of our experience that we often find it appropriate to describe our experience in terms taken from our experience of success and failure in climbing over or across some kind of obstacle. We mislead ourselves somewhat by thinking of the obstacle as some kind of thing which by its presence blocks our way from one point to another. Strictly speaking, our way is impeded, not by some kind of barrier, but by the opposing presence of some being other than our own. The barriers are the points at which competitive beings impinge upon one another without being able to overwhelm one another. Two people find it impossible to transcend one another, not because they are separated by some kind of barricade, but because they are two people. The problems of transcendence are the problems of being.

Do human beings ever have experience of God? I am taking this question in the sense of having experience of God as being in being. In raising this somewhat limited but basic question, I do not wish to suggest that we have no experience of God through an experience of absolute values or through the insights of holiness. I am somewhat artificially concentrating my attention upon our experience of the being of God. Do human beings ever have this experience? Though few of us may have the experience in any deep and unbroken way, is it an experience which is open to all men who seek it diligently? We are unlikely to have this experience of God as transcendent being, if we define the transcendent as what lies beyond the most extreme limits of human experience. We cannot hope that we may eventually know what we have defined as unknowable. And we shall be inhibited against expecting any experience of God, if we think that in order to be truly God, he must be beyond all that is in being. It is doubtful whether this notion has any clear meaning. It almost equates the being of God with some vague nothing which is somehow in being. It sounds as though nothing must be a sort of something in order to be there. We cannot but be bewildered in trying to have experience of such a vague and doubtful object. In brief, we can never experience the logical transcendent and we can have little hope of experiencing the ontological transcendent when it is curiously identified with something which is beyond all that is. The classic issue is whether there is a fundamental distinction between what is necessarily in being and what is not necessarily in being. We ought not to be too preoccupied with the adverb because it is being used analogically and contains traces of all kinds of continuances and cessations of which we have experience in our daily life and thought. The real question is whether we find this distinction unavoidable in our experience. How we describe it is another matter. As this is a question of what happens in actual human experience, it cannot be settled once and for all by a quick individual glance, as one might glance through a window to see whether anyone is at the door. I am sure that we do have experience of beings which come into existence and pass out of existence. We see the sequence of leaves on a tree, the succession of trees in a wood, we learn of the progressive changes in vegetation which follow climatical and geological change. In our own lives, we know the tremulous quality of our own existence. But do we have no sense of the unchanging beneath the changes which we see? Those who have lost effective belief in God continue to believe in Nature or the Natural Order which survives throughout all natural changes. There is here a belief in Nature as transcending all natural products. Do we have experience of Nature? We are inclined to say 'no', because we do not experience Nature as a feature of any natural scene or landscape. We are inclined to say 'yes', because, both scientifically and aesthetically, we usually believe that we can speak meaningfully of Nature, even though we find it very hard to say clearly what we think it to be. If we come to think that Nature is itself a remoter process of change, we begin to think of some still more remote conditions of change which do not themselves change. We cannot rest in absolute change. In our experience of the changing, we have also a curious experience of the unchanging. I believe that we are gradually driven towards an awareness of some being, which is variously styled pure, absolute, or transcendent. The conclusion is being itself. It is difficult to say whether one experiences this pure being or whether more usually one experiences being transcended by it. A further difficulty is that in the very moment of experience, we are using analogies to express the experience in a way which may help us to understand it and communicate it to others. We are at one and the same time trying to have the experience and to deepen and record the experience in striking analogies. These efforts of analogical explanation must always fail because all analogies are less than perfect, even in relation to quite ordinary situations. We use a whole variety of analogies drawn from a whole variety of well-known situations in everyday life. We often use at one and the same time a series of analogies including several situations which in actual life are incompatible. The analogies of transcendence are instances of analogical explanations of the being and activity of God which are useful but never final or perfect.

We must be as careful as we can in our use of analogies taken from our experience of climbing when we apply them to God as pure, transcendent being. We ought to recall that an act of climbing over or across some impediment is the act of an embodied person. Each climbing incident may be distinguished into elements which are personal and elements which appear to be impersonal. It is difficult to know what this distinction ultimately means, but it is very generally made. We must reject all interpretations of divine transcendence which suggest that God is one impersonal thing resting upon or supporting another. We must never envisage the natural and the supernatural as if they were two millstones, one resting upon another. We do not basically improve the analogy by assuming that they are in motion. We do better to take our analogical material from our experience of personal being. The manifold ways in which we find ourselves transcended and transcending in our experience of being ourselves and in our experience of being in the company of other people should be our main source of analogies in describing the relation of what is necessarily in being with what is not necessarily in being. These analogies are never adequate but I believe they can be illuminating. As they are never adequate, it is always possible to focus our attention upon the point at which the analogy is about to break under the strain. For instance, the analogies of transcendence are based upon a situation in which normally there is someone who transcends and something which is transcended. It may be useful in suggesting something of the nature of the divine being but it is misleading if taken to mean that the divine being requires something to transcend in order to be. An absolutely transcendent being can strictly neither transcend nor be transcended. But it is liable to give a false impression if we look only at the weakest points of any analogy. Each one has to be judged upon its merits and demerits.

Our starting-point was the observation, 'The language of "transcendence"...may well collapse into meaninglessness, in the last analysis.' I do not know whether the phrase 'last analysis' means the last analysis which is made before human inquiry for some reason comes to an end or whether it means that we may reach an analysis which shows with finality that the language of transcendence has collapsed or must collapse. I do not myself think that such an analysis has yet been made and I think it is unlikely that it will be or can be made.

SYNOPSIS

I. Theology must take account of the discoveries of Freud as of those of Copernicus and Darwin. The nature of Freud's discoveries. They cannot be apprehended by merely intellectual study, but demand a surrender comparable to the surrender of faith. This is in accord with what Christians believe about the Incarnation, the Passion and Resurrection.

II. The analogies in terms of which alone we can think and feel about God evoke areas of our being not subject to the discriminatory control of our discursive reason. This accords with what St John of the Cross tells us of the *via negativa*. The demoniacs of the Synoptic Gospels illustrate the same point. Cranmer's Communion Service considered in the light of his irrational reactions to God.

III. The effect of self-awareness upon our understanding of morality. Morality may be cowardice. The opposite of sin is faith. The absence of faith leads to the equation of my known self with my total self. The result is sin. The seven root sins considered in this light. The teaching of Christ upon the nature of goodness. St Paul and St John take the same view.

IV. Three further illustrations of how self-awareness can contribute to the understanding of Christian truth. The Atonement. Forgiveness. Our Lady.

THEOLOGY AND SELF-AWARENESS

'What do I know, father', *said Louisa in her quiet manner, 'of tastes*
and fancies; of aspirations and affections; of all that part of my nature
in which such light things might have been nourished? What escape
have I had from problems that could be demonstrated, and realities
that could be grasped?' As she said it, she unconsciously closed her
hand, as if upon a solid object, and slowly opened it as though she were
releasing dust or ash. (CHARLES DICKENS, *Hard Times*, chapter xv.)

I

IT HAS BEEN the fate or fortune of theological study to have been
forced to absorb into its system the assured results of other branches
of learning. In the sixteenth century, it began to be forcibly fed with
the astronomy of Copernicus, and had in consequence to abandon
the geocentric universe which the biblical writers had assumed along
with the cosmologists of their day. In the nineteenth century, theologians were made to swallow a tougher diet. The methods of
historical criticism and the discoveries of natural science combined
not only to play havoc with the accepted view of biblical inspiration,
but to necessitate the radical restatement of certain traditional
Christian doctrines. Naturally there was fierce resistance. But, on
the whole, the new knowledge was accepted and absorbed by
Christian thinkers before the century came to an end. Darwin ceased
to be ridiculed or anathematized, and it was agreed that you could
remain a Christian while believing in the descent of man from
animal ancestors.

During the final stages of the battle, however, a new potential
enemy was preparing a new sort of weapon. In Vienna Freud was
conducting his researches into human psychology. The full force of
their impact did not really hit England until after the First World
War. And not until after the Second World War have theologians

begun to appreciate the reassessments in Christian thinking demanded by the discoveries of Freud himself, his disciples and successors. 'There is a fairly close parallel', writes Lord Adrian,[1] 'between the impact of the theory of Natural Selection one hundred years ago and that of Freud's theories on our own generation...his views made the same kind of attack on our pride and met with the same passionate resentment or approval.' If the fight has not been so dramatic as in the nineteenth century, that is because resentment has largely taken the form of ignoring Freudian discoveries as ridiculous nonsense. Occasionally there has been an open attack as in C. E. Raven's Gifford Lectures[2]—'It is indeed probable that the chief effect of the remarkable outbreak of psychological and psychiatric analysis, apart from its unwholesome influence upon the post-war generation, has been to emphasize the inadequacy of analysis and to expose the fallacies so often attaching to it.'[3] Freud, Raven concludes, 'was not a great scientist or a great thinker—though he may perhaps deserve the title of "a man of genius"'.[4]

More can be made of this verdict of disapproval and the qualification at the end than its author would perhaps allow. A thinker deals in abstract concepts and makes of them a mental edifice as far removed from the warmth of human blood as the Snow Queen's palace. When Freud attempted this sort of construction in his more general non-clinical writings, his arguments could be torn to shreds by any trained philosopher. As a leading Freudian analyst, Dr Gregory Zilboorg, has observed—'It has become clear to a certain number of thinkers that the philosophical incursions of Freud could have been divorced from his psychiatric clinical opinions in the same way that the chemistry of Boyle and the physics of Newton can be looked at altogether independently of their theological digressions.'[5]

[1] *Report of the British Association for the Advancement of Science*, vol. XI, no. 42 (1954).
[2] 1952.   [3] *Natural Religion and Christian Theology* (1953), vol. I, p. 195.
[4] *Ibid.* vol. II, p. 29.
[5] 'L'amour de Dieu chez Freud' in supplement of *La Vie Spirituelle* (1953), p. 8.

As for the scientist, he is concerned to observe objective facts in the exterior world. Freud was concerned with people's subjective feelings. The discipline of natural science, by its very nature, cannot take cognizance of emotional reactions, but only of the somatic conditions with which they are accompanied. If heights make me tremble, the neurologist can investigate the nervous mechanisms which produce my shaking. But he is not equipped to discover why it is that I feel fear while other people do not.

Freud's genius, on the other hand, consisted in his discovery of a completely new system of explanation which was able to make sense of subjective feelings so far unexplained. The difficulty lies in the fact that the explanation cannot be apprehended merely by intellectual study. For there is something in it of Augustine's 'Believe that thou mayest understand'. As with Augustine, so with Freud, this is not a demand for irrational credulity (since such credulity is merely intellectual), but a demand that the risk be taken of opening oneself to a reality greater than is at present known to us. For Augustine the reality was God: for Freud, the unknown self. For Augustine the way was prayer: for Freud, analysis. And just as you cannot come to know God simply by making an academic study of prayer, so you cannot get to know your unknown self just by studying books about psycho-analysis. Of course, the academic study of prayer may lead a man to pray, without doing so deliberately or formally. And in the same way, studying books on psycho-analysis may lead a man to meet more of himself than he formerly knew. But in both cases resistance tends to be strong, and hence the almost universal necessity of applying oneself deliberately to the process. That is why all schools of analysis insist that the analyst must himself be analysed as part of his training. It is like ordinands' being made to pray. There are, it is true, some practitioners and lecturers in psychiatry who think that a man can be opened up to himself by taking the appropriate drugs. The theory is attractive. The procedure is simple and short, and it has a reassuring affinity to the idea that

71

all a man needs to make him whole is to take medicine. But there are serious objections to this view. Even if the drug, when operating, does bring up much repressed material into consciousness, is it possible for somebody to absorb so much of himself in so short a time? In the psychic realm, there is what corresponds to digestion in the physical. A person suffering from chronic malnutrition is unlikely to be cured by a single banquet of gargantuan dimensions.

More alarming, from the point of view of this essay, is the parallel with the claims made for mescalin by Mr Aldous Huxley in *The Doors of Perception*. For Mr Huxley, mescalin is a short-cut to the Beatific Vision—a view which has been fully examined and refuted by Professor R. C. Zaehner.[1] The question is whether awareness, a permanent increase of insight, can be manufactured by a drug, be it awareness of God or awareness of the self. That these two are most intimately related has been the unanimous opinion of Christian writers down the ages—'He is not far from each one of us: for in him we live and move and have our being' (Acts xvii. 27 f.).

It is therefore the opinion of the present writer that even in this age there are no supersonic flights to the Celestial City or even to the Palace Beautiful. Increased awareness can be obtained only by a journey on foot by way of the Slough of Despond, the Hill of Difficulty, Doubting Castle, and the rest. Another suggestion might be to drive through these areas on a coach trip. An attempt could be made to describe how, in the abstract, the tenets of one or other school of psychology are theoretically related to this or that article of Christian doctrine. This would be an exercise in academic psychology and would doubtless impart a great deal of information, but it would fall outside the purpose of this essay. Our concern here will be to discover how a man's knowledge of God and his attitude towards God are affected by his growing awareness of what he is and how he functions as a psychic entity. This of course will have important results in his subsequent statement of how any Christian

[1] *Mysticism Sacred and Profane* (1956).

doctrine is to be understood. But this statement of doctrine will be at a second remove. Perhaps the point can be put most clearly in Émile Mersch's words about Augustine—for him 'thinking was not so much a matter of putting concepts together as of seeking truth in himself'.[1] Freud and his successors, disciples or deviationists, have taught us how we can discover within ourselves a great deal of what was previously unknown to us, and such discoveries can tell us a great deal of how we think and feel about God. But the process is not simply an exercise in cerebration. It involves a costly surrender of what we imagine or hope or fear we are, to what in our fullness we really are. Unless we are prepared for this surrender, the new understanding of human nature which Freud initiated will tell us nothing useful about that belief in God which is the material of our theology. It is only by doing the truth that we come to the light. It is only by actually making the journey that we can perceive the nature of the country. There is a type of thinking which remains safely at home, merely receiving reports, maps, and photographs of what lies beyond the garden wall, and speculates, often with great cleverness, on the basis of such dispatches received. Thinking and living are thus divorced, or rather, thinking is made into the instrument of escape from involvement with life. Why dive into the sea, if you can talk about it so well and think about it so clearly? But in such circumstances the object of thought becomes no more than an imaginary toy. That is why much talk about God cuts no ice. What is talked about has never been lived. And that is why self-awareness cannot grow by the study of text-books on psychology. The principle of Incarnation, as Christian theology understands it, is the principle of involvement. In Christ, we believe, God involved himself totally in our human predicament. How then, with regard to our own selves and psychic make-up, can we refuse to do the same? And here Freud pointed the way. For he 'promulgated the belief... that the psychological laws governing our unconscious, affective life

---

[1] *Le Corps Mystique du Christ*[2] (1936), vol. II, p. 38.

are equally valid for all men, the mentally ill and the mentally healthy; that these laws are not violated in health or in disease any more than the laws of chemistry or physics are different in physical health or physical disease. In other words, Freud opened the road for a proper psychological identification with the neurotic and psychotic...an identification based on an actual psychological equation between ourselves and the mentally ill.'[1] This is the involvement, the incarnation, and the cross, of self-awareness. And this is why we are tempted to forsake Christ and flee, concocting for our flight the most convincing reasons possible. We cannot bear to put ourselves in the same class as the afflicted. Yet this is also the road to resurrection, to fuller, richer life. For it is our hatred of what is buried within us, our fear of it and guilt about it, which keeps it excluded from our awareness. And it is precisely this exclusion which maintains it as an enemy felt to be working against us. When received into awareness, it loses its power to hurt or destroy, and, in time, contributes positively to the well-being and depth of the personality. I may, for instance, have the habit of quarrelling with my friends and tend therefore to lose their friendship. It is easy for me to explain this fact as due either to something wrong in them or to my own circumstances, such as the necessity to overwork. I am too frightened to receive into awareness the buried child within me, who is terrified of losing his own identity by parental domination or possessiveness. It is this buried child who is losing me my friends, for he converts them into the dominating possessive parents with whom I have to quarrel in order to preserve my individuality. It is painfully terrifying to acknowledge this child and to receive him into awareness, for it looks as though, once acknowledged thus, he will make havoc of me altogether. He will make me fall out completely with everybody and everything so that I shall no longer be able to live. But this in fact does not happen. Received into awareness, the

---

[1] Gregory Zilboorg, *Bulletin of the New York Academy of Medicine* (December 1956), p. 894.

child disappears. But he leaves behind something of enormous value
—that instinct to be myself and to give expression to what I am,
from which flow all the highest achievements of human life, whatsoever things are lovely, whatsoever things are good, of which the
greatest is the capacity to give myself away in love. It is thus that I
pass through involvement with an alienated self, the cross and the
passion, to the glory of the resurrection.

II

But it is time we applied what we have been discussing to our
relationship with God. The first thing I notice is that what I think
I believe or feel about God, I am probably not feeling or thinking
about God at all. It is a theological commonplace that statements
about God are analogical. He cannot be directly described but only
indirectly indicated by means of descriptions which tell of earthly
things. I may, for instance, speak of God in terms of causality. But
what I am really saying is that in God there is something which in
some way or other corresponds to causality as we know it in this
world. That is why Kant was right in his repudiation of the cosmological argument for God's existence. When we speak of God as the
first cause we do not mean that he is the cat which began to bite
the rat. We are saying that in his relation to the world there is that
which can be hinted about by means of the image of cause, but that
the image is not the reality. So far, so good. I am using my discursive reason to discriminate. But there is a large area of myself
where the writ of my discursive reason does not run. I can indeed
generally persuade myself that it is otherwise. Smith let me down
by forgetting my dinner party. My anger with him seems reasonable
enough. But on closer inspection my anger generally turns out to be
more violent than reason would dictate. Although I do not know it,
Smith in fact stands for all the rejecters I have experienced since I
was born. And the violence of my anger is in fact being evoked by
these whole series of rejections, most of them long since forgotten.

What Smith here does to me is being constantly done by those analogies in terms of which alone I can think of God. God is my father, my king, my judge, my lover, my friend, the first cause who upholds all things by the word of his Power and who directs all things by the operation of his Providence. Since life for me is not all I think it could be, since in some way or other I am bound to be frustrated and incapable of articulating my full potency, since those on whom I depend grow ill and die, and the world itself is always on the brink of catastrophic conflict, it is inevitable that I should feel deep resentment against the almighty Father, the omnipotent king, the Person who is always claiming that he loves me utterly, but who, in terms of the language used to describe him, is ultimately responsible for all the ills from which I suffer. Sometimes this resentment breaks out into the open and is rationalized by my becoming a puzzled agnostic (if I am gentle by nature) or a militant atheist (if my nature is more violent). But if I remain a Christian believer, such feelings of resentment are both shocking and irrational. I know that the wrongness of things can be intellectually accounted for by any competent theologian. So I refuse to allow my feelings to become conscious. At all costs I refuse to meet the me who entertains them. I drive him underground, while the me I recognize and admit gives voice to expressions of grateful piety. In consequence I lose a large part of the vitality I could enjoy and use. I am only half myself. And even this half has to spend quite a lot of its energy in keeping the other half at arm's length, and this in the name of rational understanding and its demand that I should worship absolute goodness. Where in fact I am failing is in my apprehension that there are large areas of my being as yet impervious to my critical reason, and where in consequence the analogies in terms of which I think of God are evoking me by means of all those people in the forgotten past under whose control and care I have been—people who, in the nature of the case, have not yet been made perfect in love. In the Bible, God is constantly represented as making statements of a kind which belong to such imperfect people. It is therefore no wonder that as a Christian I have a great amount of irrational re-actions to him on which I have continuously to sit very hard. And the diabolical thing is that I seldom know it. All I know is that I am subject to fits of anger (finding its object in anybody or anything), depression (explained as due to vitamin deficiency), tiredness, nerves, the conviction that I have too much to do and need a holiday.

We could sum this up by saying that our attitude to God, evoked by the way in which alone we can conceive him, is like an iceberg. A small amount appears above the surface of consciousness. Below is the vast submerged mass we do not see.

The terms in which we have set this forth are new to our century. But the fact has been known by Christians for a long time.

We could take St John of the Cross as an example. Nobody has understood so clearly the absolutely earthly character of all our holy thoughts and feelings. For him who would attain to complete union with God, they have to be discarded. For whether pleasant or un-pleasant, they are not a pure reaction to God as he is in himself. They are merely our instinctive response to the earthly forms in which we try to capture and clothe him. And as such, they are misleading. They evoke our total being to what is less than ultimate Reality. Few people have understood so deeply as St John the immense emotive power of the terms in which we think of God, and the consequent pain which accompanies their loss. But, he insists, the loss is necessary; since, when we respond to them, we are responding, not to God, but to our past experience of earthly things.

Faith...tells us of things which we have never seen or understood, nor have we seen or understood aught that resembles them, since there is naught that resembles them at all.[1]...And thus a soul is greatly impeded from reaching this high estate of union with God when it clings to any understanding or feeling or imagination or appearance or will or manner of its own, or to any other

[1] *Ascent of Mount Carmel.* Translated and edited by E. Allison Peers (1953), book II, ch. 3, section 3.

act or to anything of its own, and cannot detach and strip itself of all these. For, as we say, the goal which it seeks lies beyond all this, yea, beyond even the highest thing that can be known or experienced: and thus a soul must pass beyond everything to unknowing.[1]

Faith is the gift of God. It cannot be fabricated by human contrivance. Analysis can create faith no more than reading the Bible or attending Mass. But, under God's Providence, analysis can lead a man along the negative way, detaching him and stripping him of what he once took as an experience of God, and showing him that, on the contrary, it was an experience of what eye has seen and ear heard, things of the earth earthy which enter into the heart of man. This negative aspect of analysis needs emphasizing. The analyst does not bring illumination any more than the surgeon gives life. The surgeon removes what is obstructing the natural growth and functioning of the physical organism. He does not impart the power or impulse to live. Similarly, the analyst helps the patient to cut away the thick growth of weeds which is obscuring the light of day. But he does not claim to give that light. It comes, he would say, from within a man's own nature, or, as Christians would say, from God.

To St John of the Cross we could add the stories in the Synoptic Gospels of men possessed by demons. 'Let us alone; what have we to do with thee, thou Jesus of Nazareth? I know thee who thou art, the Holy One of God.' Here we are presented with a man who has reacted strongly to the analogies in terms of which the God of the Old Testament has been presented to him. This reaction has been driven underground as irrational and blasphemous. But in the end, it has been too strong for him and has destroyed his conscious personality. This allows his non-rational self full and virulent expression. Hence the words of hatred and resentment he cries out in the synagogue of Capernaum. What Freud showed us was that every one of us, in some degree or other, has this same demon lurking inside us. We use a great deal of our

[1] *Ibid.* book II, ch. 4, section 4.

energy keeping him in fetters. What follows is the dullness and deadness of many good Christian people.

The God, for instance, of the Book of Common Prayer seems sometimes to be a merciless egocentric tyrant, incapable of love, and thus having to be manipulated or cajoled into receiving his children. It is one thing to make a straightforward confession of sin as is done in the *Confiteor* at the beginning of the Roman Mass. It is another thing to harp continuously and at length upon our utter unworthiness to approach God, as is done in Cranmer's Communion Service.[1] The general confession, with its repeated and elaborate protestations of guilt, looks like a desperate attempt to persuade God to accept us on the score of our eating the maximum dust possible. Even after the absolution we are uncertain whether we have succeeded in our project. We must be reassured by four quotations from Scripture. The words of our Saviour Christ are not enough. They must be reinforced by what is said by St Paul and St John. This repeated affirmation of what is claimed as a certain fact indicates, and must often produce, doubt of its truth. One would not, for instance, in an airliner feel very comfortable if an announcement that all was well was made twice by the pilot, then by the wireless operator, then by the stewardess. One might be excused for fearing that something was seriously wrong. It is inevitable that what looks like Cranmer's deep lack of faith in God's mercy should communicate itself to many who use his liturgy, and should produce in them that spirit of bondage again unto fear from which Christ came to deliver us. This is all the more likely with the Prayer of Humble Access coming between the Sanctus and the Consecration Prayer. Unless, to the very last, we assure God of our unworthiness so much as to gather up the crumbs under his table, he may lock the dining-room door in our face. It is not being in any way denied that, on one level, Cranmer was an orthodox believing Christian. What is being suggested is that there lurked within him, along with his

[1] Cf. my article, 'Unchristian Liturgy' in *Theology* (October 1958), pp. 401–4.

belief in the Christian gospel, belief in a celestial Mr Pontifex, unloving and incapable of being loved, who must thus be manœuvred into giving his children what they need. This will not disturb those strong in faith. But it was for the little ones who believe in him that Christ was concerned. And who knows how many of them have been caused to stumble by our incomparably unchristian liturgy? If they were aware of the harm done them, it would matter less. But they are not. They cannot diagnose their servile attitude, their inability ever to presume anything good about themselves, as that which prevents them having life, and having it more abundantly.

III

One of the most important results of what we have been describing consists in a reassessment of moral values. Not, however, a radical or basic reassessment. Christians have always everywhere agreed that God is love, and that therefore generous self-giving love is the ultimate moral value. Where the reassessment is necessary is in our understanding of how and when we give ourselves and how and when we refuse to do so. This makes it impossible to describe certain actions as wicked and others as good. For only I myself can discover in what actions I am giving myself and in what actions I am refusing to give. Our Lord, for instance, gave himself by not escaping from martyrdom. St Cyprian, we may believe, would have been withholding himself had he not escaped from the Decian persecution. Or we could consider, as an extreme instance, the act of killing other people. Given certain circumstances, such as war, a man may be convinced that the only effective way in which he can give himself is to steel himself to the task of systematic killing. Another man, in the same circumstances, may be equally convinced that he can give himself effectively by refusing to kill. Or we can imagine circumstances when to steal would be a greater virtue than not to steal. One of the unemployed, before the days of social security, having appealed in vain to all quarters, might have stolen money from a rich man in order to feed his starving family. But suppose he had played a trick upon himself. He wanted to steal the money, but was too frightened to take the risk. He preferred starving his family to the disagreeable consequences which would follow the possible discovery of his theft. His motives show him to be withholding himself. But he can persuade himself that this is not the case. He can pose to himself as a moral man who keeps the commandments. The truth, however, is that what he thinks of as his morality is a disguise for cowardice.

A great deal of what Christians often call virtue, on closer inspection turns out to be cowardice of this kind—a refusal to give myself away because I am too frightened to do it. This is most obviously true in the sphere of sexual ethics, because here more than anywhere there seems to be an enormous amount of double-think. If I am to give myself away to another person, I cannot, in any circumstances, exploit her or him. To exploit is to withhold. It is totally incompatible with giving. But this is not at all the same thing as saying that in certain specifiable circumstances I must always be exploiting and never giving. Yet this is what the Church says about sexual intercourse outside marriage. Such intercourse may be often, perhaps almost always, an exploitation, unilateral or mutual. But there are cases where it need not be and isn't. Incidents in two recent films may be taken as examples. The first is a Greek film, *Never on Sunday*, about a prostitute in the Piraeus. She is picked up by a young sailor. In her room, he becomes afraid, nervous, and on edge. This is not because he thinks he is embarking on something wicked, but because he distrusts his capacity for physical union. He is a prey to destructive doubts about himself, not to moral scruples. The prostitute gives herself to him in such a way that he acquires confidence and self-respect. He goes away a deeper fuller person than he came in. What is seen is an act of charity which proclaims the glory of God. The man is now equipped as he was not before. Can Christians possibly say that devils were cast out of him by

Beelzebub the Prince of the devils? The second film is English—
The Mark. It tells of the rehabilitation into normality of a man
strongly attracted to small girls. His abnormality, which can do
nothing but untold harm to everybody, is due to his fear of commitment to an adult woman. However, in time, a woman of his own
age inspires him with enough confidence for them to go away for a
week-end together. They have separate rooms at the hotel. But it is
clear that until he sleeps with her he will not have established enough
confidence in himself to deliver him from his utterly destructive
abnormality which tends to exploitation to the nth degree. Will he be
able to summon up the necessary courage or not? When he does,
and they sleep together, he has been made whole. And where there
is healing, there is Christ, whatever the Church may say about
fornication. And the appropriate response is—Glory to God in the
Highest. Yet each of the men in these two films might have disguised
his fear by the cloak of apparent morality. Like the Pharisees in the
gospels and many good churchmen today, they might have been the
victims of unconscious hypocrisy, keeping the law as an insulation
against the living God, the Creator.

Must not all of us have the courage of Jesus and address ourselves
in his words—'It is written, but I say unto you'? The risk is admittedly appalling. But Our Lord warned us continuously that unless
we are prepared to risk everything, we shall never find our lives.

Freud showed us that evil consists of refusing to give through fear
masquerading as morality. What he tried to do was to enable his
patients to see through the masquerade. Only then would they be
in the position to make a truly moral choice. Freud never taught
that self-control of any kind led to illness, so long as people knew
what they were doing. He did, however, conclude that most of us do
not know what we are doing, and he claimed that God and his Law
were devices to enable us to keep ourselves in as much ignorance
as possible.

Christians must admit that this is often the case. But they can also claim that it follows from a failure to apprehend the true nature of the Christian gospel. The conscious reason may give its loyal assent to St Paul's discovery that we are justified by faith, not by works. At the same time, a man may in fact organize himself as if he were justified by his works. And this, according to Christian belief, is the essence of sin. For as Kierkegaard argued in his *Sickness unto Death*, the opposite of sin is not virtue, but faith. And it is the absence of faith which constitutes the fallen state of Adam. The state of original sin is the state of non-faith. By faith here is not meant intellectual assent to a number of doctrinal propositions. It could be defined as self-confidence, except that, as we shall see, the self in which confidence is placed could be the limited superficial self, and this would make self-confidence the very opposite of faith. Perhaps, therefore, a better definition would be confidence in life, the trustful attitude of a child belonging to a loving family. Faith is not a conviction, since a conviction is the result of an intellectual process concerned with assessing evidence. Faith, on the other hand, is intuitive. It is a given (not acquired) certainty that the forces on our side are greater than the forces opposed to us. In Christian language, this is faith in God. And faith in God can perhaps best be defined in the words of Julian of Norwich: 'He said not—"Thou shalt not be tempested, thou shalt not be travailed, thou shalt not be dis-eased": but he said: "Thou shalt not be overcome"'.[1]

A man shows his lack of faith in God by his lack of faith in himself as flowing from God's creative act. The result is that he is incapable of trusting most of what he is. He trusts only a small part of himself —the self of which he is aware, the self which he can control and organize by conscious acts of will. The rest is so suspect that it is driven out of the field of awareness. Hence the belief is generated that a man is no more than the self he knows. And it is from this identification of the known self with the total self that sin arises. We are not here thinking of acts committed, but of the general state or

[1] *Revelations of Divine Love*, edited by Grace Warrack (1949), p. 169.

6-2

condition in which man finds himself. Moral theologians have attempted to describe this state or condition under seven heads, conventionally called the seven capital or root sins—pride, gluttony, sloth, covetousness, anger, lust and envy. These are the seven colours used to paint the portrait of man as sinful. Examination will show that each of them is due to the non-faith which leads me to equate myself without remainder with what I already know or feel about myself. This non-faith is a denial of God's creativity. It is an attempt to find security in the limited me of which I am aware instead of in the unlimited me which issues continuously from the fount of Being, and of which I must be very largely unaware. Non-faith is total reliance upon what can be grasped and held by conscious reflexion and implemented by conscious acts of will. This is the bogus sovereignty claimed for a small part of himself by fallen Adam.

So pride, understood as the inordinate love of one's own excellence, is inevitable if a man identifies all he is with the self he knows and can therefore organize by conscious acts of will. For the self, so organized, is a man's own achievement. If, by the use of the appropriate mental exercises, I can make myself feel a miserable sinner, I cannot fail to feel satisfied with the result. For it is I who confess my unworthiness, and the I who thus confesses dissociates itself from the rest of what I am. Implicit is the claim that the real me is the me who disapproves of myself. This is the pride enthroned (but unseen) in fervid protestation of unworthiness. Look, it says, at the me who acknowledges it has nothing good to say of itself. Surely this me deserves acceptance, the miserable me to which I have striven successfully to reduce myself. On the other hand, the self of which I am aware lives under enormous strain. For, without acknowledging it, this self is continually threatened by energies and instincts of considerable violence which must at all costs be kept shut out. Hence the known self must boost itself, try to give itself strength, by claiming an excellence it does not possess. To the degree in which I am not aware of my full self, to that degree I fabricate an artificial self. Reliance upon this artificial self is the essence of pride. When I perceive its unreality, it seems that I have nothing left. That is why despair lies close to pride, and nemesis overtakes the arrogant. The fabricated artificial self is a broken reed. A man, for instance, may equate himself with his academic intelligence and ignore the rest of what he is. Such intelligence can cope with certain things in life. With regard to many other things, it is powerless. But the man thinks it can cope with everything. He ascribes to it an undue excellence and thus artificializes it. He makes of something real in its own sphere, something unreal by extending it beyond that sphere. He trusts his academic intelligence to establish and maintain a satisfying relation with his wife and children. This it cannot do. Thus he feels disillusioned and let down. He thinks it is the fault of the others, when in fact it is the result of his own pride, the concentration of his faith upon one single aspect of himself, which shows he is in a state of non-faith with regard to the rest of what he is—a condition which springs from his unbelief in God who creates and sustains his total being.

The other six root sins are analogous to pride, arising and maintaining their strength because of my incapacity to believe that I am more than the self I know. It is easy, for instance, to see how contemporary advertising aims at inciting gluttony by contracting self-awareness to very narrow limits, so that I may give as much notice as possible to this very narrow self. I begin to see myself as little more than a person for whom living is equated with the enjoyment of food and drink. Hence they begin to have enormous importance for me. Unless I eat and drink well, I feel I am not myself. For I have equated my being with my capacity to enjoy this particular type of sensory satisfaction.

Sloth is more complicated because it has a double motivation. It arises from despair with the self I know and from fear of the self I do not know. I despair of the self I know because it is intolerable to me to be only that. Life, I feel, must be more than what I experience, and yet, apparently, it is just this and nothing more. It is therefore like being confined in a tiny dungeon. My inertia or sloth is my attempt to deaden the pain of this frustration. It is a self-generated anaesthetic. On the other hand, what is unknown is fearful. We are frightened of it as children are frightened of the dark. When the unknown within us begins to make itself felt, we are profoundly disturbed. Supposing, for instance, I feel I have something important to say. The excitement I experience is double-edged. It is both satisfying and alarming. If the alarm predominates unduly, I shall not feel like getting down to articulate my ideas. It will seem to require too much effort for one who feels as tired as I do. I shall occupy myself with trivialities. Sloth will be my anaesthetic against fear. Laziness is always only a superficial symptom of a disease far more deeply rooted, and the disease is always my inability to realize more of myself than I do.

The spring from which covetousness arises can be illustrated from the story of Naboth's vineyard. Why did Ahab grasp after a small piece of land when in fact he was king of the whole country? Because, although his conscious reason told him he was king, he could not feel he was. There was a great deal within him which disbelieved in his kingship, not being susceptible to rational evidence and argument. He might have accepted the pain of thus having to harbour an alienated self which denied what he knew he was. It is arguable that, had he done so, the alien would have remained no longer an alien. By recognition and acceptance (together with the pain it would involve) the self which denied Ahab's kingship might have been brought to believe in it. But Ahab could not deliver the self he knew, the self who was king, into the hands of this unknown, alienated, disbelieving self. Instead he tried to reinforce his conscious reason by presenting it with fresh external evidence of his kingship. The possession of Naboth's vineyard seemed to be precisely the sort of evidence which was needed. So the possession

86

of the vineyard seemed an absolute necessity. That is why Ahab grasped after it with such fanatical eagerness, and was ready to go to any length in order to acquire it. It held out the promise of enabling Ahab to enter into his kingdom, of fully realizing himself as the king he was. But the promise was illusory. For external evidence of this kind can satisfy only the conscious mind. It has no power to impress or to convince the alienated, unknown self. So Ahab acquires the vineyard he coveted. But its possession does not bring the hoped-for reassurance. The king still cannot feel that he is king, and the appearance of Elijah in the vineyard merely confirms the king's doubt, echoing from outside him the smothered voices within which he refuses to recognize or listen to. All covetousness is an attempt to reassure the self I know, by means of external evidence, against the denials of the self I do not know. And the unknown self is not affected in the least by the fresh evidence acquired. So, coming into possession of what I covet, I am driven to covet something else. For my need is not my need of possessions, but my need of myself.

Anger has been defined as the emotional reaction of an irritated self-concern. Such anger is felt to be anger against the external—people or circumstances. In fact it is anger against myself. It arises from my inability to actualize my potential. The more a man is being his full self, the less likely is he to be angry. I lose my temper with my friend because I feel he is getting away with it, pretending to be this and that when he isn't, doing this and that when he has no right to. This, of course, may well be true of my friend. We are not concerned with his behaviour, but with my anger. Why do I lose my temper with him? Because he appears to me (correctly or not) to be actualizing more of his potential than I feel I can. He is a mirror in which I see reflected my own incapacity to realize anything like my full self. His behaviour goads me with my own extremely limited awareness of what I am. Ultimately, therefore, I am angry with myself, not with him. The same is true when I am angry with circumstances. Nobody can avoid necessity. Freedom consists in accepting it. If I do not possess the wings of a dove, my freedom consists in accepting this fact and thus growing into fullness with my feet on the ground. I may think I am angry because I do not possess the wings of a dove. But on closer inspection, the wings turn out to be no more than a fantasy I have constructed as a substitute for the articulation of what I have it in me to be. The fantasy is an attempt to solace myself for my incapacity to mobilize my potential. All longings for better circumstances are fantasies of this kind. My anger with the circumstances I have is anger with myself, as a person unable to be what he is. It is anger at my limited capacity to employ what I have it in me to be.

Lust is often understood as sheer physical appetite. But this is not so. Animals do not lust after each other, and, among people, there can be overwhelming physical pleasure without lust. Lust arises because it is impossible for me to live without a sense of my own value. Such a sense of my own value *is* living. Without it, I cannot live. But to the degree in which I am unaware of myself, to that degree I shall be incapable of realizing my own value. If most of what I am remains unknown to me, and I cannot believe that I am more than what I know, then the value I can give myself is not enough. There is a vacuum which, willy-nilly, must be filled. Hence the value which I cannot give myself from my own being, I try to steal for myself from somebody else. This attempt to snatch value for myself from somebody else is the essence of lust, and it is in the cause of this enterprise that the physical appetites are conscripted. It is mistaken to say that those appetites are in control. On the contrary they are under control, and what controls them is the me, unaware of what he is and thus incapable of giving himself value, and therefore desperately seeking value for himself from somebody else. It is in this way that the sinful soul (that is, the person unaware of his potential) makes the body corrupt. There is a profound and brilliant description of lust in Emily Brontë's *Wuthering Heights*. Catherine Earnshaw is not merely in love with Heathcliff. He is her absolute obsession. For her to live is Heathcliff. Through no fault of her own, she cannot be herself. What else then can she do but try to be herself by being Heathcliff? So she says to her old nurse—'Sometimes I think he is more myself than I am. Nellie, I *am* Heathcliff.' That is lust, and in terms of the story there was no physical intercourse or intimacy. Catherine was not enough aware of her potentialities to realize that she had it within herself to be a full person. Hence she imagines that it is only by identifying herself with Heathcliff that she can begin to approach an adequate sense of her own value. But, however attractively promising it may look in prospect, such identification is impossible. I can never be another person. I can only be myself. The practice of religion can be a form of lust, and here the physical appetites are hardly brought into play at all. First of all, I make an idol which I call Jesus of Nazareth or the Ascended Lord. Then I try to give myself value by identifying myself with the idol I have made. When the living me at times bursts through, and I become more than my own idol, I consider that I have sinned. When Swinburne wrote—'Thou hast conquered, O pale Galilean; the world has grown grey from thy breath', he was describing lust masquerading as Christianity.

Envy, like lust, is founded on my conviction that I lack something which the other person possesses. But, unlike lust, envy does not seek identification with the possessor. It recognizes that what he has can never be my own. Envy faces the absolute distinction between me and the other, and leads in consequence to bitterness. We can be envious about anything. But, in the end, what makes me bitter is my conjecture that the other person is more abundantly alive than I am. I feel that he has life in a way in which I have not. The ultimate cause, therefore, of my envy is my sense of not having life. This, in turn, is due to my being unable to believe that I am more than I know, and this inability to believe has the effect of confining my self-awareness to very narrow limits, if not of contracting it still more.

89

This brief analysis of the seven root sins shows how the opposite of sin can only be faith and can never be virtue. When I attempt to make myself virtuous, the me I can thus organize and discipline is no more than the me of which I am aware. And it is precisely the equation of my total self with this one small part of it which is the root cause of all sin. This is the fundamental mistake often made in exhortations to repentance and amendment. They attempt to confirm me in my lack of faith by getting me to organize the self I know against the self I do not know. The result is that growth in self-awareness is inhibited. There is a sort of devilish perversity in this organizing me not to sin by means of the very thing which ensures that I shall. Faith, on the other hand, consists in the awareness that I am more than I know. Such awareness came to the Prodigal when he realized that he was more than a starving swineherd. What led him home was his becoming aware that he was also his father's son. Yet this awareness did not take the form of an intellectual certainty. Maybe he had forfeited his status as a son. Yet his awareness of sonship was enough to make him journey homewards. As a result of the journey, his awareness grew until, amid the music and the dancing, he knew himself fully as a son of the house. Such faith cannot be contrived. If it were contrivable, if it were something I could create in myself by following some recipe or other, then it would not be faith. It would be works—my organizing the self I know. That faith can be only the gift of God emphasizes the scandal of our human condition—the scandal of our absolute dependence upon him. I have to depend completely upon what very largely I do not know and certainly cannot control. To the degree in which such dependence is realized and accepted, to that degree I shall be less on guard against myself. This will enable me to assimilate aspects of my being which hitherto I have kept at arm's length. My awareness of what I am will grow, and the more it grows the less shall I be the slave of sin. An unwanted child in a slum will be aware of little else about himself than his instincts of survival and self-preservation. He seems to himself to be no more than those instincts. To trust or implement any other aspects of himself would seem to him to be courting destruction. So it does not occur to him that they exist. Adopted into a loving family, he discovers that he is capable of generosity. He becomes aware of an aspect of himself hitherto unknown to him. The faith generated by the atmosphere in which he lives allows him to recognize, and to act upon, those generous instincts of which formerly he was so frightened as not to see. What he once felt as a destructive enemy is now apprehended as adding to the joy and abundance of life, no longer to be kept at bay, but to be welcomed and entertained.

Freud showed us the fallacy which Greville described in his famous line—'Created sick, commanded to be sound'. He showed that the sickness was due to the claim of the conscious self to be the whole man and thus to keep the rest in absolute subservience, alienated and unknown. It is this oppressor within which issues the commands. To enlist his support in an act of liberation is self-defeating. It is to ensure that I continue alienated from myself. Freud saw in Christianity a weapon placed in the hand of the oppressor which he would use to continue and consolidate his absolute power under cover of the most respectable disguise. Many or most Christians use their Christianity for this purpose sometimes, perhaps often. Otherwise they would not continue to be proud, to covet, and the rest. So far Freud was right. What, however, eluded him was that genuine Christianity is in fact an unqualified protest against any attempt thus to reinforce the oppressor within.

This, to begin with, was the basis of Christ's quarrel with the Pharisees. Modern research has shown that the typical Pharisee was not a pious fraud. He was upright, conscientious and God-fearing, and certainly not given to conscious hypocrisy. But he attempted to make himself and others good by using God and the Law as an ally for the self which he could control and organize by conscious acts of will. This maintained and increased a division in the personality.

Thus, to take the examples used in the Sermon on the Mount, the
Pharisee could prevent himself from committing murder and adultery, and such self-control generated the illusion that he was whole
and had no need of the physician. Jesus pricked the bubble of this
consciously sincere pretension, by pointing to men's anger and their
lust. I can no more help feeling angry or lustful than I can help
feeling hungry. Jesus here concentrates attention upon an area of
my being over which I have no control, an area which can be conveniently forgotten when clothed with the cloak of good behaviour.
If, he says, I feel anger or lust it shows that I am by no means whole
without need of the physician. It shows that I am a house divided
against itself which cannot stand. If, therefore, my righteousness
consists only in the keeping of the commandments, I cannot enter
into the Kingdom of God. For such entry into the Kingdom I must
have a righteousness which exceeds that of the Pharisees. And this
righteousness cannot be contrived by the efforts of my known self.
It is the gift of God, to be compared with the wind which bloweth
where it listeth and of which nobody knows whence it cometh or
whither it goeth. The farmer does not know how the seed springs
up and grows. 'For the earth bringeth forth fruit of herself; first the
blade, then the ear, after that the full corn in the ear.' Nor does the
woman know how the leaven works in the flour. She waits until the
whole is leavened, and so is the Kingdom of God. Hence, too, the
labourers in the vineyard all receive the same wages. The effort put
in bears no relation to the resultant wage. The wage depends upon
something over which the labourers have no control—the goodwill
of the lord of the vineyard. So we shall not enter into the Kingdom
of God unless we are prepared to receive it like little children; and
it belongs to children to receive what they are without artifice or
manipulation or attempts at disguise. (It is only the child artificial-
ized by adverse circumstances who is on guard against life.) The
teaching of Jesus about riches conveys the same message. This teaching was touched off by material riches. But Jesus must have seen a

spiritual principle in the material fact, or else why did he hammer the point home to disciples who were all materially poor? My riches are the self I build and organize and master and manipulate. The rich man inside me is the self I know, bent on dominating and oppressing the rest of what I am. When I imagine I have good reason to pin my faith on this self and trust it to see me through all eventualities, then it is easier for a camel to go through the eye of a needle than for me, so organized, to enter into the Kingdom of God. For a man's life does not consist in the abundance of the things which he possesses, and of such possessions the me into which I have made myself is the most important. Hence the first beatitude—'How blest are those who know that they are poor; the kingdom of Heaven is theirs'. Self-awareness leads to the discarding of the illusion that the self who lords it over my unknown potentialities is rich in any finally important sense. When I know that as a person I have to rely on what in me is unknown and thus beyond my contrivance or control, then I also know that I am poor, and the Kingdom of Heaven is mine. The bogusly rich man inside me is also the strong man armed, keeping his goods and his palace in peace. He must be overcome by a stronger than he who will take from him all his armour wherein he trusted and divide his spoil. Far from the Kingdom of God being the ally of the strong man armed, it vanquishes him and divests him of his sovereignty. For, 'whosoever he be of you that forsaketh not all that he hath, he cannot be my disciple'. And my most cherished possession is the self I make by expropriating, and being unwilling to admit the very existence of, large tracts of my being which God is thus creating in vain.

There is ample evidence in the gospels that Jesus recognized that men were the prisoners of what they would describe as their best selves. Much of his teaching was concerned to explode the pretensions of this oppressive tyrant, and in his place to evoke an attitude of trustful receptivity to life, that is, to a me which is mysterious and unknown. The very form of his teaching worked to this end. The language of logical argument and abstract concepts confirms the oppressor in his tyranny. Such language, because it can be mastered and the significance of its statements exhaustively understood, is one of the chief weapons in the armoury of the self I know. On the other hand, the language of parable and poetry and concrete image eludes the familiar thinking mind with its technique of putting two and two together, and leaves it asking—'What does the parable mean? How can it be converted into the abstract concepts which can be fully defined and exhaustively understood?' 'What is this that he saith—A little while? We cannot tell what he saith.' 'And they were all amazed, insomuch that they questioned among themselves, saying, What thing is this? What new doctrine is this?' For the language of concrete imagery, eluding the self I know, is capable of speaking to and thus evoking a self of which I have hitherto been unaware. And it is often in this way that the strong man armed is conquered and spoiled of his armour.

St Paul and St John continue the attacks made by Jesus upon the restless, scheming, anxious pretensions of the conscious self. Justification by faith means that a man has nothing else on which to depend except his receptivity to what he can never own or manage. And this very capacity to receive cannot be the result of effort. Faith is something given, not something achieved. It is created by God's word in Christ. St John speaks of being born of the Spirit which can be controlled no more than the wind. And he insists that no man can come to Christ except the Father draw him. And the Father draws a man by the spectacle of Christ dying and dead. If the works of Jesus are seen as masterly assertions of his human will, they are misunderstood. For in fact they speak of his entire dependence on what is not his to exploit and manage. They look forward to and anticipate the surrender in death of all he owns.

However Christians may have used their Christianity there is abundant evidence in the New Testament that the Christian gospel, far from boosting the pretensions of the known and controllable self, seeks its subservience to a trustful confidence in a God who is creating what I am by means of which I am unaware.

IV

Here, briefly, are three further illustrations of how self-awareness can contribute to our understanding of Christian truth. They are brief because their aim is not to provide a comprehensive corpus of information like the lecture-notes which less intelligent undergraduates try to learn before their examinations, but to suggest possible lines of thought and inquiry which might be given fullness by the reader's own experience.

The first is concerned with the very centre of our faith and love—Christ in Gethsemane and upon the Cross. Here we are confronted with divine mystery to be adored, and, unless we worship, we shall apprehend nothing. But, from the first, Christians spoke of Christ taking sin upon himself. 'He who knew no sin, God made to be sin on our behalf' (II Cor. v. 21). Unfortunately, however, the notion of Christ as the sin-bearer has long since been conventionalized and thus fails to quicken us. A new approach, therefore, is demanded. And it may be that the general point of view of this essay may help to stir the imagination of some people. The root of sin, as we have seen, is the identification of my total self with the self of which I am aware. Two consequences follow from this identification. First of all, the known self is too narrow to be satisfyingly me and is felt in its constriction to be intolerable. Secondly, the unknown self which, for mistaken reasons of security, I keep imprisoned and in exile, becomes a savage as the result, like a man locked for life in a dark dungeon seeing nobody. What follows is not only inner conflict—the known self fighting to maintain his ascendancy against the en-savaged prisoner beating on the door of his dungeon. The situation from which the inner conflict arises produces a sense of absolute loss of value. Generally we can disguise this from ourselves. Indeed, a great deal of our activity is ultimately motivated (although we do not see it) by this very purpose—to disguise from ourselves our sense of our complete non-value. For this sense is not only death. It is worse than death. It is the final catastrophic horror. In comparison it is easy to die, especially for a cause of whose value we are assured like those, for instance, who voluntarily gave their lives in the Spanish Civil War. Such, at least, has been the testimony given by eye-witnesses to many martyrs to many ideals. The martyrdom of St Stephen, for instance, at once comes to mind. In the light of the Easter faith, we know Jesus to have given his life for the greatest of all causes, the salvation of mankind. But this does not appear to be what he felt in Gethsemane—'Horror and dismay came over him, and he said to them, "My heart is ready to break with grief; stop here, and stay awake"'—nor upon the cross when he cried aloud 'My God, my God, why hast thou forsaken me?'. It is possible that we may be given a glimpse of the inner reality of his passion if we consider it as a total loss on his part of all sense of his own value due to his oneness with mankind in its inward conflicts. When such loss occurs, it is natural to look for consolation from friends. But a Peter, a James, and a John cannot supply from without what has been taken away from within. They cannot but be asleep to the agonizing need, however genuine their goodwill. And, meanwhile, when there is a total loss of the sense of one's own value, there emerge, as an attempt at distraction, blind hatred and rage, all the worse for their having no consistent target. And then follows despair, not as a passive state of quiescence, but as something which hurls itself against a brick wall and cries aloud to the empty air. If this is a possible and legitimate way of approaching the mystery of Christ's passion, it shows us something of the meaning of the atonement he wrought. It does not speak of crimes and judges and punishments and acquittals. It speaks indeed of justice. For 'He (God) made us; He maintained us in our pain. At least, however, on the Christian showing, He consented to be Himself subject to it. If, obscurely,

He would not cease to preserve us in the full horror of existence, at least He shared it. He became as helpless as we under the will which is He. This is the first approach to a sense of justice in the whole situation.'[1] But it speaks of more than justice. It speaks of change and transfiguration. Christ's total loss of the sense of his own value, which is ten thousand times worse than physical pain or death, was the stuff and substance which God raised up in glory. In Christ, God made it into the material of a full and infinitely satisfying communion with all that is. In Christ, God took inward agony and rage and torture, and made of them eternal life which is eternal love. It is thus perhaps that we may consider the atonement he wrought in the death and resurrection of his Son. When we ourselves suffer these things, it is with Christ we suffer them. And because this is so, although the pain continues, we know it also as the glory of God.

> Who then devised the torment? Love.
> Love is the unfamiliar Name
> Behind the hands that wove
> The intolerable shirt of flame
> Which human power cannot remove.[2]

In Christ God converted the destructive fire of our human agony into the living and life-giving flame which is himself. The former contributes to and is made part of the latter. So the agony itself can now be seen in its change and transfiguration as the gift of his love. It is not therefore a surprise that many of the saints displayed symptoms of a psychopathological kind. St Paul's sudden blindness on the road to Damascus was the physical consequence of a profound psychic disturbance. It was one of the ways in which, for a period, he bore on his body the marks of Jesus.

Secondly, something may be said briefly about forgiveness —whether it be God's forgiveness of us or our forgiveness of each other. We are not here concerned with lexicographical studies of what the word means in the New Testament, but with our awareness

---

[1] Charles Williams, *Selected Writings*, chosen by Anne Ridler, p. 95.
[2] T. S. Eliot, *Little Gidding*, IV.

of ourselves as forgiven and forgiving. When I say that God forgives me, I generally mean that he accepts me, without reservation, as I am. He accepts the me who, because he is only part of himself and equates this part with the whole, is ugly, distorted, and subject (though largely unaware of it) to compulsive actions—that is, actions which, although rationalized ably enough, are in fact attempts to preserve at all costs my limited awareness of what I am. Forgiveness means that God accepts me thus, just as I am. But can this fundamental truth of the Christian gospel be more fully described? Perhaps it can be said that God accepts me just as I am because he sees that in fact I am not just this. Perhaps he can be described as seeing below the surface of my superficial self (which I consider the whole) to an underneath where lie the materials from which a being in his image and likeness are waiting for construction. And perhaps this may illuminate St Paul's idea of Christ in us, or better, Christ being formed in us. In short, when God forgives me, he receives the self of which I am unaware. His reception of the self of which I am aware is only a necessary stage in a therapeutic process. It opens me out to what I am. Certainly this is what happens in human relations. When I act compulsively (for example, lose my temper with my friend) nothing restores me to goodness and love so effectively as his refusal to believe that the me who lost my temper is anything but a superficial and unimportant aspect of my full self. Forgiveness is rooted in this conviction. Without it, there can be no forgiveness. I cannot sincerely welcome a serpent to my bosom, but only a man temporarily strangled by a serpent. All forgiveness, God's and man's, must be rooted in truth.

The final illustration of how self-awareness may contribute to theological understanding will be received by many with greater difficulty than the preceding two. For it concerns Our Lady, and the average religious Englishman feels embarrassed when she is mentioned. 'Devotional manifestations in honour of Our Lady... are suitable for Italy, but they are not suitable for England' as

Newman observed in his *Apologia*.[1] It is a pity. For since both the Roman Catholic and Eastern Orthodox Churches pay her great honour, there is little chance of moving forward towards the reunion of Christendom until those who belong to other Churches are willing to cease either ignoring her altogether (as do most of the Protestant Churches) or treating her as a poor relation it is tactful not to mention (which is the average Anglican attitude). Here no attempt will be made to identify her place in the scheme of salvation. This essay is not concerned with theological argument of that kind. Rather, we shall try to understand what it is that the figure of Our Lady supplies to the majority of Christians. What, from the point of view of human feeling, is the secret of her influence? In case those who love and honour her should consider such an approach irreverent, the writer would like to say that he himself believes her to be truly the Mother of God, and, like numberless Christian believers, asks for her prayers.

As we saw at the beginning of this essay, God cannot be directly described, but only indirectly indicated by analogies drawn from our human experience. However true it may be that the description of God as Father has the highest authority (it was used by Our Lord), a man's human experience is bound to colour his reactions to God as Father in those areas of his being not subject to the discriminatory control of his discursive reason. In consequence, the figure of God the Father may become a destructive idol. It could, for instance, be argued that this happened to a limited extent in the religious feelings of Calvin and Cranmer and, with regard to the latter, we have already observed the shadow of this idol upon the Communion Service in the Book of Common Prayer. It simply therefore will not do to say that in ignoring Our Lady we safeguard ourselves against idolatry. We are free, therefore, to continue our investigation. What, from the point of view of human feeling, accounts for the hold upon Christians of the figure of Our Lady?

[1] 1946 ed., p. 131.

In himself, God is no more a father than he is a mother. To those, like us, who do not begin to climb the summits reached by a St John of the Cross or a St Teresa of Avila, God's divine love is transmitted to us by means of our experience of human love. This human love, if it is to be properly proportioned, must be both masculine and feminine. If our love is to grow into balanced maturity, we must first be loved by both a mother and a father (or those who fill their place). Parental love, if it is to convey God's love to us, must be a sacrament in two kinds. Since God's love is transmitted to us by both and is the source of both, it was natural that attempts should be made to think of and worship God, not only as our father but as our mother. In the eleventh century, for instance, one of the greatest Archbishops of Canterbury, St Anselm, encouraged devotion to the Motherhood of God.[1] But God the Herm-Aphrodite is an emotional impossibility. It cannot but produce the most defeating confusion of feeling. Thus this type of devotion had no future and was quickly forgotten. It had nothing in human experience on which to fasten. The grotesque cannot evoke love. Hence the importance ascribed from early days to Our Lady. She is the symbol of that aspect of God's love which can be conveyed to us only by means of a feminine analogy. And this may well be what St John had in mind in the word from the cross—'Behold thy mother'. If the function of Our Lady in transmitting to us that element of God's love which the father-symbol cannot convey could be recognized, Protestants might be more willing to receive her. It could be argued that her absence can sometimes have bad results in the formation of personality. Reliable statistics are impossible to obtain, for few open their hearts sincerely to the social investigator. But it is conceivable that the absence in a culture of a friendly woman-symbol (in other words, in atmospheres where the fullness of God's love is not getting through) makes it more difficult for men to grow into emotional maturity. Certainly the goddesses of ancient Greece do not disprove

[1] See David Knowles, *The English Mystical Tradition* (1961), p. 128.

the suggestion. For they were capricious, often terrifying, and very far from good. They might well generate that fear of woman which leaves a man no option but to love his own (to him) less forbidding sex. But in Christian devotion, Our Lady has never been a forbidding figure. Always she has been associated with that love and understanding in which women excel. Freud himself, of course, as a Jew, was brought up in an entirely father-ridden religion. Could his description of religion as a psycho-pathology be partly attributable to that fact?

One further suggestion is worth making. Freud would certainly not have believed in the Immaculate Conception of Our Lady. But he did show us that a man fully and perfectly developed would have to have had a perfect mother. For Freud no such man had ever existed. Christians have always believed that Our Lord went through a normal human development, and that in him manhood came to its full and perfect expression. The Roman Church, in declaring Our Lady to have been born without taint of original sin, gave expression in a theological idiom to what Freud later discovered in his consulting-room—the overwhelming influence for good or bad which a mother has upon her infant and child.

This essay is no more than a number of concrete examples of how the new insights which Freud originated and others have carried on with this or that degree of agreement or disagreement with him, both pose problems to the theologian and suggest possible roads to an answer.

SYNOPSIS

I. Christians single out the Bible rather than, say, the *Bhagavadgītā* as authoritative. But why? We cannot any longer be isolationist, ignoring the claims of Eastern religions. It is true that some modern theology encourages us to be culturally parochial, despite contemporary revolts against dogmatism. The modern predicament poses the problem of the tests of truth in religion as between one faith and another. Its solution requires that we should gain as unbiased a knowledge of other faiths as is possible.

II. Consider the two great presuppositions of belief in Christ's divinity, namely belief in a personal God and in the importance of history. Regarding the first, Theravada Buddhism is challenging, since it is agnostic. Further, an influential form of Hinduism places the Absolute above the idea of a personal Creator. As to the second presupposition, the Judaeo-Christian view of history fits in with the doctrine of personal creation, and is suggested by Evolutionary Theory. Rejecting rebirth, moreover, weakens the cyclical view found in Hinduism and Buddhism. But such reasons in support of the presuppositions are 'soft' rather than 'hard' and clear-cut.

III. Now we can discuss Christ. The logic of theism, *via* the notion of sin and the need for expiation and sacrifice, moves in the direction of belief in the Incarnation and away from Hindu ideas of multiple incarnations. But it is not in place here to discuss actual historical evidences, partly because historical investigation *by itself*, that is, without presuppositions, does not yield hard facts about the nature and career of Christ.

These remarks indicate that other faiths contain truth and that Christian theology needs translating as far as possible into existing Eastern concepts.

I

WHEN THEOLOGIANS and preachers tell a man to hold fast to revelation, he may become distracted. Which way is he to turn? To the *Upanishads*, to the *Lotus of the Good Law*? No, these were not the books his mentors had in mind. Besides, revelation does not equal Scriptures. The Scriptures describe encounters between the Beyond and men, and it is such encounters that revelation essentially consists in. So when we are told to hold fast to revelation, we are being asked to meditate upon and to respond to the living experiences which faith can bring. But what experiences? The sudden enlightenment of Zen, the theophany vouchsafed to Arjuna in the *Bhagavadgītā*? A Christian theologian will not be thinking of these events. For one thing, the encounters (he will say) occur in and through history. But what history? That of the Aryans sweeping into the Indus valley and thereby causing that great mingling and jumbling of cultures and insights which we call Hinduism? That of the Muslims exploding into Asia and Europe? That of the distant Chinese? Christian theologians will scarcely be talking about such histories: they will be thinking of the Jews, of the Apostle Paul, of Constantine—and thereafter they will be thinking from within the parochial context of European history.

Part of the reason for this apparently narrow outlook is the fault of our schools and universities. But part is due to the way history has run. For many centuries the world was thought to consist roughly in the Roman Empire plus the so-called barbarians surrounding it; and Europe and part of the Middle East constituted a separate unit more or less cut off from the wider world. Even when that wider world was opened up, the isolationism of Europeans continued to express itself in a depreciation of the cultural and other achievements of the great Eastern civilizations, and a people nurtured on Christian orthodoxy failed to see much virtue in the religions which prevailed in distant lands.

But now things are changed, and our cultural isolationism is steadily crumbling. For now, through the devoted work of translators and commentators, and through the personal experience of those who have come into contact with other faiths, we have a far better understanding of their central teachings than our Victorian fathers ever had. But understanding may bring doubts about Christianity, for the simple reason that if we are asked to accept a revelation, it is much easier if it has no worthy rivals.

It is therefore singularly unfortunate that the type of theology that has made the greatest impact in the West outside the Roman Catholic Church in recent years is essentially isolationist. Barth's theology, of course, enshrines a great idea. Its very strength makes it retain a grip upon our thinking. At one stroke it removed our intellectual worries about the alleged unreasonableness of Christianity in a modern age and rationalized our biblical studies. Since metaphysics is useless or dangerous (for man's reason too is fallen), the attack upon it by modern philosophers could be received with equanimity. There has thus been a holy conspiracy between theology and A. J. Ayer. Where there can be no metaphysical conclusions, there can be no metaphysical doubts, and the man of intellect can keep his reason for more mundane tasks. Again, the slow undermining of fundamentalism left many in doubt, especially in the Protestant fold. For what kind of authority could the Bible possess if it were not to be taken pretty literally? And yet literally it is sometimes wrong. The new view of revelation as something which does not consist in so many propositions uttered somehow by God, but as God's self-disclosure, cut at the root of these doubts. For such reasons the new theology is refreshing. But it nevertheless is parochial and isolationist.

And why? Simply because, in its repudiation of reasons, it

presents its apologia for Christianity through a false dichotomy. It says: 'Faith comes from God: turn to revelation', as though the only live option were the choice between agnosticism and Christ. But in turning from agnosticism to faith there are many directions in which one can go.

Those who have been brought up in the small world of Europe will perhaps see only these two alternatives. But there are other living faiths apart from Christianity. And among thinking people who have some acquaintance with these other spiritual systems, there is an increasing trend towards the East. Zen, for instance, while much misunderstood among beatniks, has a powerful attraction for those who cannot bring themselves intellectually to a belief in God in the Christian sense. Vedanta too has its magnetism. It would be salutary for most Christians to read, in a dispassionate way, *What Vedanta Means to Me*,[1] in which sixteen people (mostly intelligent) give their reasons for embracing this Eastern faith. Some of them find the dogmatism of Christianity distasteful, and so echo the reaction of many Orientals. They can hardly be comforted if theology remains parochial and isolationist.

Let us transport ourselves in our imaginations to some Eastern country. Somewhere distantly to the north-west there is a little place called Palestine, and further off is Europe, glittering with automobiles. Here, in our Eastern spot, we are being asked to think of history in terms of Israel and Europe, to listen to St Augustine on the City of God trying to impose a pattern on that history. But where can the Buddha fall into that pattern? What are we to say of Asoka, the Constantine of Buddhism? Confucius and Lao-Tze: are these to be ignored? Though being chosen as a people is scarcely to be regarded as a privilege, the scandal of particularity is seen with redoubled force in Madura and Saigon.

If, then, we abandon biblical fundamentalism and interpret revelation in terms of encounters, we cannot simply ignore the

[1] Ed. John Yale (1961).

encounters which have been enshrined in the best traditions of the non-Christian religions. Yet this approach seems to leave us in a predicament. If we are so catholic in our range of appreciation, how can we know what is true and what is not? If the Buddha based his teachings upon personal experience, how can we say that they are wrong? How can we presume to judge so intimate a matter? And why should the Christian set up his own teaching as somehow superior? Superiority seems both unjustifiable and distasteful.

Our reaction to this predicament can easily take the following form. We can become hyper-protestants, and not Christian ones at that. People read the *Bhagavadgītā* and the Buddhist scriptures and they think:

These writings have something good to say; and yet religions are quarrelsome, and enshrine their quarrels in external differences. Perhaps the great teachers of the past have been misunderstood, and their teachings corrupted by fierce monks and Brahmins and churches. There must be an underlying, even esoteric, truth concealed beneath the externals—externals which form a screen between man and the Transcendent. This inner truth is the Perennial Philosophy, the true heart of all good religion; and the various 'religions' represent so many obstacles to the unity and liberation of mankind. Yet, if rightly understood, the various 'religions' may be used as so many paths to the Transcendent. They are all false, and they are all true.

This is the ultimate in religious protestantism, but it has lost any specifically Christian flavour.

It forms part of the attraction of intellectual Hinduism, of the attempts to produce the grand synthesis which will bring together and justify all faiths. The appeal to experience and encounter may issue, then, in this tolerant doctrine. Despair about the criteria of truth leads to an acceptance of all claims. The fundamental unity of all religions is the answer, the way out of our predicament. Or so it seems.

The hyper-protestantism which I have described may rest partly on the assumption that there cannot be tests of truth in religion, as between one faith and another. But though it is hard and invidious and disturbing to seek for such tests, the attempt should be made, before we come to such tolerant conclusions. But we shall probably find that any tests that there are do not operate with obvious clarity, that they are fuzzy and hard to apply, that there is no clear-cut way of saying 'This is true and that is false'. In this sense, dogmatism must perish. And this may be disturbing.

But the new world in which we are living, the East-West world, is bound to be disturbing. And further, religion is in some measure a mystery. Those who expect clear-cut tests of truth are looking at the Transcendent as though it is only a little higher than the angels. Maybe it is rather saddening for the divine consciousness to note the arrogance of those who take everything literally, who 'know' all the secrets of the heavenly realm, who presume to lay down precise rules for interpreting the structure of sacred reality.

It might further be objected that the idea of seeking the tests of truth among the great religions is un-Christian, since God judges us and not we him. Christ is the canon of truth, and the other religions must be judged in that light. Yet this objection sounds like a re-emergence of that dogmatism and isolationism which I have already attacked. But in any case if we want to follow Christ we must make him intelligible to those brought up in other faiths, and this already means talking their language to some degree. But to talk their language is in part to appeal to tests of truth which they themselves will at least recognize as relevant. We cannot, even as missionaries, escape from the modern predicament.

It may also be complained that this lays an intolerable burden upon us. Rightly to tackle the problem we have to know a lot about Hinduism, Buddhism, Islam and so forth. But Christian theology is complex enough already and the source of a flood of books (many of them, alas, in German). Is it not unbearable that we have to swell our reading-lists so, to widen our circle of acquaintance so and to expand so the time we need for reflection? This complaint is partly just; but we must recall the good authority we have for regarding the division of labour as a pattern for church organization.

Not everyone, obviously, can have the time and inclination to investigate these matters in detail. But all thinking Christians should realize the importance and general nature of the problem.

There is a last objection which I need to consider. Isn't our interpretation of other faiths bound to be coloured by Christianity? So how can we ever hope to give a fair appraisal of these religions from their own point of view? And if we cannot be genuinely fair, the exercise of trying to find tests of truth which could at least be accepted as being relevant to other faiths is pointless and uncandid. Maybe so. But though bias may not be completely eliminable, there are degrees. We must endeavour as far as possible to be warmly dispassionate.

Not long since a delightful lady missionary was driving me to a hospital not far from Banaras. We passed a shrine, and she remarked: 'I'm always very sad to see the piety with which these Hindus worship at that shrine.' I asked why. 'Well,' she said, with a sort of simple finality, 'there's no one there to hear them.' I was startled, for I wouldn't have thought about it in that way. A lot of other people would not either.

II

The investigation of the tests of truth can conveniently start from the problem of the historical nature of Christianity. We are inclined to think as follows: 'Whereas other religions have, no doubt, some insight into the Transcendent, Christianity is uniquely rooted in history. The Buddha was no doubt a supremely wise and holy man; but Christ *did* certain things, in a concrete historical situation. History, thereby, demonstrates the truth of Christianity, in a way in which it does not in regard to other faiths.'

But first, the Christian account of the events of Christ's life is not simply dictated by the evidence which we have. Far from it; for the strange nature of the events means that the historian's conclusions will depend to a considerable extent upon his presuppositions. These include belief in a personal God and a view about the importance of history. But these beliefs are absent from some important non-Christian traditions. Given the beliefs, the events of the Bible may fall into place. But without them, they hardly have the great significance claimed for them. In short, historical investigation by itself scarcely shows that Christianity is true.

Second, the events of the New Testament, even if they were established beyond any shadow of doubt (which they are not), are not quite commensurate with the cosmic conclusions that are based upon them. Christ's rising from the dead does not entail his divinity as defined in the Creeds. So the sympathetic Hindu may feel: 'This truly was a great man, of vast spiritual power; but he is best regarded as one among the great teachers of the world, not as *uniquely* manifesting the Transcendent.'

Of the two great presuppositions of Christian history, the more important, clearly, is belief in a personal God. But it is precisely at this point that Hindu and Buddhist objections are most likely to be raised. This fact is sufficiently startling to justify my saying a lot about it. For how often do we read (especially in old-fashioned books) that some kind of belief in God is to be found in all cultures? And haven't we comforted ourselves in days of doubt by the thought that the great majority of men have believed, in some sense, in God? Can this almost universal testimony be utterly without foundation? Such is the way we have been brought up to think.

But wrongly. For one great wing of Buddhism, the Theravada—that form of belief which prevails in Ceylon, Burma and South-east Asia—is agnostic about a personal Creator. Not only, according to the Pali scriptures, was the Buddha deeply troubled by the problem of evil, so that a good God became incredible to him; but further he looked on certain questions as meaningless and incapable of a proper answer: a metaphysics of the Transcendent is impossible, on his view. This tradition, seeing its central truth in nirvana, the abode of peace beyond the round of rebirth, and not in God or the Absolute, has flourished for some two and a half thousand years. It constitutes a living stream of religious experience. So we cannot shrug it off as an unimportant deviation into absurdity. Nor can we castigate it as an element in the lunatic fringe which almost invariably surrounds religion. Nor can we dismiss it (as some may be inclined to do) by saying that it is a philosophy, not a religion. For it is obviously not a philosophy in the way (say) logical empiricism is, though it may include such a philosophy. Buddhism merits being called a religion not merely because ordinary folk in the Theravadin countries tend to worship the gods and even (mistaking the doctrine) the Buddha; but far more importantly because the centre of the faith, nirvana, is something ultimately given in the experience of peace and insight, and because this experience merits comparison with that of the great contemplatives of other traditions. Only here, the experience is stripped of all but the minimal interpretation. There is no question here, among such Buddhists, of its being interpreted as union with a personal God, nor even as a merging into the Absolute, as some Hindu teachers would say. All that we have is the teaching that in some sense nirvana is a transcendent state.

It cannot therefore be said that there is any explicit belief, in Theravada Buddhism, in a personal God. Nor again can it justly be said that there is such an implicit belief—not, at least, if we look at the matter from the Theravadin point of view, for nobody within that tradition would accept that nirvana *really is* an experience of God. Christians might perhaps feel that in his own way the Buddhist saint does have some kind of vision of God. But this is not a view which can be derived from the Theravadin tradition itself. And nothing is more nauseating than that kind of apologetic which presumes to tell the other fellow what he 'really means', however strenuously he may deny it. Unfortunately, it is a theological ploy often used. It is like a Tory telling a Socialist that he really means by Welfare State a system of capitalist enterprise.

One main stream of Hindu thought and religion, moreover, while not denying belief in a personal God, relegates it firmly to second place. The highest truth is that there is one Ultimate Reality, and the world as we know it is illusory, an enchanting show which we mistake for the ultimate Reality. The religious quest is summed up in the words of the Upanishad 'Lead me from the unreal to the real'. There are, then, two levels of truth: truth about the Absolute and truths about the world, which have only a provisional and secondary significance. Belief in a personal Creator belongs to the second level, for the Creator of an illusory world shares in its illusoriness. Thus within religion itself there are two levels of truth; and the lower truth concerns a personal God who is the object of worship, adoration and prayer.

Therefore, many Hindus, and many Westerners who have embraced Vedanta, consider the Christian belief in God acceptable but secondary, true but not in the highest way, spiritual, but a sign of incomplete spiritual development. Again, it is through contemplation, which brings identification with the Absolute, that the highest truth is realized. In this the Theravada and Vedanta are at one.

But how could anyone know which of these religious systems—Christianity, Buddhism, Vedanta—is true? What tests would we apply? But before we can answer these questions it is necessary to be clear about their inner relation to religious experience. The interpretation of the great religions from this point of view which I would offer is, briefly, as follows.[1]

Theravada Buddhism is essentially a mystical religion. That is to say, it concentrates upon the contemplative experience which constitutes the assurance of nirvana. It eschews other complications. It refuses to commit itself to an interpretation of the Transcendent in personal terms. Thereby it repudiates devotion and worship as these are understood in the Judaeo-Christian tradition. The great

---

[1] This interpretation I have attempted to justify in detail in *Reasons and Faiths* (1958) and more informally in *A Dialogue of Religions* (1960).

numinous experiences of the Prophets which had such an explosive impact upon the Jews have no place or significance in the Theravadin tradition. And without genuine worship and without the experience of the numinous as a central element the Theravada has no special reason to sacrifice its essential simplicity for the complications and difficulties of a doctrine of God. In short, it centres on mysticism, but mysticism without God.

This analysis implies that we can distinguish fairly clearly between two main kinds of religious experience—the prophetic and the mystical. The religion of the holy is associated above all with the former type of experience, while mysticism may or may not be linked to such a religion of worship. I think that anyone who considers the experiences of the Prophets (not to mention Muhammad) and St Paul on the one hand, and those of Eckhart, St Teresa, the Buddha and the Sufis on the other, will recognize a difference in atmosphere which is sufficient to place them in different categories.

Thus the Hindu doctrine which I outlined can be characterized as reflecting both these strands of experience, but in such a way that the contemplative intuition of the Absolute is given overwhelming priority over the experience of the personal, holy Being.

Thus, from the Christian point of view, both Buddhism and this form of Hinduism involve an under-valuing of the experience of the personal Lord in favour of the more impersonal bliss and peace of contemplation. Once the problem is stated in this way, the main question about the truth of the rival systems becomes this: 'Which form of priority is correct?' Given that there are these two strands of experience, should we prefer those doctrines which place the Personal at the centre of the Transcendent and which interpret contemplation in terms thereof, or should we prefer those which do the opposite, by regarding the Personal as rather unimportant?

It would of course be wrong to think that because preference has been mentioned, the question of truth boils down to a matter of taste. It never does. But once we look at world religions from this somewhat Olympian standpoint, it is obvious that there is no clear-cut way of proving one to be right and the others (comparatively) wrong. Rather, the reasons which back our judgments about these things have the softness and lack of decisiveness which characterize the arguments and evidences which are used, say, in literary criticism. Perhaps some may think that this is a desperately unfortunate state of affairs. Surely there should be clear evidences for religious truth? What kind of faith is it that relies upon such 'aesthetic' judgments? But the answer to such complaints is (as I suggested before) simply that the Transcendent is no easy matter. Who really can expect the truth about it to be as plain as the truth about orchids and moons?

If we take the Personal seriously, then the following argument, based upon an appraisal of the history of religions, is relevant. Whereas, if we assign the priorities in the way in which the above form of Hinduism does, then the religion of devotion and worship becomes increasingly meaningless. The Personal is swallowed up in the impersonal Absolute. The religion of worship is at heart illusory. And we can point to an ironic state of affairs in Buddhism. For while the Theravada probably does represent, as it claims to do, the original teaching of the Buddha, the Mahayana reintroduced the numinous and the Personal in its richer, more proliferated forms of teaching. Here we find nirvana is in effect erected into the Absolute and that this Absolute is identified with the Buddha in his *dharma-kāya* or Truth-Body, that the historical Buddha—together with other Buddhas—is a manifestation of the Absolute, and that by calling on the name of the Buddha the faithful may obtain merit and salvation. There are reflexions here of the Incarnation, of belief in a personal God, of grace and even (since the Buddha showers merit on others out of his immeasurable store gained through his infinite sacrifices on behalf of mankind) of Christ's redeeming sacrifice. Buddhism thus develops beyond the rather austere form of belief represented by the Theravada into a richer and more mythological

8-2

form in which certain elements of theism are to be found. Such a fact can, of course, be evaluated in differing ways. But it may help to show that the most profound combination of the numinous and the mystical is to be discovered in orthodox theism. For here the inner vision found in nirvana and elsewhere can be seen as union with God, the object of worship, and this way of looking at it does not derogate from the peace and insight attained by the contemplative. On the other hand, the erection of contemplation into the summit of religion tends to destroy the Personal. And because the latter is regarded in such systems as unimportant, it happens too that polytheism in practice is tolerated. It is where the Holy is taken seriously that the gods are banished as unworthy representations of the Transcendent.

If this argument were rejected by adherents of these other faiths, it would be because the religion of worship and the concept of the holy and personal Creator were not taken seriously. How then can we vindicate the experience of the numinous in itself? If the Theravadin refuses to see in the Prophets and others like them the genuine stamp of knowledge of the Transcendent, how can we argue with him? It is hard to say—for we too must recognize the marvellous simplicity and serenity of the Theravada. Yet the prophetic and numinous experience is undoubtedly a form of religious encounter: and it is perhaps paradoxical for the Buddhist to appeal centrally to spiritual experience and yet to ignore or reject one great segment of such experience.

In brief, then, one test of truth which I propose is this—that a system of revealed truth or doctrine should reflect the experience of great men in particular and of all religious men in a general way. The emphasis on 'great men' may seem undemocratic. But it seems absurd to treat the lives of ordinary folk as on a par, in this context, with those of St John of the Cross, the Buddha and so on.

In the confrontation, then, of the theistic religions with those non-theistic systems which I have described, the claim of theism to represent the fullest truth initially lies in its capacity to weld together the insights both of the prophet and of the contemplative. To say this is not simply to appeal in a parochial way to revelation. And it implies that certain narrow views of theism, which neglect the contemplative strand in religion and Christianity, would destroy the basis of this claim. It may be noted that even Islam, which initially stemmed from the overwhelming prophetic experience of Muhammad, became enriched (and perhaps altered) through the Sufi movement.

I have spoken here almost exclusively in terms of religious experience and have said nothing about morality. It is sometimes tempting for Christians, and indeed others, to claim that the ethical teachings of their faith and the practical fruits of the spread of that faith are sufficient guarantee of its truth. But the heart of religion does not lie in doing good, though religion ought to *include* doing good. Further, it is very difficult to evaluate, statistically or otherwise, the effects of Christianity as compared, say, with the effects of Buddhism. Still, religions do inculcate certain attitudes towards the world; and they should be such that they harmonize with the demands of moral action. So as a corollary to what I have said about theism welding together the insights of the prophet and the contemplative, let me add that theism, by its emphasis on the transcendence of God, leaves room for the independence and reality of the world and thereby provides an attitude towards it which stimulates moral action as an independent and real part of the religious life.

So much, then, for the first great presupposition of Christian history. But what about the idea of history as a developing process in which God progressively reveals himself? This second presupposition seems in marked contrast to much traditional Oriental thought, where the cosmos has been thought vast and infinitely long in time—a way of thinking which squares well with modern cosmology: the Buddhist does not have to demythologize as much as we do, for we have had to jettison the mythological cosmology of the Old Testament.

It would take much space to write about this topic adequately, especially because in our view of history metaphysical and empirical elements are entangled together. Let me just sketch the outline of a possible answer. First, if theism be true, it brings with it a belief in creation. The doctrine that God creates (so to speak) through an act of will symbolizes well the radical transcendence of God and the dependence of the cosmos upon him. The alternative picture of emanation or of the Absolute transforming itself into the cosmos, which we find in some Hindu theologies, suggests that in some sense the creation is *necessary* and not contingent. Now an act of will is figured as being in time. The creation becomes a piece of analogical history, though not literal history, for it precedes all history. This way of describing the matter fits in with the notion that God acts too in human history. Second, the Eastern view of the cyclical nature of history is partly dependent on belief in rebirth. On empirical grounds we may well doubt whether this belief is true. Third, the way in which human history has recently been running has led, in Eastern countries, to a revaluation of the significance of time: for the drive towards political and economic freedom has introduced a secular version of 'realized eschatology'. Fourth, Evolutionary Theory, with its undertones of 'nature into history', reinforces a sense of direction (though not necessarily *progress*, that sadly battered Victorian concept).

If we were to give such reasons for the two great presuppositions of Christian history, we might well find that the adherents of other faiths will remain unmoved. But this does not imply that the arguments are not relevant. It must be remembered that rarely do religious reasonings persuade individuals to change their faith. But this does not mean that they are useless. For without reasons and evidences there cannot be such a thing as truth; and without truth there can be no belief. Moreover, we find that, as in aesthetics and in philosophy, reasonings have a long-term effect. What occurs is a kind of social dialogue. In the course of time certain views seem to gather persuasiveness while others fade into implausibility. Reasonings are by no means irrelevant to this process.

III

I have said little or nothing about Christ. This might seem a grave and indeed fatal omission in any discussion of the confrontation between Christianity and other faiths. But I have tried to show that it is not possible to plunge straight into the New Testament as though it is intelligible or acceptable to anyone, whatever his cultural background. This is one further instance of the idiocy of selling Bibles without commentaries and of identifying the Word with what you can buy for a few shillings. Before the Buddhist or the Hindu can come to grips with the Gospels he must be given an insight into the nature of Christian presuppositions about God and history. It was therefore necessary to say a good deal about them before considering the figure of Christ himself.

But it is unnecessary here to examine particular historical problems arising from a study of the texts. What I want briefly to sketch is rather the way in which (after the event) we can begin to see how the logic of theism inclines in the direction of an Incarnation. This is important both for the way in which the Christian may confront the uncompromising monotheism of Islam, which finds the Incarnation frankly blasphemous, and for the way in which he may confront the multiplicity of incarnations which the Hindu believes in.

The notion of a Holy Being carries with it a converse, namely, that the worshipper of such a Being cannot but feel himself to be a sinner, by contrast. It is a defect of much preaching about sin in the proper religious sense that it tends to concentrate upon the wickednesses of mankind, as though this harping on evil will bring men to a realization of the truth of religion. Far from it! Without the belief in a Holy One, sin is nonsense. Whom do I sin against if I am an atheist? And how can I think myself unclean if it is not by meditating on the glory and goodness of God? Remove the holiness of God, and all we can speak about is moral badness, not sin in the proper sense. First God, then sin: not vice versa. It is therefore part of the logic of theism, with its emphasis on the numinous experience of God's majesty, that men should regard themselves as sinful. In a developed form of theism, this sinfulness is of course not merely ritual uncleanness, but is intimately connected with moral faults. And there is, empirically, good evidence of such faults among the great mass of human beings. Hence men must feel responsible for their sin, even though there is something necessary about it.

But holiness can only come from holiness. Only the Holy One can remove sin, give grace, confer wholeness upon the creature. This leaves men in a predicament. On the one hand, before God men feel responsible for their sins and called upon to expiate them. Yet on the other hand, they know in their heart of hearts that only God can save. How marvellous it would be if the paradox could be resolved through God's becoming man! He could thus both expiate and save. But to do this he must truly be man: only a compatriot can be a hostage on my behalf. At one stroke we can see that the logic of theism moves gently towards the Incarnation and that it moves gently away from belief in many avatars, with their implicit docetism.

None of this argument has anything directly to do with historical facts. Whether such an Incarnation has happened in actual fact is a question which must be decided by reference to the historical evidence. So must the question whether there is any factual warrant for the belief in many avatars among the Hindus and in many Buddhas among the Buddhists. But we know how to set about answering these questions. I hope merely to have shown certain general ways of thinking about Christianity in the context of the great religions. Such thoughts are not mere appeals to revealed truth. To repeat: there are many supposed revelations, so that we cannot dogmatize *simply* on the basis of any one of them. This is not to say that revelation should be disregarded. We do not pretend to be prophets or sages who originate bodies of revealed truth or who communicate their encounters with God. But we do need to know how to evaluate the deliverances that are given to us.

Journeying into foreign lands and alien cultures can bring one to a better understanding of one's own faith. One can see certain general features of good religion which can be used as a yardstick for measuring the inessential accretions of one's own faith. And just as studying Tolstoy may throw indirect light upon Turgenev, Mozart upon Brahms, Goya upon Picasso (for widening our experience in a certain category helps us to understand better what we already know), so the gentle wonders of Buddhism and the subtle theologies of Hinduism, the poetry of the Tao and the single-mindedness of Islam, will shed some illumination upon the heart of Christianity. The early Church found good in Plato and used the 'pagans' in its own way: likewise now perhaps the Church can see the glories of other faiths and use them for its own glory.

It follows that we must increasingly ponder the problem of translating Christian theology. Not of course literally, for that's been done often enough, but more in the way in which St Augustine and Aquinas translated Christian thoughts into the terminology of the Greek philosophers. For Christianity to be really intelligible to those brought up in other cultures, the concepts of the non-Christian religions must be adapted for the purpose.

I have tried to sketch out the answers to one or two vital problems in this area. But I would be distressed if anyone, upon reading this essay, should think: 'Isn't it nice that we have a fellow here who knows a bit about Buddhism and all that and who has dealt with these Orientals? He has shown how Christianity can answer these other religions, so I don't need to worry further about it. What would the Church come to if she couldn't rely upon a few hired eggheads to keep atheists, Hindus, Marxists and all enemies at bay?' Of course, I could interpret such thoughts as a compliment to me. Would they not imply that my 'answers' were rather convincing? But are they? People ought to ponder and to be worried by these things. Reading the Buddhist scriptures may sometimes be a cure for anti-religious feelings, but it doesn't always conduce to Christian orthodoxy.

SYNOPSIS

I. *Dogmatic presuppositions in the interpretation of the New Testament*

In the English-speaking world, Jowett's essay, 'On the Interpretation of Scripture' which was published in *Essays and Reviews* (1860), opened a new phase in the debate about the meaning and authority of the New Testament. Until this period there was a broad agreement that once the meaning of any text had been established its truth could be taken for granted.

Irenaeus introduced a dangerous precedent when he appealed to the authority of the public teaching which had been current in the churches founded by the Apostles. Tradition was established as a second source of revelation and a criterion for the interpretation of Scripture. At the Reformation fresh insights were gained into the truth of the New Testament, but it came to be interpreted in accordance with a new Protestant dogmatic system. The English Deists and Continental Rationalists approached the New Testament with the presupposition that nothing which was contrary to Reason was credible. The Tübingen School used the Hegelian dialectic as a basic presumption in understanding the growth and meaning of the New Testament. Liberal theologians in the nineteenth century sought to interpret the New Testament without any dogmatic presuppositions, but it was not sufficiently realized that this virtually assumed that Christianity was the finest flowering of man's religious consciousness rather than a divine revelation.

II. *The interpretation of the New Testament today*

The authority of any document may rest primarily upon its own intrinsic character or upon its authorization by some external authority which may also claim to give the only authoritative interpretation. The authority of the New Testament is intrinsic, and is accepted by faith. Its authority can be recognized only when its meaning is understood. As we cannot dispense with presuppositions in our acts of interpretation, we must seek to be as fully aware as possible of those which we are using and we must use them as hypotheses to be tested. Our decision to accept the New Testament as the Word of God and as a guide in matters of faith and morals is an act of reasonable faith.

THE MEANING AND AUTHORITY OF
THE NEW TESTAMENT

I

THE DEBATE among Christian theologians about the meaning and authority of the New Testament entered on a new phase with the rise of the so-called 'Higher Criticism' in Germany early in the last century. The existence of this new movement had been brought to the notice of the English-speaking public by George Eliot's translation of D. F. Strauss's *Life of Jesus* in 1846, but had attracted little attention until the publication of Jowett's contribution to *Essays and Reviews* in 1860. The questions then raised are still very much alive.

Until this period it may fairly be said that while there had been acute disagreement among Christians about the meaning of certain New Testament texts (Matt. xvi. 18, for example), there had been a broad agreement that once the meaning of any text had been established its truth could be taken for granted. Statements of fact in the New Testament were historically accurate, dogmatic assertions unquestionable, commands binding on the Christian conscience. The New Testament rested on the authority of God himself, its ultimate author, and the guarantor of its veracity.

Any apparent discrepancies in statements of fact (as, for instance, in parallel accounts of the same incident in the Gospels) were explained by methods of harmonization first systematically expounded by St Augustine in his *de Consensu Evangelistarum*. Any apparent discrepancies in matters of doctrine (for example, the differing emphasis put by St Paul and St James on the relationship of faith and works) were treated in a similar fashion, being smoothed over by nice distinctions and more or less ingenious special pleading. It was always more plausible that harmonization, however far-fetched, was correct, or that apparent discrepancies concealed mysteries too deep for human understanding, than that God had permitted any error in Holy Writ.

There is nothing surprising in this. The early Christians were absolutely convinced of the truth of their doctrine, and were confirmed in their conviction by the triumph of the Gospel over the objections of the philosophers and the hostility of the Roman Empire. It was natural that they should conclude that the Scriptures which formed the title-deeds of their faith were inerrant and infallible.

Even the existence of heresy did nothing to impugn the truth of Scripture. Heresy was due only to the moral and intellectual failure of men, and never to the obscurity or inadequacy of Scripture. And even the heretics had agreed that Scripture was authoritative; they differed from the orthodox only in their interpretation of it. It is true that in the second century Marcion maintained that the moral tone of the Old Testament proved that its God was not the Father of Jesus Christ, but an inferior deity from bondage to whom Christ had come to save mankind. He further maintained that Christianity itself had been infected with Judaistic doctrines, but that he himself had purged the Epistles of St Paul, Christ's only faithful interpreter, and the Gospel of his disciple St Luke from Judaizing interpolations, and he offered the Church these as the authentic and infallible New Testament. So even he accepted the idea of an infallible Christian Scripture, and indeed gave a powerful impulse to the compilation of the New Testament as we know it. Until his time the Scripture had meant for Christians (as it had for Jesus) the *Old* Testament.

At the same time the Gnostics, whose systems of doctrine seem to us incompatible with anything that can be recognized as Christian, confidently claimed that they were based upon Scripture, interpreted according to a secret tradition handed down by Christ himself to his favourite disciples and disclosed by them to a spiritual élite. Against them Irenaeus appealed to the public teaching which had been current from the beginning in the churches founded by the Apostles. This apostolic teaching was the rule of truth, the *regula veritatis*, in accordance with which Scripture was to be interpreted. Thus tradition was established as a second source of revelation, and a criterion for the interpretation of Scripture. Against the Gnostics Irenaeus was undoubtedly right. The tradition to which he appealed was that which underlay the New Testament itself, but he had in fact established the dangerous precedent of submitting the interpretation of the New Testament to the control of dogma, and this had momentous consequences.

Christian dogma, under the pressure of heresy, became increasingly complex, subtle, and explicit, and in the process faith took on a different complexion from that which it wears in the New Testament. Assent to dogma tended to replace trust in a Person. One may fairly argue that the doctrine of the Trinity and Chalcedonian Christology were legitimate restatements of Christian truth in terms borrowed from Greek metaphysics, and necessary in their own day to safeguard the insights of the New Testament into the nature and activity of God, but they are not in fact taught by the New Testament, and the authority which the formulae that express them have acquired has inhibited the attempt to find fresh formulations that will serve a new generation, now that these old explanations have themselves to be explained. The same may be said of the understanding of Christianity as a New Law. This may have been inevitable, but it obscured St Paul's insight into the nature of faith, and prepared for a new Pharisaism.

There arose in fact a divorce between Christian experience and Scripture on the one hand, and dogma and tradition on the other. This divorce was perhaps the principal cause of the Reformation. The Reformers were led to a fresh insight into the truth of the New Testament, but this did not at once result in the freeing of the interpretation of the New Testament from dogmatic control. Instead, the New Testament came to be interpreted in accordance with a new Protestant dogmatic system. The infallibility of Scripture was common ground between the Reformers and the Catholics, and controversy turned on the interpretation of the New Testament. But an infallible Scripture was no help when there was no agreement on the criteria that should govern its interpretation.

It was to overcome this deadlock between the rival dogmatic systems of Catholic and Protestant, each relying, wholly or in part, on infallible Scripture, that Spinoza appealed in his *Tractatus Theologico-Politicus* (1670) for an attempt to study Scripture afresh, with a candid and independent mind, that is, without dogmatic presuppositions of any kind. But this anticipation of the spirit of *Essays and Reviews* bore no immediate fruit. Spinoza tacitly suggested (whether he actually believed is another matter) that once the meaning of the New Testament was understood, its authority was to be admitted. But the immediate future lay with men who denied any independent authority to the New Testament at all.

These were the English Deists and the Continental Rationalists, who made their appeal to reason as man's sole authoritative guide. They agreed that if any assertion in the New Testament was true, it was so because it was evident to human reason. As many statements in the New Testament are not of this kind, they were ascribed either to their authors' accommodation to the prejudices of an unsophisticated age, or to the machinations of priestcraft which appealed to supernatural authority to bolster its own pretensions. The Rationalists of course rejected miracles, but they nevertheless regarded the Gospels and Acts as sufficiently reliable to enable them to produce natural explanations of the incidents which the New Testament describes as miracles.

Kant's criticism destroyed the intellectual basis of Rationalism, particularly by his demonstration that the traditional arguments for the existence of God are untenable. Hegel and Schleiermacher completed his work, and the way was open for the reappraisal of the New Testament which was the work of the so-called Tübingen

School. Rejecting both traditional Christian dogma and Rationalist religion, these critics applied Hegelian dialectics to the interpretation of the New Testament. F. C. Baur used the Hegelian scheme of thesis, antithesis, and synthesis to explain the development of early Christianity: Jewish Christianity was the thesis, St Paul the anti-thesis, and St John the synthesis. This involved the wholesale rejection of traditional views of the authorship of the New Testament. All but four of the Pauline Epistles were judged to be spurious, and none of the Gospels had any apostolic author.

D. F. Strauss also utilized the Hegelian scheme to explain the history of the interpretation of the New Testament. The traditional dogmatic interpretation of the New Testament is the thesis, the Rationalist the antithesis, and Strauss's own, new interpretation the synthesis. This is that the appropriate medium for the expression of such truth as religion is capable of imparting is mythology: it is this and neither history nor philosophy that the New Testament contains and the critic's task is to discover the sources of this mythology and evaluate its religious meaning. The value of Christianity is that it is a preparation for Hegel's Absolute Idealism, a necessary but transient phase in the self-realization of the Absolute.

Thus so far the interpretation of the New Testament had been under the influence of dogma—Catholic, Protestant, Rationalist, Hegelian. It was only with the rise of Liberalism about the middle of the nineteenth century that an attempt was made to approach the study of the New Testament without dogmatic presuppositions and so to do what Spinoza had said was required. In the field of New Testament study the most typical, though not the earliest, of the Liberal theologians was Adolf Harnack (1851–1930), who made the classical statement of his position in *Das Wesen des Christentums* (1900), translated as *What is Christianity?*. It was this new movement which Jowett sought to introduce to the British public in his contribution to *Essays and Reviews*.

But excellent as were their intentions, the fatal error of the

Liberals was to suppose that in abandoning Hegelianism they had freed their minds of all dogmatic presuppositions. They had not, for they worked on the assumption that the rise of Christianity was to be understood as a purely historical phenomenon, and explained in sociological and psychological terms. Thus they virtually ruled out the possibility of the New Testament containing any revelation. At most it was the record of man's quest for God, a collection of documents for the study of the finest flowering of man's religious consciousness.

II

And so we come back to the point from which we set out. How are we to discriminate between these various methods of understanding the New Testament and various estimates of its authority, which have developed in the course of Christian history (and are still current today)? In all the intense theological activity of the last hundred years I do not discern any really new movement, but rather new combinations of the old in an uneasy eclecticism. Today most Christians, even theologians, acquiesce in either a renovated dogmatism or in a compromise between that and a modified Liberalism. Those who do the latter often seem to think one thing in the privacy of their studies, and to say another in their pulpits. The fashionable biblical theology is no real solution. It does indeed represent an earnest attempt to understand the New Testament in its own terms, but it is unable to communicate its understanding satisfactorily to men who think in terms radically different. It is self-contained and self-consistent, but out of touch with experience.

Bultmann's attempt to 'de-mythologize' the New Testament in effect would interpret it in terms of Existentialism, and so is a new example of the old *a priori* approach.

In what follows I do not pretend to answer the question how we are to interpret the New Testament or to succeed where I judge that greater men than I have failed; the most I can hope to do is to indicate some lines along which a satisfactory answer may be formulated.

I begin then by considering the relationship between the meaning of any document and the authority which it claims or which is claimed for it. This must obviously differ in different kinds of document. In some the authority is more or less independent of the meaning of the document; in others it is wholly dependent upon it. It is obvious that the authority of a document cannot be determined and subsequently acted upon unless and until its meaning is understood, even if imperfectly. A document written in an unknown language or containing nothing but gibberish cannot have any authority, but a document does not need to be completely understood before it can be recognized as possessing some authority. Some documents of unquestionable authority can be extremely obscure in parts—for example, some Acts of Parliament or communications from the Inland Revenue. But the practical difficulties which may arise from the obscurity of such documents can be circumvented because the authority which attaches to them is what may be called external to them: the existence of this external source of authority is undeniable and its rulings indisputable. Thus if an Act of Parliament happens to be obscure, Her Majesty's judges can elucidate it.

For much of Christian history the New Testament was regarded as a document of this kind. Its author was, properly speaking, God himself, and he had provided, in the bishops and doctors of the Church, or, according to more recent doctrine, principally in the person of the Pope, an authority to interpret it infallibly. The New Testament may appear to be an unsystematic collection of occasional writings, sometimes obscure, sometimes self-contradictory, but there is, in the *magisterium* of the Church, all necessary authority to interpret it, and the Christian has but to listen and obey. The contemporary Evangelical holds a view closely similar to this, in which the fundamental tenets of Evangelical Christianity replace the papal *magisterium*. But both encounter the same difficulty. How is one to recognize the claims of the external authority, papal or evangelical, to interpret the New Testament?

But there is another class of documents which do not depend for their authority upon any external guarantee, verifiable independently of the documents themselves. Their authority is inherent and intrinsic, and recognition of its existence is wholly dependent upon the proper understanding of their meaning. To this class of documents belong the writings of philosophers like Plato, and of the mystics, non-Christian as well as Christian, or of their pupils recording their oral teaching. The pupils do indeed appeal formally to an external authority, that of their masters, but this authority is itself intrinsic to the masters themselves, and depends upon their capacity to persuade or stimulate men to share their vision, accept their values, and verify their intuitions for themselves. This authority is none the less powerful for being quite independent of all external support or sanction, as is shown by the lasting influence of such men as Plato. It has lasted because men have tested his teaching in their own experience, and in consequence acknowledge his authority.

At first sight the writings of the Hebrew prophets do not seem to fit exactly into this class. They differ from Plato, for example, inasmuch as they do not come forward as men who have discovered for themselves the teaching which they impart, but as the recipients of a revelation. They are men upon whom a truth has dawned that they were neither looking for nor could have discovered by their own efforts. They do not speak in their own name, but in the name of God.

To this distinction between the philosopher Plato and the prophet Isaiah or Jeremiah corresponds the distinction between the Platonic love, *eros*, which expresses man's upward aspirations towards God, and the characteristically Christian love, *agape*, God's condescending towards man. Now there is no absolute antithesis between either element in the two pairs, discovery and revelation, *eros* and *agape*.

There is rather a necessary element of both in the whole relationship of God and man. Man seeks and longs for something which he does not realize, and God goes out in love to meet his need by his revelation of himself, and, receiving the revelation, man realizes that this is what he had really been looking for, and that he would never have found it by himself. When two human beings get to know one another, or 'fall in love', each is at once revealer and recipient of revelation. When man investigates inanimate nature, the process is almost entirely discovery. But even then the element of revelation is not entirely absent, and if one believes that nature is God's handiwork, and eloquent of the Creator, this is not a fanciful supposition. Thus revelation and discovery are really complementary, but it is not on this ground alone that the prophet is to be classed with the philosopher. There is a more cogent reason.

When the prophet says, 'Thus saith the Lord', we only have the prophet's own assurance that this is so, and if we accept it, it is by an act of faith in the genuineness of his experience. And this is consistent with the fact that the existence of God is not susceptible of proof. It is accepted by faith, and though the believer may receive subsequently what appears to him ample corroboration of his faith, in making the initial act of faith he does not know that it will in fact be justified. God is not obvious, and he does not provide objective corroboration of the prophet's claim such as to convince the indifferent. There is no means of telling, *at the time when he is speaking*, whether a prophet is in fact speaking 'in the name of the Lord'; one can only make the act of faith. And so the prophet's authority is truly as intrinsic as the philosopher's or the mystic's.

Prophecy was sometimes accompanied by signs and wonders, designed to convey an external assurance of authority. Thus Moses was enabled to perform miracles to impress the Egyptians, and Isaiah gave a sign to Hezekiah in the dial of Ahaz (Isa. xxxviii. 8). But 'signs and wonders' are in the last resort ambiguous. They may confirm or elicit an already latent faith, but they do not convince the sceptical. Pharaoh remained unconvinced, and the Egyptian enchanters had sufficient success to blunt the effect of Moses' signs.

Jesus himself did not perform 'signs' to convince his enemies—even when challenged to do so, and he made his appeal rather to his hearers' own spiritual insight: 'This generation is an evil generation: it seeks a sign, and no sign shall be given it except the sign of Jonah. ...The men of Nineveh shall rise in the judgment with this generation and shall condemn it, because they repented at the preaching of Jonah, and, behold, something greater than Jonah is here' (Luke xi. 29, 32). The Pharisees were not impressed by Jesus' teaching, and so found it easy to explain away the miracles which he did perform as the result of collusion with the Devil.

Thus prophecy, as exemplified in the teaching of Jesus, claims only an intrinsic authority, which, however compelling to the faithful, is never coercive. Similarly, for St Paul the decisive authority is that of Christ, but this can only convince those who already believe in Christ. The same is true of the New Testament as a whole, even of Revelation, which its author claims to have written by divine command (Rev. i. 11), for no one will accept this claim unless he acknowledges the intrinsic authority of the book.

It follows then that the authority of the New Testament is intrinsic, and is accepted by faith. Its authority can be recognized only when its meaning is understood, and there is no external power with authority to enforce obedience to it or to dictate a particular interpretation of it, though Christians have often succumbed to the temptation of trying to establish such an authority.

It is not surprising that this should be so. Christians may be so convinced themselves of the authority of the New Testament that it appears to them self-evident. It is then a painful and disturbing experience to find men no less intelligent and no less moral than themselves who claim that they too are quite able to understand the New Testament but are quite unmoved by its authority. It is an easy inference that the unbeliever is the victim of some insidious moral failure, and ought to be coerced into conformity, for his own sake as much as for that of those he may infect. The sin of heresy, which seems to have been a Christian invention, justified sanitary precautions as drastic as those against cholera. But the attempt to produce conformity by coercion is the usurpation by men of a power which God has not only denied to them, but renounced for himself.

Freedom, whatever its consequences may be, is essential to the Christian life in all its aspects. For compulsion is incompatible with love, and all Christians are agreed that God is love. And even Almighty God cannot achieve the impossible feat of compelling men to love him freely. It is true that the New Testament contains expressions which seem to contradict this. What is meant, for example, by, 'The love of Christ constrains us' (II Cor. v. 14)? This can, I believe, be understood from the analogous experience of love on the human level. Anyone who has ever 'fallen in love' has experienced the paradox of simultaneous constraint and freedom: he knows that he has no alternative but to give himself to his beloved, yet it is his free act, his choice. And the only constraint which God puts upon us is that of love. To attempt to supplement it in any way is a sign of fear and faithlessness, however much it may be concealed by an apparent zeal for faith. Our Lord gave the most solemn warning against causing his little ones to stumble, but he is not recorded as having authorized his apostles to prevent it by force.

It might seem then that in religion we are left very much to our own resources. How can we be sure that we are on the right road, and that our 'faith' is not self-delusion, if we have no infallible authority to guide us? What are we left with if we reject both an infallible Church and an infallible Scripture?

We can only follow our Lord's own advice implied in his question, 'Why do you not of yourselves judge what is right?' (Luke xii. 57). This may seem a very frail foundation, but St Paul assures us that the Christian's strength 'is made perfect in weakness' (II Cor. xii. 9). We have an obligation to examine the credentials even of Scripture and to exercise a proper discrimination in our following of it. We need not be alarmed if we find apparent inconsistencies in it, or examples of an occasional lapse from the standard set by Jesus.

Thus St Paul says, quoting Prov. xxv. 21 f., 'If thine enemy hunger, feed him; if he thirst, give him drink; for in doing this thou shalt heap coals of fire on his head; do not be defeated by evil, but defeat evil by means of good' (Rom. xii. 20 f.). This is in harmony with the teaching of Jesus recorded in Matt. v. 44: 'But I say to you, love your enemies and pray for your persecutors', except for the jarring note in Paul's suggestion of heaping coals of fire on one's enemy's head, which he brought in because he accepted Proverbs as an authoritative witness to the mind of God.

Again, is it true, as John xv. 13 makes Jesus say, that 'No man shows greater love than this, in laying down his life for his friends', when in fact Jesus laid his life down for his enemies? Is not the text in John rather an example of the way in which, by the time the Fourth Gospel was written, the Church had become turned in upon itself? In it there is no parallel to the Matthean command to love one's enemies, only the repeated command to love *one another*.

Then consider the seven 'words' from the Cross. Of these one only, 'My God, my God, why hast thou forsaken me?' is found in more than one Gospel (Matt. xxvii. 46; Mark xv. 34). Of the rest Luke has three, 'Father, forgive them...' (xxiii. 34),[1] 'Amen I say to thee, today thou shalt be with me in paradise' (xxiii. 43), and 'Father, into thy hands I commend my spirit' (xxiii. 46); and John three, 'Woman, behold thy son....Behold thy mother' (xix. 26), 'I am thirsty' (xix. 28), and 'It is complete' (xix. 30). These can be harmonized only on the assumption that the later evangelists were consciously supplementing Mark, but there is little warrant for this assumption. Luke borrows a great deal of his material from Mark, and when he deserts Mark, it is because he prefers an alternative source. John seems to have known of Mark, but not to use his

---

[1] This verse is omitted by an important group of manuscripts, headed by B D* W Θ.

Gospel as a source for his own. He seems to intend to supplant rather than to supplement Mark, and the same may be true of Luke. Yet Mark's 'word' is the one with the highest intrinsic probability. No one would have made it up: its very difficulty may explain why Luke preferred to omit it.

These are only a few examples of the many discrepancies which occur in the New Testament. Though they make it extremely improbable (to say the least) that it can be accepted as inerrant, yet they do not destroy its authority. In fact they tend rather to establish its credibility. The New Testament is the work of many hands, yet there is in it a remarkable unanimity in the picture which it gives of the faith of the first Christians. The Gospels may differ in many matters of fact, and in the emphasis which they put on various aspects of the personality and mission of Jesus, but a consistent portrait emerges of the man Jesus, though it may seem tantalizingly incomplete. They may be taken as the work of honest and reasonable men, though their interests and methods are not identical with our own. We shall understand them better if we try to discover what their interests and methods were, and do not impose on them an interpretation based on our own dogmatic presuppositions, orthodox, Rationalist, Liberal, Existentialist, or any other.

In our attempts to exercise this proper discrimination in our use of the New Testament we are only carrying a stage forward the work of those unknown Christians in the early centuries who established the Canon of the New Testament. These twenty-seven books are a selection from a larger mass of Christian literature, and the Church gradually came to accept them as alone authoritative. The criterion which they used was that of apostolic authorship, but because they equated 'apostolic' and 'orthodox' they tended to assume that (unless there was positive evidence to the contrary, for example, I Clement) a book must be apostolic because it was orthodox. It is unlikely that any really apostolic work was consciously eliminated (though some letters of St Paul may have perished before the collection was made), but some mistaken attributions were made. Thus the Epistle to the Hebrews survived because it was attributed to St Paul, and II Peter was included in the Canon, though it is in the highest degree unlikely that it is the work of the Apostle Peter. Thus those who established the Canon attributed to the books which they accepted as authoritative a complete authority, and ignored or explained away what must seem to us errors or deficiencies in them. In this we must judge them mistaken, and so presume to recognize that some things even in Canonical Scripture cannot claim full authority.

In a sense the authority of the New Testament itself is to some extent dependent on that of the Church, for it is through the discrimination of the Church, operating quite spontaneously, that the New Testament was established—and we are bound to admit that neither Church nor Scripture is absolutely free of error. But in following both (and they are all we have to follow), and in exercising a careful discrimination upon what they give us, we may hope to avoid being fatally misled.

For though neither Church, Scripture, nor conscience is in itself infallible, we have *in Christ himself an infallible authority*, and can trust him to use the fallible, meditated authorities of Church, Scripture, and conscience, to keep us from error. We need not try to erect infallible authorities of our own: the infallible Church, the infallible Scripture, and the infallible conscience are nothing more than idols. Jesus himself wrote nothing, and he entrusted his work to twelve men, whom the New Testament itself shows to have been as liable to error after the Resurrection as before it. And he seems to have shown a remarkable lack of interest in many of the issues which at present divide Christians, such as the proper mode of Christian initiation, the proper method of Christian worship, and the proper ordering of the Christian ministry. Only those who approach the New Testament to find support for their preconceived notions on these matters can find in it any consistent doctrine on them. We ought to acquiesce in uncertainty in those matters which Our Lord has left ambiguous, instead of flouting his one clear law of charity in making them matters of division. We cannot even be certain that the unity among his followers which he is represented as having prayed for (John xvii. 21) is a unity of ecclesiastical organization.

Of one thing we may be certain, that the New Testament is the work of men who shared the mentality and observed the literary conventions of the first century A.D. So in studying it we must not fall into the same error of method as did the Alexandrian Fathers in the Christological controversies of the fourth and fifth centuries, who started from the premise that Christ is divine, and went on to ask how then he could be human. We on the other hand would be inclined to start from Christ's humanity, and go on to ask how he could be divine.

In the same way in discussing the meaning and authority of the New Testament I would not begin from the premise that it is the Word of God, though admitting that its impression of intrinsic authority may support this assumption, but from the empirical observation that it consists of the writing of men, and that, if it is to be understood correctly, it must be understood as such.

So it was that Jowett maintained that we must study the New Testament 'like any other book', that is, in accordance with the generally accepted rules of literary and historical criticism. In this I believe he was certainly right. 'Higher Criticism', that is, the determination, so far as possible, of the date, authorship, etc., of the books of the New Testament, is not just an interesting exercise, but essential to their proper understanding, and scholars must use all the assistance which they can get not only from grammar and philology, but from archaeological discovery and the comparative study of religion as well.

Now in enunciating this notorious axiom, which appeared so shocking to his contemporaries, Jowett did not mean that we should necessarily find it to be *no more* than any other book. But one may suspect that he did not regard it as the Word of God in anything like the traditional sense. For it was for the Liberals in general the supremely great document of man's religious quest, just as for them Jesus was the Son of God as the supreme religious teacher, the man who first fully realized, and made others realize, man's divine Sonship.

We must, however, remember that the world's religious literature was not so well known or appreciated in the West in the last century as it is today, when it is by no means so obvious as it was that the New Testament is a uniquely great religious document, and Jesus a uniquely great religious teacher. Better knowledge of Jewish literature, and particularly the discovery of the Dead Sea Scrolls, underline the contention that much that once appeared unique in the teaching of Jesus is by no means so. If then Jesus is in any way unique it is not for his teaching, but for what he was. We must therefore abandon the Liberal position here, and we can do so with less reluctance if we remember that their emphasis on Jesus the teacher was in part due to their dogmatic naturalism, which made them disinclined to tackle the thorny problems of what Jesus was and did—of miracle, for instance, and particularly of the Resurrection. We must better their instruction, and in eschewing dogmatic presuppositions, eschew theirs also; and remember that it is as dogmatic to rule out *a priori*, as it is to assume, that the Bible is, for example, in some sense the Word of God as well as the words of men.

It is, however, impossible to avoid all presuppositions. If we had none about the New Testament, it is hard to see how we could have any interest in it either. The best we can hope for is to be as fully aware as possible of those which influence us, remembering always that as Christians we have a particular obligation to follow the truth. We must, therefore, regard our presuppositions as a hypothesis to be tested rather than as a key to unlock the mystery of the New Testament. We must not regard as important only what happens to be congenial to us, or select as the 'essence' of Christianity what is consistent with our own prejudices, and try to explain the rest away. We must study the New Testament as a whole. If anything in it seems obscure or irrelevant, this probably means that we have not really understood what we suppose to be clear, though the New Testament would be unlike most of other ancient literature if it did not contain some things that are likely to remain obscure, and also some things that are now irrelevant.

Reading it in this way, we shall see that it does present a coherent understanding of man's condition, based on the conviction that God has acted for the salvation of man through the man Jesus, who in what he was and did as well as in what he taught, confronts man with a challenge to his faith and allegiance. It offers us certain surprising facts as historical—principally the Resurrection of Jesus —and the evidence for these facts. This evidence may not be conclusive, but it is enough to be at least taken seriously. We are, therefore, confronted with a choice, either to accept or to reject the faith of the New Testament, but we cannot know that the choice we make is the right one until we have made it.

If we make the choice of faith, the New Testament will seem to us the Word of God, and infallible in the sense that we are prepared to follow its guidance in matters of faith and morals, though there are some things in the New Testament that belong to faith and morals which its own central or highest testimony corrects. We shall not be surprised if it contains obvious errors and discrepancies, any more than we should be surprised at the occasional evidence that Jesus himself shared the current opinions of his time on such matters as the authorship of the Psalms or the Pentateuch. Such things are inevitable accidents of the human condition. We may see in the Scriptures something analogous to the Christian belief in the Incarnation of Christ, for the Word of God is effective in both only through the words of men—the man Jesus, and the human authors of Scripture. In both 'the Word became flesh', as St John puts it. And in both it is perceived only by faith. If our decision is against faith, we have still to account for the existence of the New Testament and of the Church which wrote it and lives by it. And in this case the great variety of the alternative explanations offered may give us pause. There is none that obviously accounts for all the phenomena, or rules out all other explanations, and whichever we accept, it is by faith of a kind. There is nothing intellectually disreputable about faith as such. 'We walk by faith, not by sight', as St Paul says (II Cor. v. 7)—even if we are not Christians.

APPENDED NOTE ON 'AUTHORITY' AND 'LIBERTY' IN THE CHURCH
By A. R. Vidler

The purpose of this note is to outline a view of the authority of the Church which is consonant with the foregoing account of the authority of the New Testament.

'Authority' means title to be believed or obeyed, as distinguished from 'power', which means ability to compel obedience. Often authority and power are combined in the same person, for example, a father or schoolmaster is morally entitled to be obeyed by his children or pupils and also has the power to compel obedience.

Human beings are manifestly at the outset of their lives entirely dependent on authority for learning what to believe and do, and they remain so to a large extent, for it is impossible for an individual to verify for himself all the beliefs on the basis of which he has to act. None of us can become 'an authority' on all subjects. We are bound in many matters to depend on the authority of those persons or institutions that are entitled to be believed, for example, the experts on particular subjects. It is reasonable for a mature man thus to be guided by authority in matters which he cannot verify for himself, because he presumes that if he had the time, opportunity and requisite expertise he could verify for himself what he thus accepts on authority.

'Authorities' are trustworthy not only according to their expertness but also in proportion as they are free and determined to reckon honestly with new discoveries that bear on their subject. Thus, the trustworthiness of a close corporation, which suppressed evidence that conflicted with received opinions or did not allow its members to put forward new opinions, would be more or less gravely impaired. The only agreement worth having is that of those who possess the right to differ.

All human knowledge is limited, and all human authorities are contingent; they are relative to the time and place in which they exist, to the amount of knowledge that is available to them, to their capacity for understanding what can be known, and to the capacity of language itself for expressing various kinds of truth.

The only unconditional authority is God himself. He alone has an absolute title to be believed and obeyed. It is the Christian faith that, in addition to all that can be perceived of God's 'invisible nature...in the things that have been made' (Rom. i. 20), God has made himself known through the prophetic testimony of the Old Testament and the apostolic testimony of the New Testament. Both these testimonies have their centre in 'the Word made flesh'. It was 'the Word *of God*' that was made flesh, and therefore he is the bearer of absolute authority, but 'the Word was made *flesh*', which is to say that he became incarnate in human existence with all its intrinsic contingencies of thought and language, and therefore there is an element of contingency even in the *ipsissima verba* of Christ himself in so far as they can be accurately recovered. Similarly, with regard to the historical facts on which Christian doctrine depends and which it interprets, while there must be a sufficiency of evidence for the facts to which appeal is made, it must also be recognized that they do not admit of demonstrative proof but that here as in all historical investigation 'probability is the very guide of life'. Thus, for example, while we may not assert that the evidence for the resurrection of Jesus Christ is as cogent as that for the death of Julius Caesar, it must needs be adequate for the support of the doctrine dependent on it; and the same is true of all other dogmas to be believed for salvation.

If these considerations apply to the incarnate Lord himself and to the credenda concerning him, *a fortiori* they will apply to the authority of the Church.

The Ecclesia, which was constituted or reconstituted by the advent of the Word and the outpouring of the Holy Spirit, has a divine commission to communicate and to commend the prophetic and apostolic testimony to all nations and has a divine promise that in doing so it will be led into all truth. This commission and this promise are given to the whole apostolic Church. At the same time, in the New Testament a special authority is assigned to the apostles for witnessing to the Gospel and governing the Church, and in a special manner they are promised the guidance of the Holy Spirit who is the vicar of Christ. They properly take the lead in proclaiming the Gospel and in building the Church. But teaching and governing authority is not exclusively concentrated in the apostles. All the members of the Church share in the gifts of the Spirit who 'apportions to each one individually as he wills' (I Cor. xii. 11). Thus alongside the apostles authority was from the first exercised by other members of the Church—evangelists, teachers, prophets, presbyters, etc.: no hard and fast line was drawn between an *ecclesia docens* and an *ecclesia discens*.

There is no clear prescription in the New Testament about how the authority entrusted to the Church was to be exercised after the apostolic age. Attempts to show that, for example, a presbyterian or a papal polity is there prescribed for the whole Church for ever seem forced and unconvincing. But it is evident that an authority corresponding to that of the apostles has been exercised in the Church throughout its history, although the organs and structures through which it has been exercised have varied in different times and places. When light dawns after the tunnel period in the second century, bishops are found to be exercising an apostolic authority in preserving the integrity of the Church's witness to the Gospel and they have continued to do so ever since, despite the variations in the form of the episcopal office. Bishops have exercised apostolic authority not only in their dioceses but through their assembling in local and general councils or synods.

But, in accordance with the analogy of the New Testament, authority has been exercised in the Church by other ordained ministers and by laymen too. Not least was this so in the early centuries, for example, Justin Martyr, Origen, before his ordination as well as when he was a presbyter, etc. Laymen, as well as the inferior clergy, have participated in the work of witnessing to the Gospel that was given once for all, and in interpreting and applying it in relation to changing conditions and advancing knowledge, and they ought to do so. For hierarchies can err and have erred, even in their most august representatives. The whole body of the faithful, who share in the gifts of the Spirit, contribute to the authority of the Church by testing and checking and verifying what at first they receive on trust and whatever subsequent directives may be given by the hierarchy. In the long run the authority of the Holy Spirit in the Church is mediated and becomes effective through the interaction of the various elements in its constitution. No single element is entitled to override the others by an *ipse dixit* or a *causa finita est*. That is to say, what is authoritative is in the long run to be ascertained from the *consensus fidelium*, which includes the testimony of the laity, as Newman emphasized in a famous passage in *The Rambler*, 'On Consulting the Faithful in Matters of Doctrine'[1] (with reference to the Christological controversies of the fourth century).

Another way of expressing the wholesome complexity of the operation of authority in the Church, and of avoiding the temptation to simplify it, is to observe that Scripture, tradition and reason each has its part to play and that none is entirely sufficient without the others. In *Scripture* there is a crystallization of the prophetic and apostolic testimony to which the Church confesses itself to be permanently bound and subject. *Tradition*, which is conspicuously expressed in liturgy and the sacramental life of the Church, represents the continuous and developing experience of the Church as it brings out of its treasure things new as well as old. *Reason* stands for the duty of all Christians, according to their abilities, to exercise their minds upon the data of Scripture and tradition and to reckon honestly with the discovery of new facts and with new ways of thinking, and thereby to contribute to the development and maybe to the reformulation of Christian doctrine. Authority embraces all these elements, and it is through the interaction of them all that the Holy Spirit is guiding the Church into all truth. The Church is responsible for seeing that all its members have the maximum opportunity of playing their appropriate parts in this process,

---

[1] This article has recently been reprinted and edited with an introduction by John Coulson (1961).

for example, by education and by giving the laity as well as the clergy a place in its councils.

On this view of authority, there is always sufficient light available to enable men to be sure what they ought to believe and practise. At any given time the Church, using the resources of Scripture, tradition and reason, through the ministry of the hierarchy, of pastors, evangelists and theologians, and through the witness of the faithful, has *adequate* authority to bring home to mankind the Gospel of God and to build up those who respond to it in the Christian way of common life and obedience. But to claim *absolute* authority for itself or for any element or organ within its constitution is to make itself into an idol and to usurp the prerogative of the Holy Spirit. By refusing to claim absolute authority for itself, the Church witnesses to the continuing activity of the Holy Spirit who is ever guiding it into a fuller understanding of that truth which will be known completely or absolutely only 'at the last day'. No definitions made by the Church *in via* are in themselves final or irreformable, however faithfully they serve to mediate to mankind the final authority of God for practical purposes. 'The secret things belong to the Lord our God; but the things that are revealed belong to us and to our children for ever, that we may do all the words of this law' (Deut. xxix. 29). It is always the case that 'we have this treasure in earthen vessels, to show that the transcendent power belongs to God and not to us' (II Cor. iv. 7). Articulated credenda may always be susceptible of improved expression in the light of theological reflexion and may require revision in the light of new discoveries. So here too 'we walk by faith, not by sight' (II Cor. v. 7). The craving for an absolute authority on the human plane is a craving to escape from this condition.

In order that the Church's teaching shall always be open to the further guidance of the Holy Spirit and shall not become fossilized or impermeable by new discoveries, it is requisite that the greatest possible amount of liberty of speculation and play of mind be allowed to the members of the Church, not least to theologians. Otherwise the Church's authority becomes like that of the scribes. The greater the Church's trust in the absolute authority of God and in the promised guidance of the Holy Spirit, the greater will be its readiness to see its received doctrines and ordinances under constant re-examination. The Church has no doubt power to suppress or to exclude those of its members who advance unacceptable opinions and may have on occasion to use it, but in view of the paramount importance of maintaining the utmost liberty of thought and experiment, and in view of the inveterate tendency of ecclesiastical as of other institutions to a blind conservatism, the Church should use this power with the utmost restraint. While there is a proper pastoral care in the Church to avoid scandalizing simple believers, there should be an equal care to avoid scandalizing the erudite and the educated.

SYNOPSIS

Just as a Christian's belief about his Lord lies at the heart of his faith, so Christology is central to Christian theology. Its task is to reduce the mystery of Christ's person to propositional form. The Chalcedonian Definition performed a useful purpose in the age in which it was written, but it raises acute difficulties today. (1) The Definition assumes that the nature of godhead and manhood are known; (2) godhead and manhood are not comparable natures to be set side by side; (3) Jesus spoke of himself in functional, dynamic terms and the Bible is primarily concerned with what God did through Christ rather than with who he is. The lack of a contemporary metaphysic results today in an intellectual impasse for theology, especially for Christology. There are, however, possible ways forward. Professor Tillich attempts to replace static essence by dynamic relation. Dr Matthews suggests relating Jesus to God by means of the concept of a 'moving pattern of activity'. Further soundings suggest that this concept is in accord with biblical revelation, (a) because the Bible is primarily a book of the Acts of God; (b) because biblical typology emphasizes the recurring rhythm of the pattern of divine activity; (c) because the biblical conjunction of creation and redemption confirms the pattern on a broader canvas. The divine activity is always and only revealed as self-effacing love. Atonement is God's loving activity in Christ enabling a man to come to terms with himself and so with the love that surrounds him. Man can only relearn to love by acceptance that he is loved as he is. This is made possible by God's identification with man in Jesus and by Jesus' loving acceptance of the worst that men can do to him. Jesus may be called divine because in him God acted to enable men to find loving relations with God and their fellow men.* Jesus' life and thought were fully human, and the divine activity was fully present in him so far as is possible in a man. The paradox of grace provides the best analogy whereby we may conceive of the union of divine and human in Jesus.

*like Arius' "God in name only"?

TOWARDS A CHRISTOLOGY FOR TODAY

I

'WHAT THINK YOU OF CHRIST?' There can hardly be a more obvious question than this for any Christian to face; for our Christianity stands or falls by our answer. And, likewise, there can hardly be a more onerous question, for it challenges us to formulate our deepest convictions and to declare our fundamental loyalties. And for those whose profession is Christian theology, the question must needs be at once more obvious and more onerous; more obvious because Christology affects every branch of Christian theology as the sap of a tree affects the quality of its foliage, and more onerous because much more is required of a theologian than the disclosure of his personal response and commitment to the Gospel. The theologian must of necessity *theologize*: his work is primarily the work of the intellect. 'What think you of Christ?' He must formulate his reply in the most apt, meaningful and precise terms, and he must be prepared to defend his formulation by reasoned argument.

He is not, of course, concerned to commend to others a particular dogma: that belongs to the apologist. He is not even primarily concerned with the exegesis and authority of Scripture, although he must use Scripture and attempt to interpret and even to evaluate it. The theologian who dares to write about Christology is concerned above all to understand and to conceptualize the faith that is in him, to relate it to Scripture and to tradition, and to submit it to the test of reason. His search is that of *fides quaerens intellectum*. And yet right at the beginning of this search, he is aware that the attempt is impossible of fulfilment. For the theologian is not, like the mathematician, dealing with puzzles; nor even, like the philosopher, with problems. He is dealing with the mysteries of God, with the relationships between God and man. Human language and human

149

thought were not fashioned for this purpose, and they must be inadequate tools for talking and thinking about God. Our words and our conceptions about God are at best analogical when we make use of them to theologize. This difficulty presses particularly hard upon us, when our concern is Christology; for here we speak about both God and man not merely in the same breath but even in the same Person. This is presumably the truth that underlies Dr Relton's remark that 'the Person of Christ is the bankruptcy of human logic'.[1]

Jesus of Nazareth was a man: that at least is plain in all the New Testament records about him, and the rediscovery of his full and complete humanity has been one of the positive gains of Liberal New Testament criticism. And 'what manner of man is this!' The synoptic gospels, even when subjected to the most rigorous tests of higher criticism, confront a reader with the Ultimate manifesting himself in human personality. (The Fourth Gospel does not so easily pass such tests, for the author mingles his own experience of the risen Christ into his account of the words and works of Jesus in such a way that the critic cannot distinguish the two.) Beyond Jesus of Nazareth there can be no advance in human personality as we know it. He challenges and inspires. There may be people with more knowledge, with stronger physical prowess and with greater technical ability than he had. There may be people so withdrawn from contact with others that their conduct seems more remote from evil than his; for he threw himself without scruple into the ambiguities of human existence so that his moral decisions inevitably brought evil as well as good in their wake. But there can be no further advance beyond Jesus in strength of will, intuitive knowledge of God and man, love of neighbour, relationship with our heavenly Father—in fact, in moral and spiritual perfection of character as we know it. This perfection bursts through the written record of the gospel pages. He was *totus in nostris*, the Proper Man. Yet the Liberalism which

H. M. Relton, *Studies in Christian Doctrine* (1960), p. 166.

equates his divinity with his perfect humanity does less than justice to the gospel evidence. Jesus made claims for himself as the One who perfectly knew and revealed his Father and who perfectly obeyed his will; as the One whose ministry was the prelude to the inauguration of God's Kingdom. He seems to have been absolutely without consciousness of any guilt or sin.[1] Although he always confessed his complete dependence on his heavenly Father, he spoke with his own intrinsic authority, he claimed to dispense from the Jewish law, and he demanded absolute allegiance and loyalty from his followers and disciples. It is not possible to accept the perfection of Jesus' character without at the same time accepting the truth of the claims that he made about himself. He was what he claimed to be: he did what he said he would. He who accepts his claims finds them vindicated and confirmed in the Christian life.

The task of Christology is to reduce the mystery of Christ's person to propositional form. Any attempt to formulate a Christology will properly start with the Chalcedonian Definition, for here was an authoritative attempt by an Ecumenical Council of the Church to put into words and into concepts the mystery of Christ's person:

Following then the Holy Fathers, we all with one voice teach that it should be confessed that our Lord Jesus Christ is one and the same Son, the Same perfect in godhead, the Same perfect in manhood, truly God and truly man, the Same of a rational soul and body; of one substance with the Father as touching his godhead, and the Same of one substance with us as touching his manhood, sin alone excepted; begotten of the Father before the ages, as touching his godhead, and, in the last days, the Same, for us and for our salvation, of Mary the Virgin, *theotokos*, as to his manhood; one and the same Christ, Son, Lord, Only-Begotten, made known in two natures without confusion, without change, without division, without separation, the difference of the natures having in no wise been taken away by reason of the union, but rather the properties of each being preserved, and both concurring into the one *prosopon* and one *hypostasis*— not parted or divided into two *prosopa*, but one and the same Son and Only-Begotten, the Divine Word, the Lord Jesus Christ....

---

[1] The records do not suggest that consciousness of guilt led Jesus to seek baptism at John's hands. In any case, if Josephus is correct, John's baptism was a ritual rather than a moral cleansing (*Antiqu.* XVIII, v, 2).

II

The long history of controversy which preceded this Definition is not the concern of this essay. The carefully worded clauses of the Definition are very far removed from the ministry, death and resurrection of him who lived and loved, spoke and suffered in Nazareth and Capernaum, Calvary and Jerusalem; but they were formulated not to describe his life but to define his person. They were 'noticeboards which warn us off false approaches'.[1] They were intended to safeguard three vital dogmas which seemed to be imperilled: the Unity of God, the Divinity of Christ and the Unity of Christ's Person. As J. M. Creed said:

Even the Chalcedonian Definition of the Incarnation, although it wrecked the unity of Christendom and bequeathed a legacy of distracting controversy to the Church, was not sheer calamity; for in the circumstances of the age it provided a certain safeguard to valuable elements in the tradition which powerful tendencies in dogma might otherwise have crushed. But our age is not theirs, and the doctrinal history of the last hundred years does not encourage the supposition that we can treat our problems in their terms.[2]

Not all contemporary theologians have agreed with such a judgment. 'When we think of Jesus Christ in himself, in the mystery of his own person, the Chalcedonian formula is quite adequate', writes Professor T. F. Torrance,[3] although he admits the inadequacy of the formula in relation to Jesus' mission to mankind. Dr Mascall is more unqualified in his allegiance. For him the Chalcedonian Definition is a 'statement which, while its explanation to the world of the present day may need patient effort of exposition, does not, I would most emphatically urge, require either apology or modification'.[4] Later even this slight reserve seems to disappear. 'To us who look back upon Chalcedon after fifteen hundred years', he writes, 'the

[1] C. Gore, *The Incarnation of the Son of God* (1891), p. 108.
[2] J. M. Creed, *The Divinity of Jesus Christ* (1938), p. 82.
[3] 'Atonement and the Oneness of the Church', *Scottish Journal of Theology*, vol. VII (1954), p. 247.
[4] E. L. Mascall, *Christ, the Christian and the Church* (1946), p. 41.

notion of unconfused union in Christ may not seem to offer any special difficulty; that this is so is a sign of the triumph of Chalcedon in our theological thought.'[1]

Yet difficulties remain, and they need to be stated:

(1) The Definition speaks of Jesus as perfect (complete) in both manhood and godhead. This might have been put negatively; that is, 'there is nothing pertaining to complete godhead or to complete manhood which is lacking in Christ'. This in turn might mean: 'I don't know what manhood really is, any more than I know what godhead really is, but I do believe that Christ is lacking in nothing that belongs to either.' Even such a negative statement assumes that we know enough about manhood and godhead to assert that both can be united in their perfection in one person. It certainly implies that 'godhead' and 'manhood' are more than mere abstractions. But in fact the Definition at this point is couched in positive terms: 'The Same perfect in godhead, the Same perfect in manhood.' This positive form assumes that we know the nature of godhead and the nature of manhood.

But the nature of God is beyond our human comprehension. How can we know him who is the ground of our life as well as transcendent to our existence? To use the language of the Schoolmen, we know *that God is*, not *what he is*. We know *that he is* in the same kind of way as we know that there is a Self transcendent over the workings of human personality, although we cannot directly experience this Self, even in ourselves.[2] We experience this divine activity which has created us and preserved us and which holds us in life, and we assert that God exists as an act of faith from his effects. We experience only his effects. If we had really known the nature of God, there would have been no need of an Incarnation to reveal him to us. As Inge once wrote: 'The controversy about the

---

[1] E. L. Mascall, *Via Media* (1956), pp. 84 f.

[2] For a detailed analysis of transcendence, see an earlier essay in this book. Its writer analogizes from common experience to show that we can meaningfully speak of the Transcendent with reference to divine activity.

Divinity of Christ has been habitually conducted along the wrong lines. We assume that we know what the attributes of God are, and we collect them from any source rather than the revelation of God in Christ.... But surely Christ came to earth to reveal to us not that he was like God, but that God was like himself.'[1] This is not to deny that we have real knowledge of God's activity apart from Christ; for without it we should have no means of recognizing the fullness of divine activity in Christ. But apart from Christ our knowledge of God's activity is obscure and confused. 'No one has ever seen God; but God's only Son, he who is nearest to the Father's heart, he has made him known.'[2]

If we do not really know the nature of godhead apart from Christ, neither do we know the nature of manhood. In the first place, our growing knowledge of the evolutionary process prevents us from drawing an absolute line between man and the higher mammals. We cannot precisely define man as distinct from other living beings. Nor can we know the future potentialities of man in the further processes of evolution. Secondly, the picture of man which emerges from the natural and human sciences is still confused and un-integrated. For example, if in some sciences man is seen as a highly complex physico-chemical structure, in others he is regarded as an organism with different aspects called body, mind and soul which are capable of free response; while the evidence of psychic research would suggest that the Self, below the level of consciousness, seems to extend beyond the limits of our physical bodies.

---

[1] *Cit.* D. M. Baillie, *God was in Christ* (1948), p. 66.

[2] Incidentally, this particular criticism of Chalcedonian Christology applies with equal force to kenotic Christologies. Kenoticism, despite its religious appeal, raises insuperable difficulties, and the gravest of all is that 'it assumes that we know, apart from Jesus Christ, what God is like, and then goes on to assume that in the Incarnation those features which do not fit in the historical picture must have been laid aside. But this assumption, despite the Christianity of those who have made it, is just paganism' (L. W. Grensted, *The Person of Christ* (1933), p. 130). The real attraction of Kenoticism, however, for the nineteenth century lay in its ability to explain Jesus' limitation of knowledge. Higher criticism of the Bible, together with a vast acceleration in the growth of all kinds of knowledge, made the question of Jesus' knowledge a primary concern of Christology.

Yet even if we did have an integrated picture of the nature of man from the various sciences, we should still be unable to define exactly what man is. We cannot say what it is that constitutes manhood. We can describe how particular men behave, for example, how they act and speak and suffer and think and will and pray. As we study the wise and the great and the terrible and the saintly, the Platos and the Pericles and the Hitlers and the Teresas, we learn more of what it is to be human and our knowledge of the human situation is enlarged. But the Self remains unknown. Dr Grensted once again has put the point against Chalcedon:[1] 'The radical weakness of the formula of Chalcedon is that, though it rightly stated the relation between the two natures, no definition is given of the natures which are so related.'[2]

(2) The Fathers who composed the Chalcedonian Definition were concerned to preserve the true insights of the two competing schools of Alexandria and Antioch. They toiled to preserve both the passionate and austere monotheism for which the Jewish prophets (and Jesus himself) had striven, and at the same time to do justice to the revelation that had been given in Christ. Within the limits of their conceptual apparatus, they did well. But they were forced to use

---

[1] *Op. cit.* p. 130.

[2] This particular criticism of Chalcedon may equally be applied to many recent attempts to give a psychological as distinct from a metaphysical definition of Christ's person. What is it that makes a person a person? His fundamental characteristic is self-consciousness, according to Illingworth (*Personality, Human and Divine* (1894), p. 28). Selfhood consists in willing, reasoning, and loving, all in relationship to other personalities, wrote Moberly (*Atonement and Personality* (1901), p. 219). W. Temple saw the centre of personality now in consciousness (*Christus Victor* (1924), p. 117), now in will (*Foundations* (1912), p. 247). Gore and those who followed him regarded a person as 'a psychological unity, defined in and by its experience, discernible through psychological analysis, rather than a metaphysical substance or hypostasis distinct from its nature and experience' (L. B. Smedes, *The Incarnation: Trends in Anglican Thought* (1953), p. 3). But the researches of the psychologists have made it clear that the unconscious is as important (perhaps more important) an aspect of human personality as consciousness. Until the human sciences can give a clearer concept of personality, it is unlikely that any Christological theory that is based on the nature of personality will prove satisfactory; and even then what God did through Christ remains more important than what Christ himself experienced (cf. J. S. Lawton, *Conflict in Christology* (1947); A. M. Ramsey, *From Gore to Temple* (1960), pp. 16–43).

the language of substance, nature, *prosopon* and *hypostasis*. 'Jesus Christ disappears in the smokescreen of the two-nature philosophy. Formalism triumphs, and the living figure of the evangelical Redeemer is desiccated to a logical mummy.'[1] Similarly, W. Temple, in a famous phrase, wrote that the Definition represents 'the bankruptcy of Greek patristic theology'.[2] Elsewhere he declared that as a solution to Christology 'it marks the definite failure of all attempts to explain the Incarnation in terms of Essence, Substance, Nature and the like'.[3] It may be that failure to realize that the Nicene Fathers were using a Platonist metaphysic has led critics to do them less than justice. Nevertheless it remains true that the early Fathers were compelled by their tradition of thought to formulate the Incarnation in terms that were sub-personal. It is as though they were trying to define the mystery of Christ's person by the same kind of procedure as when a child attempts to force together two pieces of a jig-saw puzzle. Manhood and godhead are not comparable natures to be set side by side as in the Definition; and God can be aptly described only in language that is suited to personal being. The use of these conceptual forms has resulted in a formula which reduced a mystery to a statement of a problem in paradoxical form.

A dogmatic statement [writes Professor Tillich][4] can fail in two possible ways. It can fail both in its substance and in its conceptual form.... An example of the inadequacy of the conceptual form is the formula of Chalcedon itself. By intent and design it was true to the genuine meaning of the Christian message. It saved Christianity from a complete elimination of the picture of Jesus as the Christ.... But it did so—and it could not have done otherwise within the conceptual frame—through an accumulation of powerful paradoxa. It was unable to give a constructive interpretation, although this was just the reason for the original introduction of the philosophical concepts.

It is inevitable that a developed Christology should use language that is philosophical, but the particular philosophical tradition which underlies the Chalcedonian Definition is outmoded today. 'It is a

---

[1] G. L. Prestige, *Fathers and Heretics* (1946), p. 146.
[2] W. Temple, *Foundations* (1912), p. 230.
[3] W. Temple, *Christus Veritas* (1924), p. 134.
[4] P. Tillich, *Systematic Theology* (1957), vol. II, p. 163.

truism to remark that the tendency of modern thought is to evolve dynamic concepts. We need not enquire into the reasons for this, which are complex; but undoubtedly the influence of science and of the new interest in the meaning of history has been important. One of the consequences of this has been the fading of the idea of "substance".'[1]

There is nothing sacrosanct about the philosophical categories of the patristic period. God did not reveal to us a particular philosophy: he revealed himself to us in Jesus Christ. Unless we believe that the Chalcedonian Definition is binding on Christians for all time—and the Anglican concept of authority does not encourage such a view—then we need not feel ourselves bound by the terms in which Christology is defined in the formula, although we shall be very chary of rejecting what underlies these forms of expression.

(3) The biblical revelation is not expressed in philosophical terms, because the Jews did not think philosophically. They were concerned not with ontological definition but with dynamic function and with personal relationship.[2] Basic to both Old and New Testaments, as their name implies, is the concept of Covenant, which is concerned with conduct and relationships. When we turn from the Old Testament to consider the New Testament witness to Christ, we find that its primary concern is with what Christ did for men, and with the difference that this makes to our relations with God and with one another.

III

The testimony of Jesus to himself is far more important than the interpretation that the early Church put on his person and status; for, if his claims about himself are true, he alone would have been in a position to know his relationship to his Father. Here the challenge

---

[1] W. R. Matthews, *The Problem of Christ in the Twentieth Century* (1950), p. 62.
[2] The phrase 'dynamic function', while it may suggest impersonal mechanism, is used here in the sense of activity and energy proper to persons.

of higher criticism must be accepted, and an attempt must be made to distinguish the words of Jesus from the logia of the gospels; and, although the case cannot be argued in this essay, the synoptic gospels must be set apart from the Fourth Gospel: only the former may confidently be used for this purpose. In the synoptic gospels we find Jesus speaking of himself as a man, as a prophet, and as more than a prophet; as the One whose ministry was to be the prelude to the inauguration of God's Kingdom on earth. Jesus knew himself to be the Son of his heavenly Father: he described himself as Lord and as Son of Man. Negatively, he did not describe himself as God:[1] indeed, he even seems explicitly to have denied this ('Why do you call me good?').[2] In using these titles of himself, Jesus did not make ontological statements about himself: he was using biblical *imagery* to describe his messianic functions and his relations to God and to his fellow-men. When he spoke of himself as Son and of God as 'My Father', he did not mean that he was 'of one substance with the Father'. He was using the language of relationship. The use of Father for God by the Jews did not imply an idea of God but a characteristic attitude of piety.[3] When Jesus spoke of himself as the Son of his Father, he was referring to a filial relationship between himself and God. When he spoke of himself as Son of Man he was using an Old Testament image which portrayed a man, weak in comparison with the immensity of God; a representative man who, according to Jewish tradition, after humiliation and defeat, would be vindicated by God and given the place of honour in Heaven.[4] Just

---

[1] The suggestion of E. Stauffer that Jesus claimed for himself the title *ani hu* (*Jesus and His Story* (E.T. 1960), pp. 149 ff.) raises intolerable difficulties. Cf. O. Linton, 'The Trial of Jesus and the Interpretation of Psalm cx', *New Testament Studies*, vol. VII (1961), pp. 258 ff.

[2] Mark x. 19 ('Why do you call me good? There is none good, except one, God') is a *crux interpretationis*. Whatever were the reasons which prompted Jesus to answer thus (and it is a sign of the trustworthiness of the tradition that Mark records the saying), he must have implied a contrast between himself and God. This contrast is confirmed by the references in the Gospels to Jesus' prayers to his Father.

[3] Cf. G. F. Moore, *Judaism* (1927), vol. II, p. 211.

[4] The writer considers that Jesus took the phrase Son of Man (and transformed its meaning) from Daniel and Pss. viii and lxxx.

as 'Son of Man' pointed to Jesus' coming vindication, so the title
'Lord' referred to his coming exaltation at 'the right hand of God'.[1]

The interpretation of Christ found in the rest of the New Testament is, generally speaking, in accord with Jesus' witness to himself.
Most of the Christological passages in the New Testament elaborate
gospel images or add further functional or relational titles. (Even
the Fourth Gospel, for all its seeming concern with status, speaks
of Jesus in terms which are really functional.) Very seldom indeed
is Jesus called God in the New Testament. As Gregory Dix writes:

Jewish Messiahship does not yield a Christology of *status* in metaphysical terms
of 'human' or 'divine' *origin* at all. That question is quite irrelevant to the
Jewish conception. It yields instead a Christology of *function* in terms of
history.... Once Jesus was accepted as 'Messiah' by Jews (even by himself as a
Jew) this identification of his own action in history with the action of God himself
was *inescapable* (regardless of questions of humanity and deity) simply because this
was what Messiahship *meant* to the Jews. But once Jesus was preached as
'Messiah' to Greeks, the question of his metaphysical relation to Godhead was
equally inescapably raised immediately, because that was the only way in which
Greeks could think.[2] ? p. 157

Professor Cullmann makes a similar point.

When it is asked in the New Testament 'Who is Christ?' [he writes],[3] the
question never means exclusively, or even primarily, 'What is his nature?' but
first of all, 'What is his function?'...As a result of the necessity of combating the
heretics, the Church fathers subordinated the interpretation of the person and
work of Christ to the question of the 'natures'. In any case their emphases,
compared with those of the New Testament, were misplaced. Even when they did
speak of the work of Christ, they did so only in connexion with discussion about
his nature. Even if this shifting of emphasis was necessary against certain
heretical views, the discussion of 'natures' is none the less ultimately a Greek,
not a Jewish or Biblical problem.

The biblical interpretation of Christ is not in all points infallible,
nor is biblical theology normative for dogmatics; but a Christology
which is expressed in terms of functional and personal relationship
rather than in ontological categories means a return to the biblical
perspective.

---

[1] Cf. Ps. cx. 1.
[2] G. Dix, *Jew and Greek* (1953), pp. 79 f.
[3] O. Cullmann, *The Christology of the New Testament* (E.T., 1959), pp. 3 f.

The New Testament gives us a few 'stills' near the beginning of the Church's developing Christology. As this Christology begins to develop, we see ontological definitions gaining ground. How did this happen? The Greek theologians took three basic biblical images, two of which had been used by Jesus himself, and they transformed these into philosophical concepts. The Logos was unable to bear the ontological weight which was put upon it, and it tended to become a mere title of Christ. The Son of Man and the Son of God became the *vere homo* and the *vere deus* of orthodox Christology. While Harnack was right in claiming that the Hellenization of the gospel was a process of rationalization, he was wrong to suppose that it was also a degenerative process of secularization. The Definition of Chalcedon was the only way in which the fifth-century fathers, in their day and with their conceptual apparatus, could have faithfully credalized the New Testament witness to Christ.

By and large orthodoxy reigned from Chalcedon to the Enlightenment. Since then there has been a plethora of competing Christologies. What has happened has been the 'translation' of orthodox Christology into the various changing key-ideas of their authors. Thus for Hegel the idea was the regulative category, and for him Christ was the complete expression of the divine human idea. Ritschl believed in the primacy of value judgments; and so for Ritschl Christ was God because his purpose was God's purpose, and there was a complete moral union between them. For Schleiermacher feeling had been primary, so that for him Christ was divine because he was supremely and perfectly God-conscious and was the source of religious feeling and God-consciousness for all who believed in him. 'Schleiermacher is anxious to show that, though his own doctrine is stated in different terms, he is concerned to deny what the definitions sought to deny.'[1]

So also with more recent theologians. Thornton took his key concepts from Whitehead's philosophy of organism, and thus he

[1] J. M. Creed, *op. cit.* p. 30.

held that in Christ the human organism is taken up into the divine. Most other English Christologists since Gore have grounded their theory on some form of philosophical idealism,[1] while Bultmann's Christology is the result of his deep commitment to existentialism. Most of the Christologists have taken some key analogy by which to interpret the person of Christ. Their method may be compared to that of the great metaphysicians:

> I do not believe that [they] have cast round looking for some interesting idea in terms of which they might be able to construct a theory. They have been charged with the sense of importance and significance in some spiritual and intellectual experience, and the excitement of this has driven them on to attempt to give intelligible form to other vague reaches of experience with reference to this basic insight.[2]

IV

It is easier today to speak of the great metaphysicians of the past than of the present. The contemporary relations of philosophy with theology are considered in the first essay in this volume. Most modern philosophers are not concerned with metaphysics at all, and many would deny their validity. Yet for theology metaphysics are essential, if theology is not to preside over its own suicide. Today there is a general distrust of the old metaphysical systems and no general desire to return to them except on the part of those who have never deserted them. Yet there is, at the moment, little to take their place. The impasse in which Christology (and all theology) finds itself is primarily due to this lack of a metaphysic in which it can be securely grounded. This, it should be noted, is primarily an intellectual impasse. It does not immediately or directly affect Christian faith or Christian worship or the conduct of the Christian life. God is still at work. The old formulas continue to be used: they serve in worship, they comprise pictorial imagery useful for meditation, and they mark the continuity of our faith and devotion with

[handwritten marginalia: a "power vacuum" in theology — a lack of metaphysical foundation]

---

[1] This is connected with their concern with knowledge and psychology rather than with substance and ontology.

[2] D. Emmet, *The Nature of Metaphysical Thinking* (1945), p. 198.

that of our Christian ancestors. They preserve what may be meaningless to one generation but meaningful to the next. Our search is *fides quaerens intellectum*: and so long as the search can and does continue, the insufficiency of our theology need not affect Christian faith or conduct or worship. There are times when Christian theology, if it is to be true to itself, must be silent; and this may be one of them. It is a time of agonizing strain and testing for those who search for coherence and meaning. And if the darkness lasts too long, the Church's intellectuals may lose heart and her enemies rejoice.

promising theories to fill the vacuum

Some shafts of light have already pierced through the fog which surrounds contemporary Christology, pointing the way, perhaps, towards a Christology for today. Professor Tillich has suggested that

we replace the inadequate concept 'divine nature' by the concepts 'eternal God-man-unity' or 'eternal God-Manhood'. Such concepts replace a static essence by a dynamic relation. The uniqueness of this relation is in no way reduced by its dynamic character; but, by eliminating the concept of 'two natures', which lie beside each other like blocks and whose unity cannot be understood at all, we are open to relational concepts which make understandable the dynamic picture of Jesus as the Christ.[1]

Tillich sees how vital it is that Christology should be grounded in ontology rather than psychology. But his attitude to the historical Jesus is so radically sceptical that his theology as a whole is not easily acceptable to those who do not share his scepticism. Indeed, his theology seems to have been constructed precisely in order to combine such scepticism with a full commitment to the Christ. None the less, Tillich's concern with dynamic relation rather than with static essence points a way forward.

Dr Matthews, in a book to which reference has already been made in this essay, and which deserves more attention from theologians than it has as yet received, joins together the concepts of activity and pattern, in order to do justice both to the relatively static elements in experience as well as to its dynamic elements. He

[1] P. Tillich, *op. cit.* p. 170.

sketches their contemporary use and significance in several fields of experience, and then he applies the concept of a 'moving pattern of activity' to human personality and he uses this to relate Jesus to God:

> I contend that there is no contradiction or absurdity in holding that the moving pattern of the will of God could be also the moving pattern of the behaviour events which constitute the temporal and historical aspects of a human life. The scale on which the pattern is manifested makes no essential difference. A personal life of which it could be said that it is of the same pattern as the temporal will of God would be the supreme revelation of God: it would be God manifest 'in the flesh'.[1]

He puts forward his suggestion with modesty, and does not believe that it provides a fully adequate basis for a satisfactory Christology. It might, however, be useful to take soundings a little more widely than Dr Matthews has done. Thus we might note that the concept of a 'moving pattern of activity' is in accord with the biblical revelation. In the Bible we find that God is not so much he who is as he who acts. Whatever be the semantics of the Tetragrammaton (and Professor Barr is probably correct in denying that the Hebrew verb 'to be' has primarily a dynamic signification),[2] God reveals himself to his chosen people by mighty acts in history rather than by a communication of his essence or nature. 'Christian theology has tended to think of the Bible chiefly as "the Word of God", though in point of fact a more accurate title would be "the Acts of God".'[3] Jesus' own claims concern what he *does* and what God *does* through him. Furthermore, the typological interpretation of the Old Testament suggests that there is the same pattern of divine activity in the Old Dispensation as in the New. A genuine biblical typology 'seeks to discover and make explicit the real correspondences in historical events which have been brought about by the recurring rhythm of the divine activity'.[4] To explicate these patterns of divine

---

[1] W. R. Matthews, *op. cit.* pp. 70 f.

[2] Cf. J. Barr, *The Semantics of Biblical Language* (1961), pp. 58 ff. Contrast T. Boman, *Hebrew Thought compared with Greek* (E.T., 1960), pp. 47 f.

[3] G. E. Wright, *God Who Acts* (1952), p. 12.

[4] G. W. H. Lampe, 'The Reasonableness of Typology', *Essays in Typology* (1957), p. 29. Cf. C. H. Dodd, *According to the Scriptures* (1952), p. 128.

activity in the events of the *Heilsgeschichte* lies beyond the scope of this essay. But there are certain recurring themes which run through types and antitypes, and which interpret the meaning of the salvation events: the election of God, his covenant-love for his people, and the vindication of his purpose through humiliation, failure and defeat. Such diverse examples might be chosen as the barrenness of Sarah and her subsequent pregnancy, the events of the Exodus, and the death and resurrection of Jesus.

Furthermore, the way in which creation and redemption are held together in the Bible confirms the same principle on a larger canvas. In the Old Testament, for example, redemption is spoken of as a new creation, and in the New Testament Jesus Christ is called both the first-born of all creation and the first-born from the dead. This suggests that there is the same pattern of divine activity in the work of Christ as in the work of the creation.[1] Can we define this pattern in terms sufficiently comprehensive? The divine activity is always loving; God reveals himself in Christ always and only as loving activity, manifested to men in personal being. This love is free: no one can be forced to respond to it. It is self-effacing and it is not immediately recognized, so that those who do respond to it are committed to the adventure of faith. And (to adopt Professor Dodd's provisional definition of *agape*) it is 'energetic and beneficent good will which stops at nothing to secure the good of the beloved object'.[2]

In Jesus this love showed itself as self-effacing in the hidden years in Nazareth and also in his ministry, where the revelation of God in Christ was so self-effacing that Jesus' messiahship remained a secret.[3] The love of God in Christ stopped at nothing to secure the

Again, poss. a Heb. preference for func. over prop. stmts

---

[1] Cf. Heb. ii. 10: 'It was clearly fitting that God, for whom and through whom all things exist, should, in bringing many sons to glory, make the leader who delivers them perfect through sufferings' (*N.E.B.*).

[2] C. H. Dodd, *Gospel and Law* (1951), p. 42.

[3] Cf. T. W. Manson, 'Realized Eschatology and the Messianic Secret', *Studies in the Gospels*, ed. D. E. Nineham (1955), pp. 219 ff.

good of its beloved object. In creation the same pattern recurs. God's acts of creation and preservation are (despite their distortion through the refraction of evil) his acts of love, for God has no need to create us, and our creation is the overspill of his love. His love in creation is so self-effacing that it is obscured by the terrible surds of sin, suffering and insanity. It is forced on no one (love cannot be forced) so that many are tragically indifferent to or even deny his existence. He created man to share in his glory: this is the good of his beloved which, so faith contends, he has stopped at nothing to procure.

Indeed, we may even say that the same pattern of divine activity is to be seen in the work of the Holy Spirit, both corporately in the Church and individually in Christians. He works for our good; and he is so self-effacing that we cannot distinguish his activity in us from the operation of our own personalities.

If we provisionally adopt 'the pattern of divine activity' as our key concept, we shall not speak about the being and nature of God himself—and indeed, we know nothing about this, save that God is transcendent over us. However, since God is always and only active in his world as a God of love, we might say that the inmost nature of God is love, because we must hold that God's revelation is a genuine revelation of his nature. But as we do not know the conditions of God's existence (the very phrase shows the utter inadequacy of human language and thought in this connexion) we do not add anything to our knowledge by saying that God's inmost nature is love. Instead of defining the Essential Trinity of three Persons, we must content ourselves with the experience of the divine activity in three modes. Modalism?

V

If Dr Matthews suggestion were to be pursued further, it would be necessary to reformulate the concepts of general and special revelation in such a way that the events of the Old Testament were regarded as manifesting the 'moving pattern of divine activity' in a particular way among particular groups of peoples. In Jesus Christ the pattern of divine activity was perfectly revealed in the behaviour events of a single historical life. Jesus revealed the fullness of divine activity in a human personality. 'In him dwelt all the fullness of the Godhead bodily.' This would seem a congruous way in which God should fully reveal himself to man, in so far as man is capable of receiving his revelation. For personality is both the highest form of existence which men know and also the form of life which they must needs know best. This is not to say that God himself is a person, at any rate in the sense in which we speak of human personality; for the very concept of personality involves limitation. If we were to speak of the nature of God, it would be preferable to adopt C. C. J. Webb's suggestion that there is personality in God.[1] But we cannot go so far even as that. We must content ourselves with saying that God works in a personal way.

God was active in Christ not primarily to show himself to man but to do something for man. 'The canon for the Incarnation, I have said, is soteriological. It is the work of Christ that gives us the key to the nature of Christ.'[2] The New Testament is primarily concerned not with existence but with salvation. Christ did not come to make us divine but to bring us to God. We must therefore attempt to trace and interpret this 'pattern of divine activity' in the life of Jesus, so far as this can be recovered from the gospels.

The mode of Jesus' conception and birth must remain open questions to be decided in accordance with the historical evidence and according to our view of the most congruous mode of the divine activity in these circumstances. Since Jesus himself does not seem to regard the circumstances of his conception and birth as important, at any rate in those sayings which his earliest disciples thought worth preserving, these may presumably be regarded as peripheral matters

---

[1] C. C. J. Webb, *God and Personality* (1919).
[2] P. T. Forsyth, *The Person and Place of Jesus Christ* (1909), p. 346.

for the Christian today. The hidden years at Nazareth, about which
we know almost nothing, reveal God's activity in self-effacing love;
self-effacing because Jesus was living in quiet retirement, and loving
because the Divine Compassion identified himself with all the
ambiguities and choices of ordinary human existence.

Contemporary scholarship has helped to give a more unified and
integrated conception of the ministry itself. Jesus himself, in his recorded sayings, speaks of both his ministry and his death under the
imagery of baptism,[1] which indicates the unified view that he must
have taken of his life and his death. Indeed from Baptism to Cross
we can trace a common pattern, changing in the differing circumstances of his life. In his teaching, preaching, parables and mighty
works he preached the good news of the Kingdom which he was to
inaugurate by his death. His ministry itself was a work of self-
effacing love; self-effacing because of the mystery of his person and
because, in drawing men and women to himself, he pointed them
away from himself to his heavenly Father. It was a ministry of love,
a whirlwind three years at most in which he spent himself to secure
the good of mankind.

His ministry led up to and found its climax in his death. The
Cross formed its focus and culmination. But the death cannot be
separated from the ministry, nor can the ministry be separated from
the whole of Jesus' life. The first phase prepared the way for the
second, and the second led on to the end: all show the same recurring
pattern of self-effacing love and tireless activity.

What did this achieve? It enabled man to accept himself and thereby to enter into a right relationship with God and with his fellow men,
and so to fulfil the purpose for which he was created. It is because
Jesus achieved this that his disciples began to recognize in him One
who in some way was to be identified with him who brought the
Jews out of Egypt and who fashioned the stars and the earth.

The imagery which is used in the New Testament to describe the

[1] Cf. Mark x. 39, Luke xii. 50.

work of Christ was taken from the ideas and practices of the time: the freeing of slaves, the offering of sacrifices, the acquittal of men in the law court, conquest in battle, and reconciliation between men who are estranged. The more personal the imagery, the more apt the image. And yet, by the nature of the case, there can be no satisfactory analogy to God's act of atonement in Christ. Nevertheless, as we have attempted to describe the divine activity in Jesus, so we can attempt to describe how the work of Christ affects us when we accept it.

Man is only too well aware of his conscious struggles with himself. It is the struggles of which he is not aware that he cannot face. He defends himself automatically against the pressures and calamities of daily existence. These stresses and strains often force him back, unknown to himself, to his childhood states, and they deprive him of a full and loving relationship with his family and his friends and fellow men. This takes men out of a proper relationship with God. The failure of these relationships is precisely sin; and it is this that drives man to commit actual sin. But this failure of relationship may not be in itself culpable, for man can be held responsible neither for his infancy states, nor for his unconscious regression to them. Feelings of guilt concerning them are usually unconscious attempts at self-justification, symptoms of internal conflict. Genuine guilt should not consist in a man's feelings of shame at his conduct or attitudes, but results from a refusal to accept that God has lovingly and costingly accepted him, not as he should be, but just as he is.

This regression to infantile behaviour may be classified into three main types, although individuals will not usually fit into any one category. Infantile rage may have caused compulsive attention-seeking behaviour, or it may have been inverted into mordant despair, or it may have resulted in detachment and distrust of social involvement and personal relationships.[1] This suppressed rage, which in infancy was directed against the mother-figure, becomes directed

---

[1] These three main types are conveniently described as hysterical, depressive and schizoid.

against the self, or against all those with a claim on man's affections, and especially against God, the author and source of man's being.

A study of Mary Magdalene among others would show how Jesus dealt lovingly yet sternly and certainly effectively with those who had hysterical personalities. Those with other forms of apparently incurable spiritual sickness can be brought to see the Divine Compassion identifying himself with men in their desperate plight, suffering in Gethsemane and on Calvary what they themselves have felt of dereliction and despair. Man in the depths of his being feels injustice and betrayal, denial and unacceptedness, taunting and mockery, contempt and mistrust, jealousy and spite. He can find that what he has sensed (and probably repressed) about himself has actually happened to Jesus. Before the Sanhedrin, in front of Pilate, on the Via Dolorosa and at Calvary, Jesus accepted those who inflicted on him abuse and flogging, those who raged at him and lashed him and killed him. He accepted them as they were, in all their unacceptableness, and he prayed that they might be forgiven. Even so he lovingly accepts men while at the same time he suffers the full effect of their suppressed rage and hate against him. It is God's identification with mankind and his loving acceptance of the worst that man can do to him that enables a man to accept himself and God and thereby to be set on the road towards full and loving relationships with God and men. 'We love because he first loved us.' As an infant learns to love because his parents surround him with their love, so in the estrangement of adulthood, when all men regress to some extent to their infantile reactions, they can only relearn to love by their acceptance that they are loved just as they are. This is atonement. This is God's loving activity in historical events, which enables a man to come to terms with himself and so with the love which surrounds him.

After his death, Jesus appeared to his disciples. The triumph of the Resurrection which men experienced in their hearts was the mode by which the victory of the Cross was communicated to men.

The Resurrection appearances are not dissimilar in form from other paranormal phenomena of the same general kind.[1] But they are unique in meaning, and, as Professor Dodd has shown,[2] they constitute a common general pattern, with an appearance, a recognition, and a word of command. Thus God, after Jesus' death, communicated his triumph to his friends and enabled them and others to share in it, just as, by a different mode, he still communicates that triumph to us, that we too may share in it.

As the Virgin Birth symbolizes the beginning of the moving pattern of divine activity focused in a personal life, so the Ascension marks its completion. The Second Coming symbolizes the hope that in the end the whole world will manifest the same pattern of divine activity as perfectly as it was manifested in the human person of Jesus. Pentecost marks the outpouring of divine energy in a community according to the same pattern (but not with the same perfection) as it was embodied in Jesus. Inasmuch as the body of believers (the Church) is identified with the work of Jesus, they become the Body of Christ, and the same pattern of spiritual energy is manifested in them as it was in Jesus; but since this identification is fragmentary and anticipatory, the pattern is not always clearly perceived. This same pattern is symbolically stamped on a believer at baptism; and, in the fourfold action of the Eucharist, this same pattern of divine activity is communicated afresh to the Body of Christ in Christian worship, as they identify themselves afresh with Christ. The function of ministry within the Church is to help its members to make this identification.

VI

Since Christology permeates all Christian theology, it has been necessary to range widely (and inadequately) in this essay over a vast range of the theological landscape. While Dr Matthews admits that

---

[1] M. C. Perry, *The Easter Enigma* (1959), pp. 158 ff.

[2] C. H. Dodd, 'The Appearances of the Risen Christ', *Studies in the Gospels*, ed. D. E. Nineham (1955), pp. 9 ff.

his 'moving pattern' conception 'cannot adequately describe the nature of human personality and still less the meaning of the Incarnation',[1] yet it can shed a ray of light in the present Christological impasse. But can it safeguard the Unity of God, the Divinity of Christ and the Unity of his Person?

Same as Chalcedonian Def. p 152

By asserting an 'economic Trinity' and by refusing to go beyond the known to the unknown, we do not imperil the Unity of God.

What of the Divinity of Christ? We have been careful to avoid saying that Jesus has a 'divine nature' or that he is 'of one substance with the Father'. His knowledge was human knowledge, his actions were human actions. Yet in Jesus the divine activity was fully present so far as is possible in human personality.[2] Because the early fathers held that substance was the regulative concept of Christology, they could not but credalize as they did. But if activity replaces substance, there is *metabasis eis allo genos*. By saying that the divine activity was fully present in Jesus of Nazareth, we are exactly translating the essence of Chalcedon into a different thought-form. We have not rid ourselves altogether of the concept of substance, but we cannot theologize about it, since the Being of God is transcendent to our existence, just as 'I' am transcendent to my consciousness.

Knowledge is contextual—ized, socio-logical— determined? (157, 159)

What of the Unity of Christ's person? Orthodoxy speaks of an indissoluble union of natures and infers that in Christ manhood became fully personal only because it was assumed by the Logos. What if we say that the activity of the man Jesus fully and perfectly manifested the divine activity in a human person? If the activity of Jesus was the activity of God; if the love of Jesus was the love of God; what then can be said of the union of divine and human in Jesus? D. M. Baillie, in his great book *God was in Christ*, has suggested that the paradox of grace provides the best analogy whereby we may

The activity of God in Jesus is the same as God in Jesus — thus two natures unified (163)

---

[1] W. R. Matthews, *op. cit.* p. 73.

[2] To confine this divine activity to Jesus' unconscious, a suggestion which Sanday originally made and which Matthews has lately revived, would seem to be Apollinarianism in a new guise.

conceive of the union of divine and human in Jesus,[1] while Dr Pittenger would extend the range of analogues to 'the whole range of divine-human relations experienced and known; creation, providence, co-operation of will, attention (prayer), mystical union, as well as the specific action of divine grace in the creature'.[2] (Yet surely the whole range of divine-human relations is precisely the manifestation of grace?) Does not this argument from analogy leave the union of divine and human in Christ as open as Chalcedon did? Yes and no. Yes, because in the end grace remains a paradox, genuinely experienced as reality, but opaque to human comprehension. No, because grace is an activity of God, not an ontological reality: it is a divine activity of which we have some living experience, not a bare intellectual concept unrelated to our knowledge of reality.

[margin handwritten note: Immanence, Continuum*]*

VII

We may differ in our opinion about the extent to which the technical terms used at Chalcedon are final. We may wish more explicit reference in a statement on the person of our Lord to his Messianic acts. We may well desire to use the best modern scientific terms to describe our Lord's human nature. But can we go beyond the conclusion reached here, beyond the *vere Deus, vere homo*?[3]

The intention of this essay is not to 'go beyond' the conclusion of Chalcedon, but to 'translate' it into a language more comprehensible today. Translation is not always successful and often in danger of obscuring the original. At times, however, the attempt must be made. Keats's aim in writing *Endymion* was far from that which underlies this essay. Nevertheless, like him, 'I leaped headlong into the sea and thereby have become better acquainted with the soundings, the quicksands and the rocks, than if I had stayed upon the green shore, and piped a silly pipe, and took tea and comfortable advice.'[4]

---

[1] *Op. cit.* pp. 114 ff.   [2] W. N. Pittenger, *The Word Incarnate* (1958), p. 198.
[3] J. L. M. Haire, 'On Behalf of Chalcedon', *Essays in Christology for Karl Barth* (1956), p. 111.
[4] John Keats, Letter to James Hessey, 9 October 1818 (Letter 90, ed. M. B. Forman, 1935).

SYNOPSIS

I. Christ's death and resurrection is the ultimate ground for the belief that God is love.

II. God's reconciliation of the world to himself through Christ is the heart of the apostolic preaching. The New Testament writers attempted to state the meaning of Christ's reconciling work in terms of Old Testament concepts. The Pauline emphasis is upon the paradoxical justification of sinners by free grace.

III. Legalistic religion is essentially self-centred. Man's attempt to make himself acceptable is the essence of sin. Legalism thus ministers to sin, producing a wholly wrong relationship towards God. The foundation of legalism is overthrown by the act of God in Christ, by which he declares his love for men at their most unacceptable.

IV. The Thirty-nine Articles speak of a reconciliation of God to man, thus reversing the teaching of the New Testament. The content of the gospel has thus been radically altered and it has been set within the categories of law and transgression, rather than of love. This alteration can be traced in the history of the doctrine of the Atonement.

V. Such teaching has defects. Love is subordinated to justice. Ideas of merit and reward are subtly reintroduced.

VI. The immorality of the theory of penal substitution lies less in the element of substitution than in the ascription to God of retributive justice. To ascribe the motives of a hanging judge to God is to impute to him impotence. Hell is real, not as a penalty inflicted by God and as a condition external to human sin, but as a state which man brings upon himself by his refusal to allow God to accept him as he is.

VII. It is difficult, on the basis of the penal theory, to account for Christ's own treatment of sinners before his death. His death is continuous with his ministry of love and forgiveness. It is the climax of man's attempt to resist his acceptance as a sinner. Christ takes upon himself man's hatred. His death is the miracle of love. Man enters into this as he shares in death to self-justification and rises to new life as a son of God.

THE ATONEMENT: LAW AND LOVE

I

'GOD SO LOVED the world, that he gave his only begotten Son, that whosoever believeth on him should not perish, but have eternal life. For God sent not the Son into the world to judge the world; but that the world should be saved through him.' In face of the obvious and inescapable obstacle of the evil which confronts him in the world around him and in himself and his personal relationships, the Christian is bold to say that 'God is love'. To the Fourth Evangelist there is one solid ground for that affirmation: the salvation of the world through God's decisive action in 'giving' his Son so that through him men may receive a new life, the eternal life which is the knowledge of the only true God.

The death and resurrection of the Son of God are the focal point of this saving act of God, so that it is at the Cross that God is revealed as life-giving love; and in finding the revelation of the love of God in the death of Christ, St John echoes the faith of the first Christians as a whole: 'God commendeth his own love towards us, in that, while we were yet sinners, Christ died for us.' His death is the supreme act of divine love, and by that decisive reaching out of the love of God to us who, as sinners, have no claim whatever that we can make on it, we are reconciled to God: 'If, while we were enemies, we were reconciled to God through the death of his Son, much more, being reconciled, shall we be saved by his life.'

II

The New Testament writers cannot easily find words in which to express their conviction that in Christ God has broken through the barrier of man's estrangement from his Maker and brought him into the relation of a son to a father. That God has done this, that in Christ God was reconciling the world to himself, is the revolutionary fact which has turned all human ideas about God and man upside down, and is the essence of the Christian gospel. It is, in fact, what makes the Christian preaching a message of good news. It is a tremendous fact, reversing all ordinary values, including especially the values of religion; but because it is so entirely new, and so contrary to all expectations, it cannot easily be expressed in the existing categories of religious thought, and the attempts of the New Testament writers to find intelligible language in which to set out their fundamental conviction are necessarily somewhat confused and obscure.

They realize that the ancient conception of a covenant between God and man has been at the same time fulfilled and given a new meaning. God does call men into a relationship of total dependence upon himself, he takes them as a people for his own possession, to whom he reveals himself in mercy and to whom he gives knowledge of himself through trust and obedience; but all legalistic interpretations of covenant have been overthrown. It is not a matter of the favour of God being granted in answer to the observance on man's part of the divine commandments. It is not the reward of obedience, for righteousness, or a right relationship to God, is no longer a state which man can attain by his own will or effort. The new covenant rests simply on God's acceptance of sinners. The religious axiom that God 'will by no means clear the guilty' has been dramatically disproved.

The ancient ideas of sacrifice were fulfilled in so far as they suggested the provision by God of a means for removing the obstacles thrown up by human sin, which cut men off from access to God, and suggested also the destruction of man's life in order that he may receive life at the hand of God. These things had been effected by God in Christ in a way which reduced the old sacrifices to shadows of the reality, useless in themselves except in so far as they pointed to this fulfilment, in a wholly new manner, of the aspirations which they had partially expressed. The Passover, in particular, furnished an impressive image by which to depict the Christians' conviction that they had been delivered from a state of dereliction and bondage and brought through the death of their old life into a new relationship to God as his children.

Another expressive image was ready to hand in the idea of Adam as the representative personification of humanity in its double aspect, as the creature of God, made capable of fellowship with him, in his image and likeness, yet estranged from him and in a state of enmity. In Christ man was restored to his proper character as God's son. Christ was the new Adam, the archetypal representative of humanity as accepted by God and in a state of reconciliation. The old Adam had been abolished, and man's life, as lived in hostility to God, had been put to death when Christ died and rose from the dead. The Christian believer had been transferred from the old sinful humanity to the new humanity of which Christ was the archetype and the starting-point. Here again the imagery suggested by the religious concepts of the Hebrew tradition was that of death leading to life.

These and other expressions of what God had done for man in Christ were no more than partial gropings after a set of concepts which, taken together, might convey something of the meaning of Christ's reconciliation of men to God. No single one of them, nor all of them together, were capable of furnishing more than an incomplete expression of the truth, for they belonged to a realm of religious belief which had been radically transformed. St Paul, in his wrestlings with the problem of the relation of faith in Christ to his native Pharisaism, came to realize the nature of this transformation more fully and clearly than most Christians of the apostolic age. He saw that the reconciliation of the world to God, effected by Christ, meant that the principle of law had been replaced by that of spontaneous and undeserved love. God's acceptance of man is not conditional upon anything that man may do. It is unrelated to justice, and it takes no account of merit or demerit. It is entirely paradoxical and contrary to all ordinary notions of reward and punishment. It means the abandonment of all the basic principles of legalism in men's relationship to God and their attitude to one another, for the essence of such legalism is the belief that man is treated by God on the ordinary principles of human justice and within a relationship like that of a master to a slave or a judge to a defendant, so that if man obeys orders he will find favour, if he is innocent he will be acquitted, but if he is disobedient or guilty he will incur displeasure and be punished. According to these principles, man's achievement is the basis of his standing in the sight of God. Hence his religion will be concerned with finding ways and means for securing his acceptance by God, and it will move in the sphere of commandments and prohibitions, duty and transgression, merit and guilt, reward and punishment.

St Paul realized the essential truth that the act of God in Christ had taken the whole question of man's relationship to God out of this area. It had done so because that relationship was now determined solely by the love of God. His gracious approach encountered man, not in the state in which he ought to be, or in which he would like to be, but where he actually is, in a condition of alienation and enmity.

III

Legalistic religion is essentially self-centred. It is concerned with the efforts of man to justify himself to himself and to God. It is the attempt of man, with or without the help of God, to make himself acceptable. But to seek to make himself acceptable is the very essence of sin. It is what prevents him from accepting God's acceptance of him as he is. It is what produces disharmony within himself, and the failure to face his own nature and come to terms with himself; and it is the impassable barrier which interposes itself between him and God, for it is the outcome of that self-centredness which is sin. The quest for self-justification is the basic expression of what St Paul calls 'the mind of the flesh'; it is the motive of a life alienated from God and therefore also from a man's proper being. Legalism (which for St Paul was summed up in Pharisaic confidence in the Law of Moses) cannot but minister to sin, for it expresses and generates that attitude to God which consists either in confidence in one's own achievement and the belief that one can become acceptable to God by virtue of one's own merits, or else in the overwhelming sense of guilt which indicates hatred of oneself and either despair and hatred of God or the fear of God which seeks for some means to propitiate his wrath and satisfy his justice.

If man cannot justify himself, because this would contradict the whole basis on which God in fact has chosen to accept him, and if God accepts man when he is in himself totally unacceptable, the whole foundation of legalism is overthrown. The gospel has replaced the law, for justification comes from the free and unmerited grace of God and has only to be accepted. So St Paul abandoned that 'righteousness which is in the law', by which he had formerly been 'found blameless', so that he might be found 'in Christ, not having a righteousness of mine own, even that which is of the law, but that which is through faith in Christ, the righteousness which is of God by faith' (Phil. iii. 9).

This depth of insight into the nature of the gospel is peculiarly characteristic of St Paul. The united witness of the New Testament, however, is in full agreement with his central conviction that in Christ God has declared his love for men at their most unacceptable and shown that he is truly their Father and not a master or a judge, unless they themselves insist on treating him so. 'God is love', and the death of Christ is the point at which his love encounters man supremely and decisively.

IV

When we turn from the New Testament to read what the Thirty-nine Articles of the Church of England tell us about the death of Christ we find ourselves abruptly plunged into a very different atmosphere. Christ 'truly suffered, was crucified, dead and buried, to reconcile his Father to us, and to be a sacrifice, not only for original guilt, but also for all actual sins of men'. Something has happened to the good news of the love of God. It was once a gospel: that God has reconciled men out of their self-centred endeavour to justify themselves and into a simple faith in his acceptance of them in the depths of their estrangement from him. Now it has become a message that the estrangement was on the side of God. God was at enmity with us, rather than we with him. He has been reconciled to us by the death of Christ. Man was guilty, but the guilt of his original transgression of God's will and all the actual offences against God's law which spring out of that state of being a transgressor has been annulled by the death of Christ as a sacrifice which expiates guilt. The work of Christ is now seen, not as effected from the side of God towards men, reconciling them to God, but from the side of man towards God, reconciling him and causing him to acquit the guilty. We are back again in the realm of justice and transgression of law. The favour of God must still be won, if not by men, then for men. It is, of course, clear that it cannot be won by man for himself. There is still a gospel of a kind here, for we are assured that what we could never hope to achieve has been done for us by Christ as man; but it is not the gospel of the free love of God. The categories of thought in which the death of Christ is interpreted are those of law, and legalism is no longer done away with.

Behind the language of Article II there stands the long history of the attempts of Christian thought to formulate a doctrine of the Atonement. Much in that history has been profitable and enlightening. Irenaeus, for instance, contributed much in his insistence upon the self-identification of the Son of God with humanity and upon the way in which Adam's sin—the attempt to gain independence for himself by denying his sonship to God and to set himself up in the place of God, living for and to himself—was reversed by Christ's human dependence upon his Father and his total obedience, so that the power of human sinfulness was broken, and, more mytho-logically, the devil who held man captive was defeated. The develop-ing theology of the Atonement was, however, vitiated by its departure, in a matter of fundamental principle, from the New Testament's gospel of the paradox of God's love for sinners: it tended to interpret sin in a legalistic fashion as a transgression of commandments instead of as a deep violation of personal relation-ship, and it found difficulty in acknowledging the essential truth that God accepts men as they are, without conditions.

At least as early as the time of Tertullian, man's relationship to God was being put back into the sphere of justice. Sin becomes transgression, and the sinner is one who has lost merit through his guilt. The regaining of his sonship towards God has to be obtained at the price of satisfaction. Sin is not a state of estrangement and disharmony, in which man finds himself through his effort to escape from the reality of himself and his Creator and take refuge in an artificial self which he constructs in order to bolster up his self-assurance; it is a matter of the breaking of commandments. The Christian who commits transgressions after his baptism falls away from the grace of God; but he may work his passage back into the divine favour. He may make satisfaction to the offended deity by works of penance that serve to offset his sins. His relationship to God is not that of a son to a father, but of a debtor to a creditor; and his object must be to keep his account in credit by a surplus of good deeds over bad. This theory of satisfaction, if it were applied to the parables of Jesus, would make the father exact compensation from the prodigal son before killing the fatted calf for him: so much work as a hired servant would have to be performed before the sinner could justly look for the restoration of his privileges as a son.

It is no long step from the application of the idea of satisfaction to sins committed after baptism and compensation for them by penance to the interpretation of Christ's death as the supreme satisfaction for original sin. By his life of total obedience and by his supremely meritorious death (its merit being in proportion to his own innocence and his voluntary acceptance of it), Christ made a full satisfaction in the place of sinful men. God's justice, which necessarily demands satisfaction for sin, has been satisfied and his wrath has been appeased, so that, having been propitiated and reconciled to men, he is now able freely to exercise his love in forgiving them. The difference between the initial remission of sins in baptism and the forgiveness of post-baptismal sins is simply that in the former case men cannot offer satisfaction, and only the Son of God is 'good enough to pay the price of sin' vicariously on their behalf, whereas in the latter, with the help of God's grace, men can perform prescribed works of penance and in due course may hope to merit reinstatement as sons of God.

This disastrous translation of personal reconciliation with the Father through the acceptance of free justification into terms of debit and credit has gone far to reverse the true meaning of Christ's death. In much of the traditional teaching the Atonement has come to be seen as an act by which God's attitude to sinners has been changed, and by which he has been enabled to forgive them without violating the ordinary principles of justice. The Cross is no longer the point at which the paradoxical love of God embraces men at the moment when they are supremely unlovable; it is rather the scene of an apotheosis of law and justice. It is where we see justice enthroned as God. There is still a revelation of divine love in the death of Christ, for God, in the person of the Son, undertakes, out of his own spontaneous love, to satisfy the demands of his justice; but love has to serve the ends of justice, and justice remains the higher principle, inhibiting the free acceptance of sinful men until full satisfaction has been made on their behalf. God is justice. He is also love; but only secondarily. It is not surprising that the interpretation of the Atonement in terms of satisfaction and propitiation has so often been accompanied, at least in popular theology, by a conception of the relation of the Son to the Father in which the former is subordinated to the latter, for if the Son reveals and is love he is subordinate to the higher principle of justice.

We find this type of thought about the saving work of Christ in Athanasius, along with other and better conceptions. The justice of God has pronounced sentence of death on Adam and his race. God's dilemma is that either he must allow those whom he created in his own image to perish, to his own dishonour, or he must deny himself by tearing up his own just decree, which he would be doing were he simply to forgive them. The mission of the Word is to take a body capable of dying, so that by offering himself to death on man's behalf he may save the consistency of the divine sentence against sin and discharge the debt of life which man owes to God.

This principle of law and justice, debt and its discharge, is, however, especially characteristic of Western theology. As it was formulated by Anselm it is certainly preferable in many respects to the theory of a ransom paid to the devil, which was so popular in much patristic thought. Anselm tries hard to emphasize the initiative of the Father in the work of redemption, and to show that his love is the motive of the entire action; but he is using categories of thought which are fundamentally unsuitable. His thinking is ultimately controlled by the idea of compensation offered from the side of man to God, sufficient not only to repay the obligation of obedience due from men to the Creator, which they had withheld from him, but also to satisfy his offended honour. The divine justice is still enthroned as supreme, and God's love is displayed in the working out, for man's sake, of a means whereby its demands may fittingly be met.

V

Such theories exhibit two fundamental defects. They subordinate love to justice, and so resolve the principle of the gospel into that of law, on the supposition that God's action takes place within a framework of law and that what he has done in Christ is to meet the demands of law himself, instead of exacting them from the sinners for whom Christ is a substitute. They also bring back into the gospel of reconciliation a subtle form of the idea of merit and reward. God does not reconcile sinners to himself freely and spontaneously. His favour is still proportional to desert. He does not simply accept the unacceptable on the sole condition of willingness to be accepted; he looks to man to make himself acceptable, and, since man cannot do this, it is done for him vicariously by Christ. Man has still something to offer to God from his own side; he need not utterly abandon his pretensions to self-justification or the idea that he may have some merit to plead. He possesses it vicariously. What he offers is, indeed, not his own but Christ's; but the merits of Christ are credited to him and Christ is justified in his stead. He is still able, because of vicarious merit, to plead something before God. He can, as it were, clothe himself with Christ's achievement as his substitute, and need not stand utterly naked in the presence of God. He can plead innocence before God because his guilt has been transferred to another, and need not throw away the last vestige of his self-justification by accepting the free gift of sonship, given to him without conditions, just as he is, guilt and all. In respect of man's relationship to the Father, as well as of the Father's attitude to man, the theology of satisfaction sets the Atonement within the sphere of law and perverts the central message of the gospel.

The medieval conception of the sacrifice of the Mass made the transition which had taken place in the theology of the Atonement more explicit. Instead of being the act of God in Christ reconciling the world to himself, it was the act of the God-man, from the side of man, appeasing the wrath of the Father and satisfying the demands of his justice. The priest who offered Christ on behalf of the living and the dead set his vicarious death between the people's sins and their just reward. It was an act directed towards God as the judge who avenges transgressions of his law, rather than as the God who declares his acceptance of sinners at the cost of the death of the

God-man at their hands. In popular piety even Christ the mediator came to be thought of primarily as the judge upon his throne; the terrible judge against whose sentence of condemnation the intercession of the saints, and especially of his Mother, must be entreated in order to propitiate him and induce him to be merciful.

The reaction of the Reformers was violent against this last belief, and it was their main concern to repudiate the 'blasphemy' of the Mass in which man presumed to satisfy the demands of God by repeating, or re-enacting, the unique sacrifice of Christ made once for all at Calvary. They were aware that man cannot justify himself before God, and that all that is required of him is to accept the sonship that is given freely to him as a sinner. They knew that God accepts sinners by grace alone and that he does not wait until they become acceptable, nor even until he has made them acceptable. Justification has simply to be received: it is taken by faith alone, not by faith plus virtue of any kind. The gospel is good news of God's love, not a rehash of legalism. They did not, however, carry their doctrine of justification far enough. It was still set within a framework of merit and satisfaction: not the merits of men, including the saints, nor any satisfaction made to God by man, but the merits of Christ and the satisfaction offered by him to the Father. Justice and law were still enthroned as a false god in the place of love, and the free grace of God to sinners was still inhibited by the prior demand that compensation for sin must be paid before God can forgive. They failed to realize that forgiveness after satisfaction has been fully made is no forgiveness at all, even though in this case it is God, the forgiver, who undertakes to pay the compensation to himself. They envisaged a dichotomy in God, justice being set over against love.

It is true, of course, that the Reformers' teaching on Atonement was not confined to the idea of satisfaction. Luther, in particular, held strongly to the belief that in his redemptive work Christ had fought the power of evil on man's behalf, and he shared the insight of Irenaeus and St Paul into the central importance of the doctrine of the Second Adam. Christ as the true and representative man had reversed man's disobedience, defeated the principle of sin which is man's self-centred desire to secure his independence against God, and restored fellowship between man and his Creator. This is true and important doctrine: a vital element in our understanding of the work of Christ, both in his earthly life of dependence on the Father and in the death which is the moment of climax when obedience is pressed to the point of death and beyond it.

Nevertheless, the Reformers' interpretation of the Atonement was too largely formulated in terms of the reconciling of a wrathful God to guilty sinners; and this was emphasized, in a manner which contrasts with the teaching of Anselm, by the stress which they laid on the concept of vicarious punishment. God is, in this view, a judge who declares his righteousness in punishing sinners. Sin merits death, and God cannot condone sin or acquit the guilty without exacting retribution for their transgressions. The love of God is shown, not in a paradoxical acceptance of the guilty, but in himself providing a substitute for the guilty, to whose shoulders their guilt is transferred and upon whom the righteous vengeance of the divine law may be expended in place of those who deserve to suffer it. The Son takes upon himself the sentence pronounced against sinners by the Father. So far as they are concerned, it is a sentence, not simply of physical death, but of eternal torment in hell; and Calvin was prepared to push the theory of vicarious punishment so far as to assert that Christ in some sense suffered the pains of hell for the sinners whom his propitiatory death rescued from them.

VI

The theory of penal substitution has often been criticized as immoral. The immorality generally alleged against it is its representation of God as one who inflicts punishment upon the innocent. Transgression has been committed; the penalty must be paid for transgression; and it does not matter who pays it, the guilty or the innocent, so long as abstract justice is satisfied. This is true, however far the crudity of this conception may be modified by the qualification that in inflicting the penalty upon Christ God himself finds the means to satisfy his own justice, and in the person of the Son takes the punishment upon himself. Much more serious, however, even than this caricature of justice is the blasphemy of supposing that God inflicts retributive punishment like a hanging judge. Retribution is impersonal; it considers offences in the abstract rather than either the offender or the person offended against. It assigns to every crime a fixed retributive penalty, without regard for the reclamation of the criminal or the rehabilitation of his victim. It is a legalizing of revenge, and the ideal or typical form of retribution is the death penalty.

In human society punishment is necessary. In a sinful world it is not possible for every individual citizen to be treated according to the true principles of love. Turning the other cheek cannot be enforced as a binding principle in social life. The task of the State is to make civilized life possible and to create tolerable conditions in which the individual can go peacefully about his business. It must necessarily act in accordance with the principles of justice, assimilating these so far as may be to the ideal of love, but recognizing that they inevitably fall far short of it and that in an imperfect world justice, even when informed by love to the extent that this may be possible, is only a second best; it is a rough and ready principle for making organized society workable.

In this respect, the restraint of offenders and the compulsion of law have some resemblance to war in international relations. Before the atomic age, war, too, could be justified on some occasions as a rough and ready method of restraining an aggressor and making possible conditions for progress towards a firmer state of peace. Similarly, it may be recognized that it is necessary for society to restrain wrongdoers, sometimes by force, and, for the sake of preserving order and deterring potential criminals, to inflict punishment upon offenders. Even so, punishment ought to aim at reformation, and in a civilized community there ought to be some regard for the offender as a person; and it is becoming increasingly clear that the extent to which the criminal can properly be held to be directly and personally responsible for his offence is narrowly limited. Many would therefore hold that to inflict the purely retributive and deterrent penalty of death, treating the criminal as one who bears the sole and complete responsibility for his crime and ruling out all possibility of his reclamation, is itself criminal.

Whether they are right or wrong in this belief, it is certain that we ought not to ascribe purely retributive justice to God. He does not deal with sinners in such terms. In the first place, it is impossible to assign direct personal responsibility to each individual who shares in the sin, that is the alienation from God, of the world at large. Sin is not mere transgression of law. It is a personal condition of estrangement brought about by man's desire for self-justification. Every human being is born into a world deeply permeated by this sinfulness, and he is, as it were, absorbed into this environment of hostility to God and disregard of him, so that every aspect of its sinfulness affects him. Racial hostility at the present time is an obvious example of one such aspect; the whole of humanity is in a sense involved in this particular expression of man's basic sinfulness, but it cannot be said that every individual, or perhaps even any individual, is directly responsible for it through his own deliberate choice, so that he is to be reckoned personally guilty.

Secondly, we must not make a God in the image of sinful men, who, through lack of love, have to control their social relationships by means of a rough and ready justice. God, the Father of mankind, does not deal with his children on the basis of deterrence and retribution. Not even a decent human father does this. To condemn the offender to death may possibly be necessary in the conditions of sinful society; but, if so, it signifies the bankruptcy of justice through the failure of love. It is a short way of dealing with an unsolved problem; but it is no solution, and, if God were to adopt the same method and consign sinners to destruction in hell, he could no longer be called Almighty, for he would have given proof of his impotence. To hang the criminal is to admit defeat at the level of love, and a God whose dealings with his creatures end in their condemnation to hell is a God whom evil has defeated. The traditional picture of the Day of Doom is of a God who is powerless to save and redeem to the full; and the picture is not greatly improved if we place in the centre of it, not sinners being thrown into a flaming pit, but Jesus suffering torture on the Cross as their substitute. In either case God is imagined as a judge who exacts revenge. It is high time to discard the vestiges of a theory of Atonement that was geared to a conception of punishment which found nothing shocking in the idea that God should crucify sinners or the substitute who took their place. It is time, too, to stop the mouth of the blasphemer who calls it 'sentimentality' to reject the idea of a God of retribution.

This is by no means to deny the reality of hell. Hell is all too real. It is the state of those who refuse to be accepted freely by God, and who try to escape at once from their own true selves and from their Father. Hell is separation from God; but God does not decree any such separation, nor does he make a hell and thrust men into it. Hell is made by man, and only man can consign himself to it. So, too, the death of Christ was inflicted as a punishment, not by God but by sinners in the attempt to justify themselves, to secure their own righteousness and hence, though without realizing it consciously, to reject God to the uttermost; in fact, to kill him with every accompaniment of contempt and hatred.

VII

To interpret the Atonement in terms of satisfaction or punishment raises another serious difficulty. The parables of Christ have much to say about the love of God and his acceptance of sinners by sheer grace. In his own dealings with sinners, the paralytic, Levi, Zacchaeus, the woman taken in adultery, he declares the divine forgiveness and receives them into fellowship with himself. The father in the parable welcomed the prodigal without conditions. Zacchaeus was not called upon to make restitution before Christ entered his home; he repented and made amends because Christ had already accepted him as a sinner. To suppose that this manifestation of the love of God was made possible only because Christ was afterwards going to offer satisfaction to the divine justice on behalf of these people by suffering death is absurd. If the words and deeds of Jesus had only a proleptic or provisional significance, the gospel stories make no sense.

If Christ's death is the supreme expression of the love of God which, in him, had already reached out to some men and touched them, it is continuous with all that he did and said on earth. In his life and death, alike, God was acting towards sinners, breaking through their self-centred resistance and reconciling them to himself. His suffering and death are the climax of man's attempt to justify himself in hatred towards the God whom he fails to recognize as such, to rid himself of his sense of guilt, which is both a symptom and a form of his self-justification, by killing the one who spoke and acted in God's name, even as the prophets had been persecuted of old (as Christ himself reminds us), and to resist with fury and violence God's acceptance of him without merit or achievement of any kind being credited to him. The Cross is the ultimate sign of man's hatred; and in that very focal point of hatred the love of God accepts him despite the worst that he can do, in his most extreme sinfulness and bitter enmity. Christ takes upon himself man's hatred, to the point of sharing in man's own sense of estrangement and despair. It is the paradox and miracle of love, whose triumph, and with it man's reconciliation, is sealed in the Resurrection. The sinner is saved by the blood of Christ which his hatred shed. The death of Christ is the fulfilment of the ancient hope of expiation, the taking away of sin, for by it sin is removed out of the way in the only manner in which sin can be removed, by the acceptance of the sinner into sonship. Christ's death means the death of the old Adam, whose life is centred upon self; and in this aspect it is a representative death in which all those are sharers who are accepted by God through him: a death to sin and self-justification, leading to life as a son of God, reconciled to him through faith responding to love.

9

THE GROUNDS OF CHRISTIAN MORAL JUDGMENTS

BY

G. F. WOODS

SYNOPSIS

I. *Moral judgments*

1. Moral judgments not reducible to judgments which are not moral.
2. The conditions and occasions of moral judgments.
3. Grounds for moral judgments.

II. *Traditional grounds for Christian moral judgments*

4. Biblical grounds.
5. Theological grounds.
6. Natural law.
7. Inadequate alternative grounds: (i) natural science; (ii) moral philosophy.

III. *Moral grounds and metaphysical grounds*

8. The analogical use of the word 'ground' in the phrase 'moral ground'.
9. Moral judgments on the ground of: (i) what is the case; (ii) what ought to be the case.
10. Moral grounds always include metaphysical grounds.

IV. *Grounds of Christian moral judgments*

11. Christian moral judgments on the ground of: (i) what is the case; (ii) what ought to be the case.
12. The ultimate unity of 'what is' and 'what ought to be' in God.

THE GROUNDS OF CHRISTIAN MORAL
JUDGMENTS

THIS ESSAY is not concerned with the disparity between Christian profession and Christian practice. This must be the constant concern of Christian pastors and teachers, but my concern is with the element of bewilderment in the minds of many Christians today about the content and justification of Christian morality. This is a fact which deserves quiet study. On quite a number of moral issues the minds of thoughtful and responsible Christians are perplexed. They seriously desire to live as Christians but they find it difficult to know what a Christian ought to do, or, when they are sure what a Christian ought to do, they find it difficult to offer grounds for their convictions which they find convincing. We have, for instance, the agonizing questions of pacifism and euthanasia. These questionings and misgivings are not the outcome of moral irresponsibility and carelessness. They are most keenly felt by those whose Christian moral sensitiveness is most acute. Even so, we must not lose our sense of perspective. Christian moral perplexity is not a wholly new fact. Christian moral decisions did not begin to be difficult in the present generation; it has always been harder to define the Christian life than to recognize it. When the world has been dark and bewildering, Christian conduct has continued to shine by its own light. We must not assume that uncertainty about the content and justification of Christian morality is only a modern problem. At many stages in the history of the Christian Church, particularly in periods of social change and striking advance in the various fields of human knowledge, many thoughtful Christians must have found themselves somewhat at a loss. And, even in morally more stable periods, no sensitive Christian has been without moments of genuine uncertainty about the application of Christian standards to particular cases. We need not idealize the past in order to emphasize the gravity of the present situation. We cannot meet the present challenge by moral dogmatism or moral scepticism and we must be on our guard against accepting superficial solutions which happen to be expressed in a contemporary terminology. However, I see no reason why Anglican moral theology should not work gradually towards a solution of some of our moral problems. Resolute pessimism is as tiresome as foolish optimism.

My purpose in this quite tentative essay is to study the grounds of Christian moral judgments. I certainly have no neat solutions to all our problems but I hope to show how our present bewilderment has arisen and to suggest some of the ways in which we may gradually move towards greater clarity and assurance in our Christian moral judgments. I shall consider the way in which we make moral judgments and seek to show that we cannot avoid relying upon metaphysical grounds both in secular and in Christian judgments. The fact that I do not make much use of the traditional vocabulary of Christian morality must not be taken to mean that I think this whole vocabulary is obsolete. My desire has been to accept the discipline of avoiding conventional terms in the description of our Christian moral experience so that I might look at the experience itself. And the best way to rehabilitate many of the terms may be to discover that we really need them to express what we want to say. This mode of approach is rather cumbersome but it is, I believe, justifiable if it helps us in understanding the grounds on which a thoughtful Christian should now make his moral decisions.

I

We have no doubt about the fact that we often make judgments which we call moral, but are we quite sure that in the last resort these may not be reduced to other types of judgment which are not moral? For instance, if we say that something is right, do we ultimately mean no more than that we are saying that it is right?

Is it just a fact that we are making the judgment as it may also have been a fact that it was a wet day when we were making it? Are moral judgments no more than the opinions customarily held by some social group at some period of time? Are Christian moral judgments simply the moral judgments which have been made at some particular period by those who professed and called themselves Christians? I believe myself that we cannot eliminate the distinction between judging what is the case and judging what ought to be the case. I find in my own experience that there is an irreducible distinction between seeing that something is so and seeing that it ought to be so. The two judgments are not the same. I find the distinction extremely difficult to understand but I have no doubt that it exists. I cannot eliminate it by discarding the vocabulary in which it has been expressed. If I did cease to describe certain judgments as 'moral', I should have to find another word to do the same work. But to affirm that we do make judgments which are legitimately and irreducibly called 'moral', does not determine whether we all make these judgments in the right way nor whether we all agree in the judgments which we make. Though the study of moral judgments necessarily includes the study of moral language, it must include the study of the situations which continue to make the use of moral language useful. There are no purely linguistic questions in the study of moral behaviour.

How do we come to make moral judgments? This may mean either, 'What are the conditions which make it possible for us to make them?', or 'What prompts us to make particular moral judgments in the conditions where it is possible for us to make them?'. I cannot believe that it is possible for moral judgments to be made where there is no moral agent. If in the last resort we are transitory collocations of entities which are utterly impersonal, I do not see how moral action can be conceivable. The various forms of impersonalism preclude moral conduct. In a moral act there is a moral agent who acts; who knows that he acts; and who knows some kind of distinction between what is done and what ought to be done. In these conditions, moral judgments may arise. They may be about many points in the moral case. They may, for instance, be primarily about the responsibility of the agent or primarily about the rightness or wrongness of the moral act. In this essay I am concerned with the grounds of moral judgments concerning moral acts. It is a nice point to decide whether there are any human acts which have no moral significance. For instance, when one is about to light a cigarette, is there any moral difference between selecting one match rather than another from a box of matches? In normal circumstances I see no place here for a moral judgment, but, in some intricate piece of espionage, it might be that the careful selection of an exceptionally thin match might be an agreed sign leading to an act which would be considered to be moral or immoral. Fortunately, most of our actions are so simple that we are hardly, if at all, conscious of making a moral decision. We pay our fare on the bus without making an agonizing reappraisal of the moral justification of private property and the ultimate vindication of public transport. But in hard decisions, we are conscious of being in moral doubt both before and after the act. These are the occasions when we are prompted to make explicit moral judgments and to become aware of the moral grounds on which we are basing our decisions.

When we reflect upon the grounds of our moral decision we may come to see quite clearly that we were not at the time fully conscious of all the factors which led to our decision. Through private and public criticism, we can be made aware of influences which have affected our moral judgment without our being conscious of their influence at the time. We act on unconscious and conscious grounds. For instance, on some question of social justice, we may think that we are judging impartially when in fact we are simply voicing the traditional social outlook of the social class to which we happen to belong. But this well-known fact does not relieve us of the duty of responsible decision. It is our duty, when we are made aware of these unconscious grounds, not to despair of making well-grounded moral judgments but actively to examine whether we can morally approve or disapprove of the factors which have unconsciously influenced our decision. I think it is convenient to distinguish between the causes of our moral judgments and the reasons by which we seek to justify them. It may well happen that our accounts of the conscious grounds of our moral decisions may be far more coherent and articulate than what actually took place when we were in the throes of making the decision. What we say afterwards is usually somewhat edited to explain and justify what we chose to do. Our smooth reports are not unlike the accounts of battles given in retrospect by successful, and unsuccessful, generals. It is convenient to distinguish the conscious grounds for our moral decisions into two groups: those which concern our knowledge of what is the case and those which concern our knowledge of what ought to be the case. For instance, if a man says that he did give a half-crown and not a two-shilling piece to the shopkeeper, and if we believe that people ought to tell the truth, we may direct our attention either to the facts of the case or to the obligation to tell the truth. We can make an immense variety of judgments either about the facts or about the obligation but, in so doing, we are conscious that there is an important difference between the two classes of judgment. What is the case differs from what ought to be the case. In making our moral judgments in moral cases, we are clearly aware of a distinction between basing our judgment upon the facts of the case and basing our judgments upon what ought to be the case. Our moral grounds are both factual and evaluative.

II

For a number of reasons some of the traditional grounds for Christian moral decisions have lost something of their former stability. I shall select three of the traditional grounds for Christian moral judgments which no longer possess unquestioned firmness and seek to show why some of the modern alternative grounds are also proving unreliable.

The tradition of biblical ethics is not functioning easily. The progress of historical criticism has overwhelmed biblical literalism but its ghost still influences the popular view of Christian ethics. There is still a tendency to use the New Testament as a store of proof texts, with supreme authority given to any words of Christ which appear in the canonical Scripture. But not all the sayings which are reported of Christ are easily understood. For instance, what is really meant by the saying, 'Whosoever shall smite thee on thy right cheek, turn to him the other also' (Matt. v. 39, *A.V.*)? And even apparently plain statements of Christ may be difficult to interpret in practice, for example, 'What therefore God hath joined together, let not man put asunder' (Mark x. 9, *A.V.*). Moreover, this understanding of Christian ethics is at a loss about matters such as atomic warfare to which no direct reference is made in the New Testament. A more thoughtful approach to the New Testament Scriptures advances beyond an unhistorical study of single texts in isolation and considers Christian principles and the mind and spirit of Christ. A deeper study displays the close interrelation between Christian conduct and Christian doctrine. A fine example of this kind of study is to be found in Dr C. H. Dodd's book, entitled *Gospel and Law* (1951). All these acts of deepening interpretation are based upon the conviction that the New Testament still offers a substantially reliable account of the life and teaching of Christ. Where this confidence is lost, it is hard to see how the New Testament can be useful as a ground for Christian moral judgments. Generally speaking, the advance of biblical scholarship has enabled Christians to make a better use of the Scriptures as a guide to Christian living, but serious problems remain about the use of the historical method because much more is becoming known about the ways in which the metaphysical presuppositions of an historian affect the manner in which he interprets the available evidence. The old appeal to the bar of history is now a rather complex matter of competing jurisdictions. For these and many other reasons, the appeal to the Bible as the ground of Christian moral choices is recognized as being less simple than used to be supposed.[1] But the fact that it is an instrument which has to be handled with care by no means implies that it is now useless.

Some of the present hesitations about using the Bible as a ground for moral judgments are probably due to various misgivings about the whole conception of theological ethics.[2] These doubts spring not so much from a direct disbelief in God as from moral objections to treating God as the ground of moral distinctions. It is asked how we can discover the will of God in a moral case. And, even if we know how to discover the will of God, are we in danger of doing what is right simply for the sake of some divine reward? Is our Christian duty being reduced to a matter of prudent calculation? And is the distinction between what is and what ought to be simply accepted and recognized by God or is it the result of his will? If it is simply recognized by God, it is not grounded in God but in some foundation other than God. If it is a result of the will of God, are we being asked to obey a divine will or command which is itself inscrutable by our criteria of right and wrong? Can we be morally justified in obeying an injunction which morally we cannot understand? Are theological ethics an infantile way of thinking about the grounds of moral action which we ought gradually to discard as we grow older? These are not new questions. They have been asked for many generations but they are being asked afresh. They occur to the minds not only of critics of Christianity but also to those of thoughtful Christians. While these questions remain unanswered in the minds of the critics or the Christians, the use of the

[1] William Paley, *Works*, ed. D. S. Wayland (1837), vol. I, p. 41: 'Now, there are two methods of coming at the will of God on any point. I. By his express declarations, when they are to be had, and which must be sought for in Scripture. II. By what we can discover of his designs and disposition from his works; or, as we usually call it, the light of Nature.' This is a simple but not thoughtless appeal to Scripture.

[2] Cf. W. G. Maclagan, *The Theological Frontier of Ethics* (1961).

Bible as a guide to moral conduct is liable to decrease. Thus a variety of factors have combined in a confused way to lower the prestige of the Bible as a moral authority. Whether this decline is warranted is another question.

The tradition that grounds for moral action may be found in a body of Natural Law has also lost some of its effectiveness, though it remains very influential. There are several reasons for this decrease. In an age of faith, the natural world is viewed as the creation of God. Nature is understood as a hierarchy of beings, each possessing its own nature. Impersonal natural beings follow their own nature automatically. Personal beings have a rational knowledge of their true nature and are free to live or not to live in accordance with it. But in an empirical age such as our own, the order of nature tends to be understood as what is open to the investigations of natural science. The supernatural is overlooked or denied. Natural processes are explained by natural law. Natural law becomes a statement of what happens, not of what ought to happen. It comes to mean a convenient expression, particularly in some agreed symbols, of some natural uniformity which has been observed. The view begins to prevail that nature simply takes its course and offers no moral guidance to mankind. In an evolutionary process, the survival of the fittest means no more than that those who in fact survive have shown themselves capable of survival. It is as though the sole indubitable significance of passing an examination consisted in the fact of the candidate's name being included in the pass list. Whether he ought to have passed is another matter. Even when the ethics of naturalism are resisted, those who believe in a natural moral law find it difficult to discriminate between what is natural and what is unnatural. Is, for instance, family planning natural or unnatural? And, if we do know what is natural, why should we do what is natural? In what sense does the natural world include both what is the case and what ought to be the case? Can any natural fact or facts be the ground of the distinction between right and wrong? How can we use the word 'natural' in any clear sense if we are not clear what we mean by 'Nature'? I mention these points and questions, in passing, only to show that the tradition of Natural Law as a guide to right living is somewhat puzzling but, once again, as in the case of the Bible, we ought not hastily to discard an instrument as useless because it is hard to use and may be misused. All ordnance survey maps are not useless because some of them urgently require revision. But it is obvious that acts of revision are more easily undertaken when the method of revision is known and accepted.

However, the business of living does not wait for the publication of perfect ethical systems. Moral decisions cannot be indefinitely postponed until the traditions of biblical ethics, theological ethics, and natural law have been revised and commended to the popular mind. It is not surprising that when traditional moral guidance is not trusted, an appeal is made to alternative moral authorities. For instance, in view of the present prestige of the natural sciences, it is quite understandable that moral guidance should be sought from the scientists. They offer so much control over what is that it is assumed they must be equally competent to say what ought to be. But the scientists usually decline the office of moral tutors on the ground that their professional duty is limited to a study of the facts of the natural order. They have often said that the use which is made of their discoveries is not their responsibility, but they have shown an increasing tendency to emphasize the need to use our power over nature for the welfare and not for the destruction of mankind. But, when they speak in this way, they are speaking as morally responsible men, who happen also to have outstanding scientific qualifications. In so far as they are making moral judgments on the grounds of their scientific knowledge, they are not speaking as scientists. In the realms of individual and social psychology, when an analysis of human behaviour is being made, it is most valuable to have a dispassionate study of what takes place which is devoid of moral approval or disapproval. In such studies and statements, the psychologist is not professionally engaged in passing moral judgments but he remains under an obligation to act in accordance with his scientific conscience during his investigations. This repression of any moral judgment upon the behaviour under analysis is possible and justified as long as the act of analysis continues but, when some kind of psychiatric treatment is proposed with a view to the restoration of mental health, the psychiatrist must begin to act on the basis of some notion of what ought to be the case. He need not have any precise conception of what is involved in mental health. He may have only a general confidence that human personality will develop well when various psychical obstacles are removed. He may claim not to be imposing any rigid pattern of behaviour but simply allowing the human personality to develop its proper powers. Yet he cannot avoid the moral judgment that it is somehow better for people to develop well than to fail to develop, or to develop in unfortunate ways. He may, however, hold very definite views about the shape which individual and social life should assume. He is then acting as a moralist even if he rejects the title. But he may claim that he is no more than a kind of social engineer who uses his skill to fulfil social projects which he has not himself chosen. He may claim that he is doing no more than promote the kind of social health which is admired in the society in which he happens to live. But, as a person, he cannot ultimately escape the moral responsibility for using his professional capacities in the service of a particular purpose, for example, in advising a propaganda ministry in a totalitarian regime. The general outcome is that natural science can never of itself provide adequate grounds for moral decisions. The natural scientist and the scientists of the mind, while rightly rejecting any so-called natural or revealed moral standard which ignores scientific knowledge, must inevitably find it impossible to base their moral judgments, either in reference to their own actions or in reference to the guidance which they may give to others, on purely scientific grounds. There are no purely scientific grounds for moral decisions.

When the moral agent finds that the sciences cannot offer him grounds for his moral judgments, he may turn hopefully to philosophical ethics. He is likely to be disappointed. In an age of metaphysical diffidence and disintegration, it is only to be expected that systems of ethics should be under suspicion. Without a generally agreed view of the world and human nature, there is no frame or context within which a fully articulated system of right conduct may be constructed. This loss of metaphysical confidence is not due to any lack of philosophical ability but to the sheer awareness of the complexity of the natural order and of human history. In this situation, the classic ethical theories remain in being but are seldom the primary concern of the contemporary moral philosophy. The intuitionist theory that by some kind of moral intuition we know what to do in particular circumstances or that we know what moral principles are self-evident has lost ground because in fact we disagree about what particular acts ought to be done and because the proposed principles seem to conflict or to be so abstract as to be of little or no use in practice. Whether this recession from intuitionism is fully justified is another question. In our empirically disposed age, utilitarianism which advises us to look at the consequences of our actions as the ground for our moral decisions remains more attractive. But even when the calculation of the consequences is reasonably practicable, it remains necessary to decide whether they are good or bad and what their just distribution is amongst the people immediately and remotely concerned. The philosophical spirit has turned to a more modest task than the elaboration of ethical systems. It has concentrated upon an exact study of the use of language in moral discourse. The aim is to give an illuminating analysis of the way people talk when they are engaged in moral conversation. It is believed that the analyst should be able to give a disinterested account of moral linguistic behaviour without divulging his own moral convictions and without allowing them silently to influence his report. It thus becomes a professional virtue in a moral philosopher to refrain from offering any detailed guidance upon particular moral problems. He remits the duty of giving such guidance to moralists and theologians. There can be the implication that really no one is justified in offering moral guidance which claims to be authoritative. The broad result is that a Christian facing the serious moral problems of everyday life is not now given by most moral philosophers either a system of ethics or detailed guidance in particular moral cases. I am by no means unsympathetic to this view of the proper task of the professional moral philosopher but it does mean that Christians who find deficiencies in their traditional instruments of moral guidance will not usually find an answer to their moral problems by turning to what is written by the majority of contemporary moral philosophers. They are primarily engaged in a different enterprise.

Though a philosophical concern with detailed moral problems has receded in England, the amorphous existentialist movement on the Continent has been seriously concerned about practical moral issues upon the basis of a fresh exploration of what it means to be a human being. These views are often given somewhat obliquely through novels and plays, because the existentialist holds the view that man has no unchanging essence but fashions his own being in his daily existence. Man is not a given substance with a set of powers which he may, as occasion permits, recognize and exercise. He is a self-creative being who is always more than what he has so far become. He is not imprisoned in his past. He is open to the future. His inventiveness is more than making public what has always been included in the unpublished inventory of his own possessions. He is creating his standards in his actions. As there are almost as many existentialisms as there are existentialists, any generalizations are very hazardous, but without somewhat bold generalizations an outline discussion cannot advance. The existentialist mood might appear to lead straight to a quite anarchical view of morality but, in fact, both Heidegger and Sartre make a distinction between a way of living which is authentic and one which is unauthentic; between a way of living in good faith or in bad faith. The basic misconduct is to live without sincerity and integrity. To submit by choice or by thoughtlessness to any form of social or mental totalitarianism is to lose genuine existence; personal life lapses into an anonymous and impersonal functionalism. It looks as though the old distinction between what is and what ought to be has been rediscovered in novel forms. In any case, a sheer emphasis upon sincerity and integrity, while supremely relevant in assessing praiseworthiness and blameworthiness, does not provide any clear ground for distinguishing between acts which are good and those which are bad. A man may quite sincerely do an act which is wrong. An emphasis upon moral integrity, while rightly emphasizing the importance of making responsible decisions, does not in itself show us what we ought to do. Sincerity alone is not a sufficient guide for moral judgments. I do not think that existentialism is consciously affecting the moral decisions now made by ordinary Christians but I think that, if it were better known, it would speak to the condition of mind in which many people now find themselves when they are in the act of making moral decisions. Moreover, I believe that existentialism is a valuable protest against the various forms of impersonalism which are threatening us today.

The purpose of this cursory report has not been to give any full account of present-day thinking about moral issues nor to estimate the adequacy or inadequacy of the ways of thinking which have been described. The primary purpose has been to give some insight into some of the reasons why a thoughtful Christian of today often finds himself somewhat bewildered in making moral judgments. His position might be compared to that of a navigator of a ship who has lost confidence in the reliability of his compass and the visibility or even dependability of the heavenly bodies and is puzzled to find that what he took to be alternative direction systems seem to be full of ingenuity and knowledge of the natural world but somehow unable to give any particular guidance about the particular course to follow on any particular occasion. As an interim solution, he may revert to the less sophisticated practice of taking soundings by hand. These are not infallible but they may be the start of more assured orientations.

III

In speaking of the 'ground' of a moral judgment, we are using an analogy. Like all analogies it is less than perfect. In becoming identical with what is being analogically described, it would cease to be an analogy. It can never reproduce without some measure of distortion the thing which is being explained. Ground commonly means the ground, for example, upon which a house stands. But a house does not simply stand upon the top soil. It rests upon the firm ground which is some distance below the accidental surface of the site. The real foundation may be the rock which supports the ground. On what is the rock grounded? This question becomes foolish within the context, because for practical purposes the ground is the layer of firm material which bears the weight of the house. There must always be something hazardous, and possibly misleading, in taking the way in which one physical thing supports another physical thing as an analogy for the reasons which support our deliberate moral judgments. The analogy may not be too inappropriate in describing the factual basis of our judgments but it is under very great strain when it is used to describe the basis of what ought to be the case and the way in which our judgments rest upon what we accept as obligatory. There are so many kinds of grounds and so many kinds of support which the various grounds may offer. Though the use of open and concealed analogies is virtually unavoidable in moral philosophy, we must learn to be on our guard against becoming imprisoned within the analogies which we use. Our analogies must remain subordinate to our insight.

What we believe to be the case is the first type of ground on which we base our moral judgments. A distinction is here assumed between ourselves and the case; between what we believe to be the facts of the case and the actual facts of the case; between the case as known and the case in itself. This distinction cannot arise if there is no one to know the case. To whom can a moral case be known? It can be known only to those in some way involved in the case. They may be distinguished according to the standpoint from which they have an opportunity of studying the case. Whether as groups or individuals, they occupy the standpoint of the agent; of the patient, that is, the person primarily affected by the moral act; of the spectator who observes the act but not as agent or patient. Each one possesses a certain mobility in time and space in relation to the case. What they can see of the facts of the case is affected by their viewpoint. But what they can observe is not always the same as what is in fact observed. The special concerns and interests of the observer vitally influence what he notices. He attends to a restricted field within the general field of possible observation. Those who attend to a moral case are primarily interested in those facts which have some moral significance. They study the material facts. From any of these typical standpoints it may often be difficult to determine the point at which the observable facts cease to be morally relevant. In *The Mikado*, the flowers that bloomed in the spring had obviously nothing to do with the case but they might have been a vital matter in a bitter dispute between two market-gardeners. And we are unlikely to assume that a theft at Hampstead has anything to do with the fact that at the material time there was an exceptionally high tide at Liverpool. A ruthless dictator may ignore as morally irrelevant the fact that his policy will incidentally cause the death of some innocent people who are unimportant to him. Their death does not matter for him. It is not for him a morally material fact. The important point is that when we make our moral judgments upon what we take to be the facts of the case, we judge only the case as known. What is known of the case is always less than the totality of the case. The known case is an abstraction. The form and content of the abstraction is deeply affected by our standpoint in relation to the case and our estimate of what we believe to be morally important.

But ascertaining the facts of a moral case for use as a ground for our moral judgment is far more than viewing from a variety of standpoints in space and time the collection of facts which are taken to be of moral importance. A moral case is not like the Albert Memorial, which can be photographed from many points of view in order to provide a complete record for some catalogue of ancient and historic monuments. In observing the facts of a moral case, there is an intricate interplay between observation and interpretation. It is extremely doubtful whether there are any pure facts. An observer always has his own view of what can be the case.[1] He has some notion that each actual case is somehow composed of its form and its content. Its form is almost a kind of container which can hold many particular collections of particular facts. The forms do not change but the contents are subject to change. No two moral cases are quite alike but each shares the common form which is characteristic of a moral case. In the commonsense view, the form of the case is a number of entities involved in a moral action. These entities have the form of things and people. They have an impersonal or a personal form. Both types of entity have an appropriate form of being and acting. This working model of a moral case is itself

[1] John Oman, *The Natural and the Supernatural* (1931), p. 96: 'We know a reality not, as some seem to suppose, when we do not think about it, but only when we think about it rightly, which is when our meaning corresponds to its meaning. Thus a vast amount of thinking and valuing, which is a kind of science, is embedded even in our perceptions. And, in the same way, a vast amount of thinking and valuing, which is a kind of theology, interpenetrates our higher intuitions. For this reason we can argue ourselves out of any experience and, without right thinking, we cannot rightly receive the plainest facts...theory...always in time works back into our experience and comes to determine the kind of experience of which we are capable.'

A. J. Ayer, *Philosophy and Language* (1960), p. 21: 'For my part I have no wish to disown the verification principle, though it suffers from a vagueness which it has not yet been found possible to eradicate. I doubt, however, if it is a wholly effective means of distinguishing questions of analysis or interpretation from questions of fact. The trouble lies with the assumption that it is possible to supply a neutral record of facts, which is free from any taint of theory; a common bedrock for divergent interpretations. But this is highly dubious.'

included in a larger working model of the world. The totality of the moral case is enclosed in the totality of what is the case. The whole model is an attempt to do justice to what is changing and to what does not change in the world of our experience. The observers of a moral case, whatever standpoint they may happen to occupy, are perpetually accepting and understanding the observable facts in terms of what they believe can be the case. Their view of a moral case and their view of the world determines what they are willing to accept as factual. Their view of the world is the constant censor of what can be accepted or rejected as news of the world. This censorship becomes conscious when the observer is presented with a series of alleged facts which he finds questionable. A conventional scientist is unlikely to believe that an illness is actually due to witchcraft, because this is not a type of cause which he accepts as a fact. The accepted view of the world is also the pattern in accordance with which an observer constructs his view of the facts of the case when, for some reason, the available evidence is insufficient or conflicting. What an observer takes to be the real facts of a case is always affected by his view of reality. And any effort to verify the facts publicly must take place within some generally agreed view of our own being and capacities and of the nature of the world in which we find ourselves. It follows that disputes about the form and content of moral cases are frequently disguised disputes about incompatible world views. In short, there is no neutral account of the facts of a moral case which is uninfluenced by the standpoint, interests, and view of the world held by the observer. No one is without a world view. He may be unaware of the view which he holds but, if he is aware of it, he ought to avow it openly. And he has no right to insist that no alleged facts are to count as genuine facts if they are unacceptable to the world view which he happens to hold.

What we believe ought to be the case is the second type of ground on which we base our moral judgments. Again, I think we are conscious of a distinction between what we *believe* ought to be the case and what truly ought to be the case, irrespective of whether we recognize it to be so. We seek to formulate our view of what ought to be the case in many ways. We find these formulations useful as a rough guide to conduct and as a rapid way of explaining or justifying what we have done. They are also immensely useful in moral education. The formulations are by no means all verbal. We have notions of types of human character which are admirable and worthy of emulation. We can think of a moral policy which ought to be followed. We can speak of moral virtues. We can devise and use moral principles which cover a number of cases. We can talk of moral laws and moral standards. All these formulations can on appropriate occasions be used as grounds for our moral decisions. But I suspect that, beyond or behind these formulations, we have confidence that there is what truly ought to be the case. We have some fluctuating insight into this and we know that it is sovereign over all our imperfect efforts to express it and to comprehend it. Although we may be convinced that it is there, we are at a loss when we try to think of its manner of being. People incline towards an impersonal or a personal interpretation of its being. As long as we remain convinced that what truly ought to be cannot be inferior in being to the facts of the case which it criticizes, we are bound to seek some understanding of what truly ought to be in terms of what truly is.

IV

The Christian in making moral judgments should act on grounds which include both his knowledge of the facts of the case and his knowledge of what ought to be the case. He shares, with all other responsible moral agents, the duty of ascertaining the facts of the case to the best of his knowledge and belief. He must take all reasonable steps to overcome his ignorance of the relevant facts. He must use and gratefully acknowledge expert knowledge and advice from those who are best qualified to give it. For instance, in matters which are determinable by some established method of scientific inquiry, he must obviously accept the duly ascertained results. This point is often of great importance in social and international questions where the pertinent facts are only available in official reports and surveys of one kind or another. Frequently the expert advice will be taken from experts who make no profession of the Christian faith. But it is essential that the authority of the expert should not be allowed to transcend the field in which he is expert. On grounds other than his expert knowledge he may be a very wise adviser but his professional advice remains authoritative only within the field of his expert knowledge. The assessment of the nature and range of these sources of expert knowledge and advice is one of the most important matters on which Christian moral judgments need to be made. When, for example, the facts of human nature are being examined, a shrewd and experienced parish priest is entitled to compare what are said to be the scientifically established results with what he has himself learnt from his own trained insight and study. The literature of Christian saintliness must not be ignored. But the view taken of the facts of any moral case is bound to differ when the observers take different views of the world. Though a sincere materialist and a convinced Christian may agree about the more crudely manifest facts of a case and about the more obviously foreseeable consequences, they will unavoidably differ about deeper levels of fact. In assessing the facts of a moral case, the Christian will always be influenced by his view of the totality of what is the case. He will view the case in the light of the Christian doctrines about God, the world, and man. In so doing, he is not gratuitously distorting the facts by introducing metaphysical considerations which are happily absent from all other accounts of the facts. He is being conspicuous because he is aware of his view of the world and because he is publicly acknowledging the view which he holds.

The Christian should also base his moral judgments upon what he believes ought to be the case. When he judges upon what he believes ought to be the case, he is bound to rely upon some kind of formulation or expression of what ought to be the case. The obligation must present itself to him in some kind of noticeable form. It may quite often take a form which is other than verbal. There is the image which a Christian has of the life and teaching of Christ. There is the idea of the mind and spirit of Christ. There is the general impression of the Christian way of life which is gained from a study of Christian history, particularly the history of the Church in New Testament times. There are classic catalogues of Christian virtues. There are more general formulations in terms of rules and law and standard. These are all useful and justifiable ways of expressing what a Christian believes ought to be the case in a form which enables him consciously to use them as a ground for his moral judgments.

Christian moral principles are an outstanding example of a verbal formulation of the Christian conception of what ought to be the case. Their discovery, formulation and use are all quite mysterious. They are not facts in the sense in which tables and chairs are facts but it is a fact that we discover, formulate and use them. Each principle has to be used on its merits. They can be so wide as to offer virtually no particular guidance when we are faced with a moral decision in a difficult case. That a Christian should do what is Christian is undeniable but not very helpful. The principles may, however, be so qualified by reference to particular circumstances that they apply only to a very narrow range of cases. The bulk of Christian principles which are useful fall somewhere between extreme generality and extreme particularity. In the hope of attaining a complete rational system of Christian ethics, it is customary to justify any exceptions to the known principles by reference to further principles. In this way a conflict between two or more principles may be reconciled without abandoning the principle that all particular cases must fall under some moral principle. But it remains true that the principles which are most used are neither extremely general nor extremely particular. They are sometimes called middle axioms or directives. We need more formulations of such principles as a guide for bodies of Christians who pass their daily lives in broadly similar occupations. We need revised formulations of vocational ethics for Christian men, after the style of Thomas Gisborne's *An Enquiry into the Duties of Men in the higher and middle classes of society in Great Britain, resulting from their respective stations, professions, and employments* (Two volumes. The third edition, corrected. London, 1795). We need fresh principles of situational ethics which are easily seen to be broadly relevant to the types of situation in which men find themselves in contemporary society. Such principles would never cover all cases but their formulation and use would sharpen and assist the Christian conscience in making well-grounded moral decisions.

But I believe that Christians who use these formulations of what ought to be the case are aware that all these expressive forms fall short of what is to be expressed. There is a deep Christian conviction that somehow there is a realm in which what ought to be is what is. This is the never adequately or exhaustively formulated ground which is the ultimate justification of our moral decisions. It is not taken to be an ultimately groundless ideal but an ultimate fact. The Christian rejects the view that ultimately what is and what ought to be stand in unexplained and accidental juxtaposition. He rejects the view that what ultimately is must simply be accepted as a brute fact which is either devoid of all the characteristics of personal being or altogether beyond the range of meaningful discussion. He knows as well as anybody else that what is real has the last word and that if ultimate reality is devoid of any kind of personal characteristics or beyond the limits of all personal analogies, the end must be utter moral silence; a silence of what has never spoken and never could speak. If this is so, it is so, and we cannot make it not so. But the point at issue is not whether we have the moral courage to say, with Bishop Joseph Butler (1692–1752), 'Things and actions are what they are, and the consequences of them will be what they will be:

why then should we desire to be deceived?',[1] but whether in fact what ultimately is has no relation to what ultimately ought to be. It is a matter, not of moral courage, but of the truth. Belief in God, as the august affirmation that what ultimately ought to be is what ultimately is, can be held with confident faith but never without trepidation. In view of the many genuine difficulties which now cause thoughtful men to hesitate before making such an affirmation, it is our plain duty to remove any avoidable impediments to an act of faith in God. As Christians do not believe that what ultimately ought to be is impersonal, it is not surprising that they try to think of its being in personal terms. But a host of problems arise if God is understood as though he was a human person, even a perfect human person, dwelling in a natural and moral environment just like our own. We can ask whether God himself is subject to what ought to be the case. We can ask whether what ought to be the case is really so or whether it simply happens to be what God wills or commands. We can ask whether God experiences moral struggle and failure. The puzzles are endless but I believe that they can be reduced if we realize that we must think analogically. But from whence ought we to draw our analogies? If we are to think of God as personal, we must draw our analogies from our own experience of being personal beings. This is the kind of being with which we are most closely acquainted. And, in our moral experience, we are aware of the mysterious tension between what we are and what we ought to be. We do not do justice to this tension if we seek to eliminate it by denying either of its two sides or by saying that the two sides stand in simple juxtaposition. We have experience of a unified personal being in which moral unity is not fully attained. In momentary acts of sheer Christian charity, we know that this tension is overcome. From these mysterious experiences of our own personal being we may draw analogies which may go some way in assisting us to

[1] Joseph Butler, *Fifteen Sermons*, no. VII, § 16 (*The Works of Joseph Butler*, ed. W. E. Gladstone (1897), vol. II, p. 114).

think of the being of God in whom there is no tension between what is and what ought to be. This by no means solves all the difficulties but it removes some pseudo-problems in philosophical moral theology.

This very limited study of the grounds of Christian moral judgments has led to an emphasis upon the essential bond between Christian morality and Christian doctrine. This conclusion may be disappointing to some readers for whom, on one ground or another, the traditional Christian doctrinal structure has ceased to be a living faith. There is a widespread belief that the form in which we have received the doctrinal tradition has been largely influenced by historical factors which should lose their influence as human history advances. Cosmologies become obsolete. The social order changes. Philosophical speculation passes through alternating periods of confidence and diffidence. Analogies acquire and lose their popularity. To sort out what is sound and what is unsound in these views is an immense task which virtually remains to be undertaken. Though any re-statement of Christian doctrine must begin from a scholarly study of the tradition, it is not sufficient simply to repeat the biblical phraseology. Re-statement is more than repetition. This task of translation is easier to demand than to fulfil. Translation is delayed when a new language is being sought into which the translation may be made. In the long run, it is wasted labour to define and undertake the problems of doctrinal translation in terms of languages which are obsolescent. It may be that for a period sensitive Christian theologians may be more clearly aware of views of the world which are felt to be incompatible with the Christian tradition than of any clear and systematic re-statement of the Christian faith. Somewhat as natural scientists continue to do magnificent scientific work without demanding an immediate definition of the ultimate nature and structure of the natural world, practical Christians may have to persevere in the Christian way of life without waiting for a classic reformulation of Christian doctrine about God, the world, and man. But such a reformulation remains the duty and task of Christian theologians.

10

CHRISTIAN PRAYER

BY

JOHN BURNABY

SYNOPSIS

I. Prayer: a universal element in religious behaviour. In its 'mystical' type, it is self-justifying and looks for no effects in the external world. Yet if Christian faith is distinct from the religion of mysticism, its distinctive character should be reflected in Christian prayer.

II. Prayer in the New Testament. Both in the teaching of Jesus and in the practice of the Apostolic Church, prayer means primarily asking God for what we need.

III. Naïve belief in the effectiveness of prayer raises difficulties for thought. These are due to varying assumptions in regard, for example, to divine providence, natural law, and human freedom. They may lead us to suppose that prayer can have no effect except upon him who prays.

IV. A Christian theology of prayer must be grounded not on metaphysical assumptions but on the nature of the Gospel. The revelation of God in Christ, and the gift of the Holy Spirit, signify the doing away of 'apartness' as between God and man.

V. Consequences for our understanding of God's saving work as the work of love, taking effect through men who are united to God by the Spirit of Christ. Prayer is affirmation of this union, not appeal for God's action conceived as separate from all that men can do.

VI. Consequences for the practice of Christian prayer. Union of will with God must have specific and particular expression. Un-Christian elements in traditional forms of worship.

CHRISTIAN PRAYER

I

THE WORD 'prayer', used in a religious reference, may cover any and every human activity of which the conscious purpose is to enter into communication with a being or beings not normally apprehensible by the senses but believed to be no less real and (generally) more powerful than human beings themselves. The communion with 'the divine' so attempted may take very various forms. It may be simple request for the exercise of this superhuman power for the benefit of the petitioner or of others on whose behalf he prays. It may be the humble acknowledgment of action or failure to act, believed to be such as to offend the deity addressed and to incur the loss of its favour. It may be the return of thanks for benefits supposed to have been conferred, and praise of the goodness so displayed. Or the act of prayer may have no purpose outside itself; it may seek nothing more than an intensification of awareness, a concentration of thought and affection upon the invisible reality. In this last form, the communion sought need not be conceived in terms of personal intercourse. 'The divine' may be approached as an infinite sea, in which the solitary being of the individual can be embraced or even absorbed—in which the restless consciousness of isolated existence is at least for the time extinguished by the peace of union. The astonishing similarity in the language with which experts in this kind of prayer, belonging to religious traditions which appear to have little else in common, have described their experience, has encouraged the belief that 'mystical' religion is the only one that can aspire to universality. Moreover, the fact that mysticism can flourish with little or no dependence upon particular dogmatic or doctrinal systems has seemed to give it an immunity from sceptical criticism such as none of the (so-called) 'positive' religions can claim. The experience on which it rests may even be accepted by the philosopher as evidence, so far as it goes, for the reality of the invisible world to which it believes to have found an entry.

Friedrich Heiler, in his classical work *Das Gebet*,[1] distinguished and contrasted two types of prayer—the 'mystical' and the 'prophetic'; and Protestant theologians have been inclined to deny the right of the mystic as such to domicile in a pure and reformed Christianity. Yet within the Christian Church a great tradition of mystical theology has thrived upon the genius and the teachings of some of the noblest examples of Catholic sainthood. The vast literature of Christian prayer has been predominantly occupied with the technique of contemplation and the 'practice of the presence of God' to which the saints have shown the way. The consequence of this preoccupation has been to suggest that the use of vocal prayer is no more than an elementary stage in the Christian life, and in particular that petition is an act or attitude which *ought* to be superseded, as we come to know better what it means to lift up our hearts to God. If this is true, our inherited forms of Common Prayer, which are both vocal and to a large extent petitionary, will not serve to train us in these higher reaches of communion with God. We shall either acquiesce in the existence of a double standard in the life of prayer—one for the expert and one for the ordinary believer—or we shall be tempted to abandon the practice of both public and private prayer as we have known it, and take the easy way of reducing our devotions to a vague and planless meditation. In these circumstances we may find reason for considering afresh whether the distinctive character of Christian faith may not be expected to introduce a distinctive element into the prayer of Christians—whether it is possible to discern a theological foundation for Christian prayer by which its practice may be guided. The purpose of this essay is restricted to inquiry into the nature of this foundation.

[1] F. Heiler, *Das Gebet* (5th ed. 1923). E.T. (abridged), *Prayer: a Study in the History and Psychology of Religion* (1932, reissued 1958).

II

Such prolegomena to the theology of Christian prayer will naturally begin by observing the way in which the Christian Church in its beginnings was accustomed to pray. And it is plain enough that prayer in the New Testament means quite simply that part of our communion with God which consists in *petition*. No doubt the life of Christ was (in the famous phrase which Origen applied to the life of sainthood) 'one great unbroken prayer'.[1] But his recorded teaching assumes that when we pray it is to ask God for what we need. 'Ask, and it shall be given you' (Matt. vii. 7; Luke xi. 9). 'Ask, and ye shall receive, that your joy may be full' (John xvi. 24). 'Whatsoever ye shall ask in prayer, believing, ye shall receive' (Matt. xxi. 22; Mark xi. 24). 'If two of you shall agree on earth touching anything that they shall ask, it shall be done for them of my Father which is in heaven' (Matt. xviii. 19). 'Whatsoever ye shall ask the Father in my name, he will give it you' (John xvi. 23). Every clause in the Lord's Prayer is petition; and if the parables about persistency and importunity in prayer (Luke xi. 5 ff.; xviii. 2 ff.) must be read in the light of the discouragement of 'vain repetitions' and the heathen belief that much speaking will secure hearing (Matt. vi. 7), we cannot think that St Paul's exhortation to unceasing prayer was out of harmony with Christ's own teaching (I Thess. v. 17).[2] Of the prayers of Christ himself, indeed, we know less than is often assumed; but in the little that the Gospels have to tell us, petition and intercession, with thanksgiving, make up the whole (see Mark xiv. 32 ff.; John xii. 27 ff.; Luke xxiii. 34, 46; xxii. 32; John xvii; Matt. xi. 25 f.; John xi. 41).

All the evidence of the Acts and the Epistles goes to show that

---

[1] Origen, *De Oratione*, 12.

[2] J. Jeremias (it should be noted) has argued in *The Parables of Jesus* (pp. 115–18) that the parables of the Unjust Judge and the Unwilling Friend were originally spoken to enjoin faith in God—who is *not* an unjust judge or an unwilling friend—and that the application of them to persistency in prayer is due to Luke.

prayer in the primitive Church was what we should expect it to have been—in St Paul's words, the making of our requests known to God, requests which there was no thought of confining to 'spiritual' blessings (Phil. iv. 6; cf. e.g. Acts i. 24; viii. 15; xii. 5; Rom. i. 9 f.; xv. 30 f.; II Cor. i. 11; xii. 8; Col. i. 3, 9; Eph. vi. 18 f.; Jas. v. 13 ff.; I John v. 14 f.). This at least was what the early Church meant by *proseuché*, though we can be sure that thanksgiving and praise had their due place in its devotions. We may think of the Common Prayer of the first Christians as naturally continuing the inherited usages of Jewish synagogue worship, to which all that the remembered teaching of Jesus had added was the spirit of absolute trust in the Father, who cannot but give good things to them that ask him. Petition is present everywhere in the most important part of the Church's liturgical inheritance from Judaism—the Psalms; and petitionary prayer has continued to be the dominating element in Christian worship, both Catholic and Reformed: witness the long series of Collects for Sundays and Holy Days in the Book of Common Prayer.

III

For the present we need only note the complete simplicity or *naïveté* with which the Apostolic Church did its praying. To make 'in everything' our requests known to God was for St Paul the cure for all worldly worry (the *merimna* which Christ forbade); and no more for Paul than for Jesus himself was the belief that the Father knoweth what things we have need of, before we ask, the least discouragement to prayer. It went without saying that if God *would* grant our requests, he *could* do so—until the restless minds of Greek Christians began to ask questions. This questioning begins at least as early as the third century, when Origen opens his treatise *On Prayer* by attempting to meet it. The questions with which he finds it necessary to deal are prompted by the apparent inconsistency between accepted Christian practice and certain *a priori* notions about God and man. It is *assumed* that God's omniscient providence covers all happenings in time: if then the whole course of events is already ordered for the best, what can be the use of our asking God to do this or that? Again, it is assumed that the only real goods are of the spirit: how then can we be justified in asking for the satisfaction of our desires for material things? Both these questions have continued to be asked ever since; yet Christians still pray as they have always prayed, both that God will hasten the coming of his Kingdom, and that he will give us such things as are requisite and necessary, as well for the body as the soul. In particular, the belief in what is commonly called 'the power of prayer' is held today perhaps more widely than ever. Faith is nourished by accounts of wonderful 'answers to prayer'—wonderful, presumably, only because they cannot be explained by chance coincidence; and the multiplication of petitioners, for ends small and great, is diligently organized, as though God were indeed the unjust judge or the lazy friend in bed who must be pestered into activity.

The thoughtful Christian is likely to find here a grave abuse of prayer. He will be repelled by the apparent implication that prayer is a force, quantitatively measurable, taking effect in proportion to its magnitude in the direction of events. But he will often be no less puzzled than he was in Origen's Alexandria to understand what kind of difference it may make whether he prays or not. He will perhaps be less worried by the ancient antinomies of prayer and predestination, and he will be less disposed to depreciate material goods. But he will have his own assumptions. He will have learnt to take for granted the observable uniformities of the natural world, and to attribute the unpredictable character of human history to the existence in men of a real power of deliberate choice and effective action. He will regard human freedom and moral responsibility as a necessary corollary of belief in a God whose relation to men is to be conceived in the terms of Christ's teaching; and he will recognize that such freedom could only have purposeful exercise in the stable environment of a world whose processes are subject to an order that is discoverable. He will be disposed to think that if God has given us both freedom and the means of controlling our environment, he intends us to use both. Yet he will find in the Church's prayers what seems to be a disavowal of this freedom, and an appeal to God to replace it by action of his own. These ancient prayers, of which the Collects for Easter Day[1] and the First Sunday after Trinity[2] are typical examples, are very generally inspired by the thorough-going Augustinianism which reaches its logical extremity in the Collect for the Tenth Sunday after Trinity, where God is besought to put the right prayers into our mouths, so that they may be sure of acceptance.[3] But St Augustine himself was able in his own day to appeal, in defence of his doctrine of the necessity and the all-sufficiency of grace, to the Church's universal and unvarying practice of prayer.

The prayer for grace, the prayer that God will put into our minds the good desires which still will need his continual help that we may bring them to good effect, was for St Augustine no more than the acknowledgment that (in the words of another collect) the Lord of all power and might is the author and giver of *all* good things.[4] If that is true, the acknowledgment itself must be good for those who make it; for it will be a continual check upon the besetting sin of the 'religious'—the conceit of superior goodness. It is easy to believe that such prayer, if it is made sincerely, will have its effect upon him who prays. But we may equally easily slip from there into the general supposition that the *only* effect of prayer is reflexive, that the act of asking to be made better is the sufficient cause of any improvement in our moral and spiritual condition that may ensue. And then we

---

[1] 'We humbly beseech thee, that as by thy special grace preventing us thou dost put into our minds good desires, so by thy continual help we may bring the same to good effect.'

[2] 'Because through the weakness of our mortal nature we can do no good thing without thee, grant us the help of thy grace, that in keeping of thy commandments we may please thee, both in will and deed.'

[3] 'Let thy merciful ears, O Lord, be open to the prayers of thy humble servants; and that they may obtain their petitions make them to ask such things as shall please thee.'

[4] Collect for the Seventh Sunday after Trinity.

shall find ourselves sooner or later asking whether the God to whom our prayers are addressed has any part in the business—whether our belief in his activity may not be illusory. Prayer whose ultimate purpose is self-directed, whose only effect is upon the condition of the self, does not need the Christian's God. The argument for the truth of religion so often drawn from the close similarity of mystical experience in widely differing religious traditions cannot take us far towards faith in the God and Father of Jesus Christ. If we are to pray as Christians, we must be able to pray for others, and to believe that our prayer can help them. Here again, the suggestion may be made that if my prayer does help my friend it is because he may be affected by it, consciously or unconsciously, in the manner of tele-pathic thought-transference. But even if it should prove that the faculty for 'paranormal' communication between persons is after all a common capacity of the human mind, the Christian intercessor will insist that he is not trying to 'get into touch' with the person for whom he intercedes, but asking God to act for that person's good. We cannot 'explain' intercession by telepathy, any more than we can 'explain' prayer for ourselves by autosuggestion; for the heart of all Christian prayer is faith in *God*.

IV

We should not be surprised, then, if our perplexities about prayer were due to imperfect understanding of the revelation of God in Jesus Christ, and of the difference which that revelation must make to our understanding of human life. If we are to set our theology of prayer upon a secure footing, we must first have as clear a notion as may be of the change in men's thoughts of God and of their own relation to him which resulted from the events recorded in the New Testament. And this will not be a digression from our subject: it will be the necessary preparation for its advancement.

The Hebrews were not alone among the peoples of the ancient world in speaking and thinking of their God in vividly personal—

which means human—terms. But they reached an awareness of the *distance* between the divine and the human which in combination with this anthropomorphism was unique. 'I am God, and not man' (Hos. xi. 9). 'Thou thoughtest that I was altogether such a one as thyself' (Ps. l. 21). 'As the heavens are higher than the earth, so are my ways higher than your ways, and my thoughts than your thoughts' (Isa. lv. 9). This 'otherness' of God in Hebrew thought discovers its ground in the essential difference between Creator and creature; but it is transformed by man's act into the disastrous moral opposition between divine holiness and human sin. Old Testament religion hopes for an end to this opposition, but it can only conceive that end as the establishment of God's kingdom—his rule over a repentant and obedient people. The symbol of sovereignty, acknowledged and accepted, does away with opposition but does not eliminate distance. If the high and lofty one that inhabiteth eternity, whose name is Holy, can be believed to dwell with him also that is of a contrite and humble spirit, the real 'apartness' remains no less than it was when in Ezekiel's vision Jehovah returned to dwell in a restored and purified, but scrupulously fenced, sanctuary (Isa. lvii. 15; Ezek. xliii). So in the Messianic hope the Messiah is God's plenipotentiary but not God's presence; and when Peter claims Messiahship for the risen Jesus before the Jerusalem crowd, it is for 'a man approved of God by miracles and wonders and signs' (Acts ii. 22). What most demands an explanation is the fact that Jesus came so soon to possess for the Apostolic Church, led as it was by devout Jews, the significance of deity. We are likely to come nearest to a clue in what the Church called the gift of the Holy Spirit. For the 'power of the Spirit' in the lives of believers was the central fact of the Church's experience; and this power was bound up with the believing relationship to Jesus Christ, through whom the Spirit flows in an inexhaustible supply. If then the manifest working of the Spirit was proof (as St Paul could say) that 'God is in you of a truth', it must *a fortiori* be true that 'God was in Christ'

(Rom. xv. 13; Acts ii. 33, 38; John iii. 34; iv. 14; vii. 38 f.; I Cor. xiv. 25; II Cor. v. 19; Rom. viii. 1–11). Hence St Paul's equation of life 'in the Spirit' with life 'in Christ'. The Johannine theology of incarnation—the Word become flesh—does no more than draw out the implications of Pentecost.

The Church found God in Christ because it had already found God present in its own life; and it is probable that Christian faith must always go this way; men will discover the doctrine as they find God's will being done in themselves (John vii. 17). 'No man can say that Jesus is Lord, but by the Holy Ghost' (I Cor. xii. 3). That is to say, a man must know something of what it means to have God in himself, before he can confess that he owes that presence to the union of Godhead and manhood in Jesus. To believe in the gospel of the Incarnation is to believe that God's way of ending the separation between himself and sinful man was not to wait till men should return to him, but to go where they were *and to stay there*. That of course is as 'mythical' a manner of speaking as the story of the Virgin Birth. Let it serve to express the Church's faith that since the risen Jesus parted from his disciples the following of him in the Christian life is possible only in the measure in which the human spirit is united to the divine. This is not to say that when we speak of the divinity of Christ we mean no more than when we speak of the presence of the Holy Spirit in the Christian. The Church has never been satisfied with a Christology that reduces incarnation to the level of a supreme instance of grace. No wonder that attempts to define the difference have never been wholly successful. But the difference itself is one of which saint is not less but more acutely conscious than sinner. Perhaps the union between human spirit and divine, except in Christ, is insuperably 'asymptotic': it can never reach identity—just as the unity of love between two human persons can never abolish the ultimate personal distinction. Nevertheless, we may still find in the divine-human person of Christ the pattern as well as the source of all Christian life 'in the Spirit'.

V

What is the bearing of this upon the theology of prayer? It means a revision of our assumptions. We shall not begin by taking for granted particular notions either of God's providence or of man's freedom, either of the insignificance of material things or of the immutability of natural processes. We shall assume only, as a belief to which we are committed, that what we call the salvation of the world has been wrought—by God indeed, yet not (as it were) in man's despite, by an act of overriding omnipotence, but through the freely willed self-devotion of a man; and that God's kingdom must come on earth through the operation of human wills which by the acceptance of the Spirit of Jesus have become one with the will of God. Prayer, then, will be the means of affirming and confirming this unity—a means whose effectiveness will be in proportion to the sincerity of its utterance. To pray 'Thy will be done' is not to cease from our own willing, in a passive abandonment of our own desires: it is to *desire* the accomplishment of God's will. To pray for the gift of grace is not to ask that the infallible power of God may be substituted for our human weakness: it is to confess the constant falling away of our will from the unity of the Spirit, and in the same act to make a beginning of return to it. Needless to say, it will always be possible to repeat prayers without meaning them, to think that we are praying when we are doing nothing of the kind. Just because so much of our praying is little more than 'vain repetition', we need the prayer for the Tenth Sunday after Trinity, that the Spirit may teach us to pray as we ought. That prayer itself, if it is to be real, must be the expression of a 'hearty desire to pray'; and there are times when we may be unable to get further than the hearty desire, when that is the only thing that holds us to the Spirit. Real prayer, however, can never be without the minimal act of will that intends to embrace and further the purposes of God—and even by so intending does so embrace and further them.

Christian thought and speech has never been able entirely to rid itself of that conception of God's will which John Oman used to parody as 'the force of omnipotence directed in a straight line by omniscience'.[1] We know that we ourselves cannot always get a thing done by willing it, and we feel that the will of God cannot be subject to the same possibility of frustration. But if God's will is to unite us his children to himself in love, its strength must be of a different kind from that of the 'strong-willed' man who drives his own way through opposition. God's reconciliation of the world to himself will not be perfected by other means than that which was put in action on the cross of Christ—the charity which endureth all things. That is the labour of love which the disciple of Christ is constrained to share; and whether his *Kyrie eleison* invokes the merciful love of God upon himself or upon his neighbour, his prayer will seek nothing but the increase of charity—and will find no other answer. Because charity is the power of God, the only power by which his kingdom can be extended among men, it will only be when we doubt the power of charity that we shall be troubled by the question, 'Can our praying make a difference?'.

We may still ask, *how* is the difference made? Is it, after all, nothing more than a difference in ourselves? Can the course of events outside our personal history be affected in any way by what we do on our knees before God? Such questions may naturally arise if we assume that the anthropomorphic conception of a 'rule of law' is in some way or other applicable to the world of God's creation and ordering. We may find it difficult to suppose that God would 'break his own law' by action in response to our prayer; and if a miracle is defined as a 'breach of natural law', an event for which no extension of our knowledge could find a place in a pattern of regular sequences, we cannot know whether a miracle has ever been or ever will be wrought by God. For we can never tell what a future extension of our knowledge may bring within the 'rule of law'. But

[1] J. Oman, *Grace and Personality* (3rd ed., 1925), *passim*.

231

one may be willing to credit the possibility or the actuality of miracle in this sense, and yet rightly refrain, as did Jesus in the wilderness, from asking God to work a miracle even for the most apparently desirable end. Alternatively, one may believe that God is really active in the world's history, without supposing or expecting him to 'interfere' in the order of nature more radically than we do ourselves every time we strike a match. But have we any right to assume that the power of God to change the course of events is of the same kind as our own, differing from it only as the greater from the less? We have learnt to face the possibility that human decisions based on knowledge of the properties of matter may bring upon the world a cataclysm once supposed to be at the sole disposal of the Almighty. Probably no one's faith is simple enough to prompt the hope that God would frustrate such decisions, if they were made, by suspending the physical processes of chain reaction. It would be equally naïve to think of the divine power as that of a super-scientist, whose knowledge of nature's potentialities must so far exceed that of any human being that he could always so apply them as to prevent men from destroying themselves. Yet our tendency is to suppose that the God to whom we pray is a source of causative action in the world of phenomena to be reckoned as additional and external to those agencies which he has brought into being in the wills of men; and then our prayer must take on the appearance of an attempt to make up for our own deficiency in power or wisdom by calling that other more reliable Agent into operation for the accomplishment of what seems to us good. It is this sort of notion that exposes us without defences to the unbeliever's question: 'Why is our God to all appearance so impotent?'

What has here been suggested is that the only answer to that question is a re-statement of the implications of our Christian faith. The Christian faith implies (so it has been contended): (a) that the kingdom of God is to be promoted in human history by no other power than the power of love, and (b) that the power of God's love takes effect in human history in no other way than through the wills and actions of men in whom that love has come to dwell. To pray is to open the heart to the entry of love—to ask God in; and where God is truly wanted, he will always come. 'What happens when I pray' is, to begin with, an encroachment of the love of God upon the defences of my self, my hard heart and laggard will. But it is not possible that the effect of such encroachment should be confined to the place where it has been made. If it were so, if prayer could have no other effect than an improvement in the spiritual condition of the person who prays, why should we not frankly admit as much, and confine our prayers to the request for our own growth in charity in the terms of the Collect for Quinquagesima? The answer lies in the nature of charity as a birth of the divine in the human. Wherever a human will suffers itself to be invaded by the will of God, it cannot remain a passive prisoner, but must take service with its divine captor. Or, to use a better metaphor, the life that is released in the soul that has consented to the wooing of God's grace is no longer a life *of* the soul, but the life and power of its union with God. And by that union the universal working of the love of God has increase. My prayer is not good for God's work in the world because it is good for me; it is good for me because it is good for God's work in the world. Whether its effect will be seen in the particular form to which the prayer has been directed, is something that we must be content not to know. It is not easy to believe that prayer is either always or never 'answered' in the way desired. It is possible— indeed necessary—to believe that true Christian prayer is always the service of God.

VI

What further guidance for the practice of prayer will result from the acceptance of these principles as its theological foundation?

It should be clear, in the first place, that we need not regard contemplation and petition as two essentially different ways of prayer between which we must choose. Heiler's 'prophetic' and 'mystical' types are not so distinct as he supposed. The aim of all our petitions must be the alignment of our own will with the will of God; and conversely there can be no real union of the soul with God that is not *active*. The 'prayer of quiet' can help us in the Christian life only in so far as it strengthens us to work the works of God. And Christian petition must itself be a 'practice of the presence of God'.

All Christian prayer is 'in the name of Jesus Christ', and asks for fulfilment 'through Jesus Christ our Lord'. Not only, then, should our prayer seek what Christ sought in life and death, but it should look to be answered in the way that Christ pursued, by the means that he chose. We shall continue to pray for the health of body and mind which Christ gave to the sick, as we pray for the peace of the world which Christ could not promise—not doubting that God wills our health and the world's peace, not knowing whether, things being as they are, he is able to give us either, yet sure that our prayer 'makes a difference', in so far as it is an embodiment, however tiny and feeble, of charity. It would indeed reduce our theology of prayer to an absurdity if it followed that the most instinctive and universal cry of the troubled soul—'Lord, help me!'—could not, since charity seeketh not her own, have the true character of Christian prayer. The disciple is not above his master, and it should be enough to recall the prayer of Gethsemane. It is certainly true that the prayer 'Lead us not into temptation' is not fully Christian if it is evoked by failure of faith; and that the prayer for help in adversity ought always to be at the same time a prayer for strength to meet adversity with the persuasion that it cannot separate us from the love of God. Still, the first rule in prayer is sincerity. Our desires and our needs are the most vital part of us; and God's children may not approach their Father with a feigned devotion, fearing to tell him what they really want. If I am to learn to want what God wants, the way to do it is not to disown the inmost desires of my heart, but rather deliberately to spread them out before God—to face with all the honesty I can achieve the real truth about my desires, to wrestle with the sham of professing desires which are not really mine, and *then* to pray. Then, no doubt, I shall find that there are things, desirable in themselves, which the Christian who prays in charity cannot ask God to give him, because neither love of God nor love of neighbour would be served by their possession. For prayer itself will be the schooling of desire.

The pattern prayer, however, is spoken in the first person plural. It is *we* who pray, the Church of Christ, not the *ego* in its isolation. We ask for daily bread and the forgiveness of sins, not as private needs but as the needs of the family of God. It is to be noticed that many if not most of the prayers of individuals recorded in the Bible are intercessions, and that these prayers for others are seldom for the general welfare of those who are prayed for, but rather for particular people in particular situations. Indeed it is the particularity of these prayers in the Bible, as of Cranmer's great Litany in the Book of Common Prayer, that gives them most value for us as models. It costs but little effort to pray for all men according to their needs— men and needs alike unnamed and unknown. Sincerity in prayer demands the effort to concentrate upon the particular. We must pray for the needs we know in the brother we know. So our private prayers can model themselves upon the common prayers of the Church, translating the Church's prayers into terms of the particular place that is assigned to each of us in the service of God's kingdom on earth. *My* prayers can be made, just as *my* duty can be done, by no one but myself. If I neglect them, they will not be made at all: I shall have deserted the post where no one can replace me.

There is certainly more than a little in our traditional forms of worship that corresponds but ill to the essential character of Christian prayer—if that character is best seen in the great saying of St Paul, that 'God has sent forth the Spirit of his Son into our hearts, crying Abba, Father!' (Gal. iv. 6). Of this incongruity the Psalter, taken over as it stands from the worship of the pre-Christian synagogue, is the most conspicuous example. The Psalter owes its place in the Church's liturgy primarily to the ease with which it lent itself to interpretation by the early Church as prophetic of Christ. It has established its hold by the supreme beauty and truth of many of the Hebrew hymns and prayers which it contains. But the type of *Klage-lied*, of complaint or expostulation, to which not less than a quarter of the psalms belong, is animated by a temper which even the most reckless allegorizing can scarcely baptize into Christianity. The authors of these psalms are no less sure of their own piety than of the power of the God on whom that piety makes its demands. They are the 'righteous poor', oppressed and down-trodden by the godless and prosperous, the self-conscious 'saints' crying to God for vengeance upon their enemies. It is the urgent appeal of one of these distressed suppliants which we use in versicle and response at the opening of our Morning and Evening Prayer.[1] On the other hand, Christian worship has been only too deeply coloured by the conviction of the great Hebrew prophets that human prosperity and adversity are the manifestations of God's proven character as the rewarder of righteousness and the punisher of sin. Our liturgical confession of sin too often seems inspired rather by fear of God's implacable justice than by sorrow for the wounding of divine love. Prayers like the Collect for the Fourth Sunday in Lent,[2] and still more the sentences, as terrible in meaning as they are grand in diction, which for innumerable mourners have accompanied the committal of a beloved body to the grave,[3] strike tones not easily recognizable as those of the Spirit of God's Son.

It is, unfortunately, as inevitable that traditional forms of worship should resist change as that the praying of the Christian, when he

---

[1] 'O God, make speed to save us; O Lord, make haste to help us' (Ps. lxx. 1). The words of Ps. xxii, which broke from the lips of the dying Christ, express just that despairing sense of separation from God from which Christians believe that they have been delivered by the Christ who died for them.

[2] 'Grant, we beseech thee, Almighty God, that we, who for our evil deeds do worthily deserve to be punished, by the comfort of thy grace may mercifully be relieved.'

[3] 'Man that is born of a woman', etc. (Order for the Burial of the Dead).

enters into his chamber and shuts his door, should be influenced in both form and content by the prayers in which he has joined in Church. But there is at least in the Church's central act of worship, the memorial of the precious death and passion of God's dear Son, a safeguard against misunderstanding or misuse of the act of prayer which no defects in verbal expression can altogether remove. 'When in the sacrament we plead the sacrifice of Christ, and in union with him offer ourselves to God, the whole of that process is a giving and receiving in one. . . . The very giving of ourselves to God is a receiving of him, and the very receiving of him is already a giving of ourselves. There is no other way of receiving him except by giving ourselves to him; and there is no other way of giving ourselves to him except by receiving him.'[1] In other words, the significance of the sacrament is to represent and realize that oneness of life into which the taking of our nature by the Son of God, its bearing through cross and resurrection into the heavenly places, and the coming of the Holy Spirit to be its strength and stay, have brought the Creator and his creatures. All Christian prayer is the activity of that oneness of life.

[1] D. M. Baillie, *The Theology of the Sacraments* (1958), p. 122.

Is the Church satisfactorily regarded as a religious organization?

I. F. D. Maurice emphatically repudiated this idea and held that the Church was a deliverance from religion.

II. D. Bonhoeffer, in his fragmentary *Letters and Papers from Prison*, said that a proper consequence of man's 'coming of age' was that he should outgrow religion, and that what was needed now was a 'religionless Christianity'.

III. An anonymous correspondent asks whether the organization of Christianity as a religion was not a mistake from the start.

IV. Organization is inevitable: it is also inevitable that organization, and traditional doctrines, are outgrown.

V. A look at the Church of England in the light of these questions. Despite its archaic appearance, it may be better qualified to be open to the future, and less in peril of becoming a mere 'religious denomination', than other churches. Even its anomalous relation to the state is worth preserving for the time being because of its advantages to both church and state.

RELIGION AND THE NATIONAL CHURCH

'THE CHURCH is primarily a religious organization, and the Christian gospel caters for the religious needs of men', says a confident contributor to the lively young Anglican journal, *Prism*.[1] 'Religious' is a word of many meanings, but he explains what he means by it. 'It is the job of the church to preach, to pray, to sing hymns and to encourage and develop the pious feelings of its members....Religion is not concerned with the whole of life, but with a part of life.' He complains that the Church of England is not nearly religious enough. 'It has failed to cater to those religious feelings, needs and desires which are present in human nature.' I take these statements as my starting-point because I want to ask whether 'religion' is so good a thing and so obviously the *raison d'être* of Christ's Church as this writer assumes it to be and, then, whether we should desire the Church of England to become more—or less—religious.

I

I observe, in the first place, that there are reputable Christian theologians who have been far from regarding religion as a good thing. F. D. Maurice, for instance, writing to Charles Kingsley in 1849 apropos of J. A. Froude's book *The Nemesis of Faith*, said: 'Religion against God. This is the heresy of our age.'[2] He did not say this only in his private correspondence. Though he did not explain systematically what he meant, there are frequent allusions in his published works not only to the ambiguity of the word 'religion' but to what he looked upon as its deplorable associations. The word, he said, 'is a peculiarly ambiguous one, and one that is likely to continue ambiguous, because we connect it with the study and treat-

---

[1] David Nicholls, 'Your God is Too Big', *Prism* (July 1961), p. 22.
[2] F. Maurice, *Life of F. D. Maurice*[3] (1884), vol. I, p. 518. He said he derived the idea from Edward Irving.

16   241   V S

ment of the Bible, though the Bible itself gives us no help in ascertaining the force of the word, apparently sets no great store by it or any similar one. So far as I am able to make out, it is best used to denote certain processes or habits or conditions of our own minds.'[1] Again, he said that 'the worst cant of our days comes from those who wish by all means to uphold a Religion, and have no faith in a God who upholds justice and truth'.[2] 'I find Evangelists and Apostles speaking not of Religion, but of God.'[3]

By 'religion' Maurice meant the various opinions, schemes, systems of belief and practice, which men devise and by which they seek to establish some meeting-point or reconciliation between themselves and God, whereas 'the Gospel is the news that God is reconciled to man in His Son, that in Him there is a meeting-point between God and man'.[4] The Gospel is the revelation or manifestation—not of another religion but—'of Him who is the Living Centre of the Universe, the assertion that all men are related to Him; the destruction of every wall of partition between Man and Man; the admission of all who desire it into fellowship with the Father of the whole family in Heaven and Earth'.[5]

We are turning the Gospel into one of the religions of the world, which is to be proved by endless argumentations and confutations to be better than other religions, when, if it is a Gospel of God, it should meet all other religions, it should satisfy all their cravings, it should sever them from those dark fantasies and superstitions which must spring up in every land and every heart when the creature who is formed in the image of God fashions God after *his* image.[6]

Religions separate men from one another and tempt them to boast of what they possess and other men do not; the Gospel is the proclamation that they already belong together as children of the one God and Father of all, and the Church is the Kingdom or

---

[1] *What is Revelation?* (1859), pp. 239 f.
[2] *The Commandments* (1866), p. xvi.
[3] *What is Revelation?*, p. 181.
[4] *The Kingdom of Heaven* (1893), p. xv.
[5] *The Prayer-Book and the Lord's Prayer* (1880), p. 109.
[6] *Tracts for Priests and People*, no. XIV (1861–2), p. 75. I owe this reference to Mr J. W. Cox, Jr.

Family in which their unity is to be realized—'a City that hath foundations, whose Builder and Maker is God,—a Temple in which they themselves are to be living stones'.[1]

It seemed to Maurice that Christians, especially the Christians of his own time, with their rival and separating denominations, sects, systems, and schools of thought, had turned the Gospel into that from which it came to deliver them. They sought to press people to accept their own version of religion, instead of witnessing to the God-given unity in which their differences were overcome and which could 'redeem the divine truth (in each separate system) from the husk in which it is hidden, and...unite it with all from which it has been separated'.[2] As early as 1844 he wrote to Macmillan the publisher, 'the one thought which possesses me most at this time and, I may say, has always possessed me, is that we have been dosing our people with religion when what they want is not this but the Living God'.[3] He knew this temptation in himself and did not only observe its effects in other people.

It must be remembered that in Maurice's time there was in England an intense and bitter rivalry of competing religious parties with their several organizations, periodicals, Exeter Hall meetings, etc. In the present century there has been a considerable abatement of this fanaticism, of which the ecumenical movement is the sign. But has Maurice's protest lost its point? It is open, of course, to anyone to define religion as he will, and we are not bound to accept Maurice's use of terms.[4] He has, however, put to succeeding generations the searching question whether Christians are not constantly inclined to substitute for the Gospel of the universal love of God and the unity which it creates their own narrowing and partial misrepresentations of it.

[1] *What is Revelation?*, p. 183. [2] *The Prayer-Book, etc.*, p. 111.
[3] *Life of F. D. Maurice*, vol. I, p. 369.
[4] The word 'religion' is obviously used in other senses elsewhere in this volume.

16-2

II

Dr Karl Barth and Dr Emil Brunner are theologians who in a different idiom have said in our own time much the same as Maurice about religion as man's most subtle substitute for God's own revelation of himself.[1] Dietrich Bonhoeffer, on the other hand, in the letters which he smuggled out of prison during the last years of his life, carried the critique of religion a good deal further. If Bonhoeffer had lived, he might have given German theology quite a new direction after the Second World War: indeed, it has been said that he 'would probably have become Germany's greatest theologian...He would certainly have become its most revolutionary'.[2]

Before the war he had acquired considerable influence in the opposition of the Confessing Church to Nazism as well as in the ecumenical movement. He was deeply involved in the plot to overthrow Hitler and in consequence was arrested, imprisoned, and finally executed just before the end of the war.[3] When his *Letters and Papers from Prison* were published, their importance was widely recognized, but they seem now in danger of being forgotten, perhaps because their contents are too disconcerting for Christians to live with. To Bonhoeffer it seemed that Barth had opened up the idea of a 'religionless Christianity' but, instead of proceeding to its logical conclusion, had arrived at a 'positivism of revelation' which was essentially a restoration, not a growing up, and which engendered in its preachers a 'take it or leave it' attitude.

Bonhoeffer's own soundings were much more radical. He said himself that he was often shocked by the things he was moved to say, and it is of course possible to dismiss them as the desperate paradoxes to which a near-demented theologian was driven by im-

[1] See e.g. K. Barth, *The Epistle to the Romans* (E.T., 1933), *passim*; E. Brunner, *The Misunderstanding of the Church* (1952).
[2] C. C. West in *Theology* (January 1954), p. 33.
[3] See the memoir by G. Leibholz prefixed to the 1959 edition of Bonhoeffer's *The Cost of Discipleship*.

prisonment and persecution. But I do not see how anyone who reads the *Letters and Papers from Prison* as a whole can doubt Bonhoeffer's essential sanity, the profundity of his Christian faith, or the extraordinary penetration of his intelligence. Admittedly, his thoughts were tantalizingly fragmentary or inchoate, and we are not in a position to say how he would have developed them.

He spoke of the world's coming of age.[1] 'The movement beginning about the thirteenth century...towards the autonomy of man (under which head I place the discovery of the laws by which the world lives and manages in science, social and political affairs, art, ethics and religion) has in our time reached a certain completion.'[2] Christian apologetic had hitherto attacked the adulthood of the world as the great defection from God, and had sought 'to prove to a world thus come of age that it cannot live without the tutelage of "God"'. Edged out of the main concerns of the world, Christians had fastened on metaphysics and individual salvation, guilt, suffering and death, as the questions to which only 'God' could furnish an answer. Like the existentialist philosophers and the psychotherapists, 'they make it their object first of all to drive men to inward despair, and then it is all theirs'. There was the 'priestly' snuffing around in the sins of men in order to catch them out. Christianity as 'religion' had seen God in the interstices or on the boundaries of man's life. God was thought of as a stop-gap. He was brought in as a residual explanation of what could not otherwise be explained. This is what religion had for the most part come to stand for in the eyes of believers as well as of unbelievers.

Instead, 'we should find God in what we know, not in what we don't...he must be found at the centre of life: in life, and not only in death; in health and vigour, and not only in suffering; in activity, and not only in sin'. That was where God was found in the Old

---

[1] For a British theologian's exploration of this idea, see R. G. Smith, *The New Man and Man's Coming of Age* (1956).
[2] All quotations are from *Letters and Papers from Prison*, which is now available in Fontana Books.

Testament and by Christ too. 'Never did Jesus throw any doubt on a man's health, vigour or fortune, regarded in themselves, or look upon them as evil fruits. Else why did he heal the sick and restore strength to the weak? Jesus claims for himself and the kingdom of God the whole of human life in all its manifestations.'

Therefore, it is in the thick of the world, and not apart from it, that the meaning of Christian faith must be found. So Bonhoeffer wrote on 21 July 1944, when he had just received the news of the failure of the attempt to assassinate Hitler:

During the last year or so I have come to appreciate the 'worldliness' of Christianity as never before. The Christian is not a *homo religiosus*, but a man, pure and simple, just as Jesus was man, compared with John the Baptist anyhow. I don't mean the shallow this-worldliness of the enlightened, of the busy, the comfortable or the lascivious. It's something much more profound than that, something in which the knowledge of death and resurrection is ever present.... It is only by living completely in this world that one learns to believe....I mean by worldliness—taking life in one's stride, with all its duties and problems, its successes and failures, its experiences and helplessness. It is in such a life that we throw ourselves utterly in the arms of God and participate in his sufferings in the world and watch with Christ in Gethsemane. That is faith, that is *metanoia*, and that is what makes a man and a Christian.

Bonhoeffer believed that this idea of a 'religionless Christianity' or of a 'holy worldliness', as I have described it elsewhere,[1] would involve an incalculable transformation of the Church, of preaching, of worship and prayer, in so far as they have hitherto been directed to religious interests. He was confident that this transformation would take place, though he could not say how it would do so. Thus he wrote to a godchild:

Our Christianity today will be confined to praying for and doing right by our fellow men. Christian thinking, speaking and organization must be reborn out of this praying and this action. By the time you are grown up, the form of the Church will have changed beyond recognition....Until then the Christian cause will be a silent and hidden affair, but there will be those who pray and do right and wait for God's own time.

'A secret discipline must be re-established', he said, 'whereby the *mysteries* of the Christian faith are preserved from profanation.'

[1] *Essays in Liberality* (1957), pp. 95–112.

Christians should restrain their spate of words, their pious and theological jargon, and keep quiet until they have proved in their commerce with the life of the world which of their words ring true. For the Church to take this recommendation seriously would in itself be revolutionary. Perhaps Bonhoeffer's message for the Church is best summed up by Professor Ronald Gregor Smith:

The Church cannot stand over the world with a whip; nor can it get behind it with a load of dynamite. The whip and the dynamite, where available, would be better used on itself. The world is not...'hungry for God' in the sense of popular conservatizing evangelists, who really mean by that a hunger to hear their own words in the old accepted terminology of their fathers....The world is very suspicious, and rightly so, of those who cry 'The temple of the Lord are these', for it has had long experience of the unbridled ambitions of the Church over against the world. What the world would really see gladly is an honest and complete recognition, without any ulterior motives, by those who claim to carry forward the message of Christianity, of the existence of the world with all its own principles of movement, hopes and possibilities.[1]

III

While I was brooding on the subject of this essay, I received an entirely unsolicited communication from an Anglican missionary overseas which seemed to step straight into what I was thinking about, and stepped in not from the study of an eccentric professional theologian but from an area that is almost as much in the Church's front line as Bonhoeffer's Nazi prison was. I therefore asked my correspondent's permission to incorporate in this essay what he had written to me, and he kindly consented.

The Church is patient with its critics, in so far as they criticize details here and there, but not so patient with those who put a question mark under the whole show. Yet that is what those outside have been doing for a long time now, and perhaps it is time that some of us who are inside also gave it more thought.

Christianity has inherited from Judaism the Law and the Synagogue, the lawyers and the rabbis. We call them by different names, but that is in essence what they are. We take them for granted. We find it hard to imagine a Christianity without a sabbath day, and buildings in which to keep it, without rules

---

[1] R. G. Smith, *op. cit.* pp. 68 f. See also D. Jenkins, *Beyond Religion* (1962).

for the churchman, without doctors of the law, and professional priests. It may be that we were right to do all these things. It may be that God intended these things to be re-established in 'the new dispensation'. Or, to put it in another way, they may be such necessities of the human condition that they will always re-assert themselves in some form or other, and therefore God tolerates them, and in so far as we permit him, uses them. But Jesus was thrust out of the synagogue, was very careful to lay down nothing that could be construed as a law, was finally got rid of by a zealous and righteous collection of theologians and priests. We can hardly therefore make the *a priori* assumption that these things must be....

When I was a zealous young curate, nothing annoyed me more than people who said, 'I don't believe in organized religion'. It is easy to make some such answer as 'What is the good of disorganized religion?', but in fact it is a question that angers the promoters of organized religion just because we are half afraid that there may be something in it. Dislike of 'organized religion' is in its essence a Christian protest against 'Christianity', and one that I believe we shall have to take more seriously. Some of our prophets, like Bonhoeffer, have already said that the age of religion is over. It does not look like it at the moment. But then if a Christian prophet had said in 200 A.D. that the age of slavery was over, he would not have been readily understood. Certainly, there is no immediate cause for the bishops to tremble on their thrones. Even if it has not got God behind it, organized religion has enough weight of vested interest behind it to roll on for another few hundred years. And I am not saying that it has not got God behind it: I am only asking that we look at the whole question with an open mind.

It is obvious from any study of missionary results that the more primitive a people are, the more readily they respond to religion. Catholicism, the most religious of religions, tends to have more success than Protestantism among primitive peoples, and less in countries like Japan.

Certainly, Jesus accepted the religion of his day. But then he accepted tax farming, colonialism, slavery, and everything else of his day, except certain attitudes of mind. If it is the attitudes of mind of churchpeople that seem to have attracted his attention most, that is only because it was there that the things he hated were most evident. It is an exaggeration to say, as some have, that he came to destroy religion. He had more important aims. It is surely truer to say that it just did not concern him very much. When he says, 'If you are offering your gift at the altar...' or 'When you fast...', we must not construe this as orders to take gifts to altars or to fast, any more than his citation of Jonah provides a charter for fundamentalists. He left no instructions about public prayer. Whatever the Last Supper may have been, it does not convey the impression of a religious service. When his disciples, feeling one down in relation to the proficient Pharisees, ask him to teach them to pray, he says in effect, 'There's nothing to teach: it is as easy as saying "Our Father..."'.

Modern scholars are agreed that 'Jesus intended to found a church', and I do not wish to quarrel with them, as long as we do not pre-suppose that we know what 'a church' is. It does not automatically follow that Jesus intended to found anything like any of the existing denominational organizations or a re-unified combination of them.

My correspondent, whom I will call 'Tertius' since he wishes to be anonymous, went on to point out that the improvisation that we see going on in the Acts and Epistles shows that Jesus had not said anything that could be used as directions for founding an organization. Naturally the apostles modified, simplified and adapted the institutions of Judaism for their own purposes. We do not have to infer that the ecclesiastical institutions which began to take shape in the New Testament period and were subsequently solidified are permanently necessary for Christ's work in the world. The Spirit of Christ can set men free and enable them to become their true selves without requiring their dependence on any particular religious organization. 'We all know people,' Tertius writes, 'who without ceasing to be agnostics, Confucians or Hindus suddenly hear the words of Jesus and start thinking and acting in a new way. Do we perfect them, or corrupt them, by making them into churchmen? Any missionary who is honest about his experience will not be in a hurry to answer.'

The fact that Christ can set men free from fear and frustration and self-centredness without the Church as a religious organization, or by speaking to them in other terms than those that have been canonized in the Christian tradition, has ecumenical implications of a larger kind than those at present envisaged in the ecumenical movement. So Tertius concludes:

This way perhaps lies a solution to the problem that Arnold Toynbee has pressed in 'Christianity among the Religions'—the intolerance implied, and the quarrels inevitable, when 'Christianity' claims to be the only true religion. If we are content to admit that Christianity is more or less indistinguishable from the other religions in matters of theology, priests, prayers, sacraments, etc., and that a man can as well become a disciple of Jesus and use his words to interpret the Five Principles of Confucius as he can use them to interpret the Ten Commandments, if we have the courage to leave the appeal of Jesus to the conscience and the aesthetic sense—to the Holy Ghost—then we have what? We have apostasy, heresy, horror—everything that the true churchman instinctively recoils from—but that does not mean that we do not have Jesus Christ, if only he were sufficient for us.

IV

I suspect that Maurice, Bonhoeffer and Tertius all have things of great importance to say to the churches. I am not going to take up all the points they raise, but only some of them, with a view to seeing how they may bear upon the present condition of the Church of England. It is clear that all three use the word 'religion' to denote elements in historical Christianity which they regard as dubious or deplorable, but none of them defines at all precisely the sense in which he uses the word nor how much he includes in it. None of them apparently would deny that prayer and worship, which are usually regarded as characteristically religious activities, are proper to the new life in the Spirit which the coming of Jesus released into the world. Maurice and Bonhoeffer, and possibly Tertius too, would not deny that liturgy and preaching, hymnody and pastoral care, the labours of theologians and spiritual directors, the consecrated devotion of evangelists and monks and nuns, have at their best promoted, nourished and sustained that communion with God and one another in which men become their true selves. Were they then concerned only to assert that these religious activities and institutions have too often been treated as ends instead of as means of the spiritual life, or that they have been so organized and elaborated as to turn into instruments of spiritual bondage what should have subserved 'the glorious liberty of the children of God'?

No one was more aware of this danger than St Paul. It is the point of the contrast he drew between bondage to the Law and the freedom of the Gospel and of the war that he waged against legalism. But although the Judaizing legalists were defeated, it is all too true that the Christian movement has ever since been beset by other and no less insidious legalists. From time to time there have been protests and revolts against this perversion of the gospel of Jesus and of Paul, to which the Church was felt to have succumbed, and many of the schisms in or from the Church have been inspired by the quest for forms of Christian community in which the freedom of life in the Spirit, that was perceived to have been the mark of the earliest Christianity, could be recovered. Unfortunately, these newly formed churches or sects have as a rule been themselves soon beset by the legalism against which they had revolted, and frequently in a narrower and more rigid form.

Maurice, Bonhoeffer and Tertius all stand in the tradition of protest against legalism, but they have all learned the lesson that there is no way out to be found in starting another religious organization. The message of Maurice, who was most occupied with this aspect of the matter, was indeed that the institutions of the historic Catholic Church, when rightly understood, are the true safeguard against legalism, systematization and the narrowing of Christian community into an exclusive and intolerant sectarianism. He worked this idea out at length in his book, *The Kingdom of Christ or Hints to a Quaker respecting the Principles, Constitution and Ordinances of the Catholic Church*.

The fact is that religion is a form of human activity which readily lends itself to the ambitions of organizers, and organizers are always with us to fasten upon it. Even J. H. Newman once avowed his belief that 'freedom from symbols and articles' was 'abstractedly the highest state of Christian communion, and the peculiar privilege of the primitive Church'.[1] But, as Dr Brunner has said, 'it is so much easier to secure the life of the fellowship, its coherence and its indispensable hierarchy by means of solid legal forms, by organization and offices, than it is to allow the life of communion to be continually poured out upon one, to allow oneself to be rooted in it by

[1] *The Arians of the Fourth Century* (1833), p. 41.

the action of the Holy Ghost. You can handle and shape as you please such things as law and organization, but you cannot act thus towards the Holy Ghost.'[1]

Christianity, in so far as it is or appears to be a religion, comprising doctrines, officials, meetings and regulations, offers to the organizers, and to the organizing proclivities in any of us, an alluring field of operation. There is a parable for all churches and for all churchmen in E. M. Forster's description of Mr Pembroke, the schoolmaster, in *The Longest Journey*:

Here (at Sawston School) Mr Pembroke passed his happy and industrious life. ...He organized. If no organization existed, he would create one. If one did exist, he would modify it. 'An organization', he would say, 'is after all not an end in itself. It must contribute to a movement.' When one good custom seemed likely to corrupt the school, he was ready with another; he believed that without innumerable customs there was no safety, either for boys or men. Perhaps he is right, and always will be right. Perhaps each of us would go to ruin if for one short hour we acted as we thought fit, and attempted the service of perfect freedom. The school caps, with their elaborate symbolism, were his; his the many-tinted bathing drawers, that showed how far a boy could swim; his the hierarchy of jerseys and blazers. It was he who instituted Bounds, and Call, and two sorts of exercise-paper, and the three sorts of caning, and 'The Sawstonian', a bi-terminal magazine. His plump finger was in every pie....

His last achievement had been the organization of the day-boys. They had been left too much to themselves, and were weak in *esprit de corps*; they were apt to regard home, not school, as the most important thing in their lives.[2]

I need not pause to interpret this parable.

One question therefore before us is how the Church as an embodiment of Christian community can be kept free from the domination of organizers and legalizers. Maurice thought the solution lay not in discarding or making light of ecclesiastical institutions and sacramental ordinances but in interpreting them in a manner that at every point rebuked and corrected the disposition of men to lord it over God's family and God's gifts. Tertius seems to be much less sanguine about this possibility. Though he does not expect any sudden change in the existing churches, he does contemplate with

[1] Brunner, *op. cit.* p. 53.
[2] *The Longest Journey* (Penguin Ed.), p. 48.

equanimity, and almost with enthusiasm, the emergence of a Christianity in which 'organized religion' has only a peripheral or optional role to perform, even if it has so much. For my part I would say that I used to believe—and would still hope—that Maurice was right, but like Tertius I now find myself wondering whether he was not trying to marry incompatibles. Certainly like Tertius I would not now attempt to vindicate organized religion with the confidence and facility that I did once upon a time.[1] I do not want to see the questions at issue in this debate looked upon as foreclosed in the church to which I belong. We have here a perennial problem that has not yet been resolved. Perhaps it never will be resolved, since it is inevitable that a faith which is to be shared and to draw men together, for example, in common prayer and worship, must in some measure be attended by organization, and at the same time it is equally inevitable that organization will be productive of legalism.

Bonhoeffer, however, poses not a perennial but a genuinely novel problem when he speaks of the world's 'coming of age' and the consequent need for a 'religionless Christianity'. It is consistent with accepting Bonhoeffer as a prophet for our time to acknowledge that, like other prophets, he saw things too much in black and white and also that he foreshortened the realization of what he expected, as when he told his godchild that, *by the time he was grown up*, the form of the Church would have changed beyond recognition.

As regards the world's coming of age, I would distinguish between what has been happening to educated and sensitive minds, to the intellectually and emotionally mature, on the one hand, and the persistence and recrudescence of infantile passions and superstitions in contemporary societies, on the other. Who indeed will venture to claim that he has wholly attained to intellectual or emotional maturity? It is to be hoped that the present state of the world is not a register of man's coming of age.

[1] See my book, *A Plain Man's Guide to Christianity* (1936), ch. XIII.

What Bonhoeffer had in mind, I take it, when he spoke of man's or of the world's coming of age was the potentially typical man of today—the man who has experienced and absorbed the effects of the scientific revolution—post-renaissance, post-Darwinian, post-Freudian man—who cannot go back, and ought not even if he could: men, for example, for whom the questions discussed in this volume of essays are inescapable if they give their minds to inquiring about the tenability of Christian faith. For such men traditional religious symbols and mythologies, dogmas and doctrines, have for the most part lost their power to signify and to move. It is possible of course that religion in this broad sense may yet be invested with new life, but Bonhoeffer was surely right in urging us to reckon with the likelihood that the Christianity which has been preoccupied with the boundaries of man's life and which thought of God as a stopgap has had its day. It must give way to a faith that finds God in the centre of the world and at the heart of our present human needs and relationships. It will be a faith that finds God not in a special area that can be labelled 'religion', but wherever the fruits of the Spirit can be touched and tasted: 'the fruit of the Spirit is love, joy, peace, patience, kindness, goodness, faithfulness, gentleness, self-control' (Gal. v. 22 f.). All traditional doctrines and institutions must be subject to this test, and there is no obligation on Christians to promote or to preserve what does not survive it.

Many of the religious elements in historic Christianity and much that has gone under the name of religion may thus be outgrown, or survive chiefly as venerable archaisms or as fairy stories for children, and we cannot tell in advance how they will be replaced or which of them will need to be replaced. We are at the beginning of a period in which we must be willing to prove all things and to hold fast only to what is good. It would be foolish to discard what is old until it is manifestly otiose, or to suppose that new forms of Christian spirituality and community will develop and commend themselves quickly. The qualities mainly called for are openness to the future, a willingness to travel light or in the dark, patience and imagination in experiment, a large toleration of variety and diversity based not on indifference but on trust in the continued guidance of the Holy Spirit.

V

However, my purpose in this essay is not to discuss these questions in general terms but to ask how they bear upon the Church of England. It is for the members of other churches to inquire into their own estate. I speak of the Church of England, not of the other churches of the Anglican communion. They are set in such different environments and are at so many different stages of development that what applies in England need not apply to them. For instance, in parts of Africa the first task of the Christian mission is to liberate animists from belief in and fear of evil spirits not only by enabling science to dissolve superstition but by proclaiming the gospel of the love of God and by building up liberated communities. Here, in order to serve this purpose, the present problem may be how to provide a sufficiency of Christian organization. And in England itself there are no doubt many individuals and groups that need not less but more religious and moral discipline if only that they may learn to do without it or to discriminate between the wheat and the chaff. Persons can enter into the freedom of the Gospel only when in one way or another they have experienced the discipline of the Law.[1] Though this is not its proper work, the Church has to provide a *praeparatio evangelica* if that is not being provided by other agencies, just as Christian missions start schools when and where governments have failed to do so.

But our main question is: What prospect is there that the Church of England may have a continuing mission in a society where the traditional forms of religion are being outgrown? Does this church look like being able to welcome and foster new ways of discovering

[1] On the various uses of the Law, see my book, *Christ's Strange Work* (1944).

and nourishing the life in the Spirit? Is it a closed or an open church, backward-looking or forward-looking, in bondage to legalism or a school of freedom?

At first sight, the Church of England is one of the most archaic of the churches of the West and one of the least amenable to change. It has not revised its forms of worship (The Book of Common Prayer) since 1661, though some of its members have to a modest extent taken the law into their own hands and introduced modifications and innovations. But by and large the language and thought-forms of the church's liturgy are what they were in the seventeenth century. As regards doctrine, the sixteenth-century Thirty-nine Articles continue to be the official standard, though the assent to them that is required of the clergy was made less rigorous in the nineteenth century. The Report, *Doctrine in the Church of England*, which was produced by an Archbishops' Commission in 1938 and might have led to a more contemporary statement of the church's faith, was quietly shelved and is seldom referred to. The Church of England struggles to maintain a territorial parochial system that covers the whole country: in spite of a greatly diminished man-power in proportion to the population, the system remains what it has been from time immemorial.

This church continues to be established as all churches were once, though few are now. The form of its relation to the state is a survival from the time when church and commonwealth were regarded as in principle one society. The admission of dissenters to parliament in the nineteenth century, and correlative changes, constituted an implicit recognition that the principle no longer held, but the old formal relation was maintained without the articulation of any new principle to justify it. Thus parliament, no longer restricted in its membership to churchmen, retains legislative control of the church: the setting up of the Church Assembly in 1920 modified only the process of legislation. The higher officers in the church are nominated by the Sovereign on the recommendation of the prime minister, who may now be, as is said, 'of any religion or none'. The solemn mockery of the 'election' of diocesan bishops by cathedral chapters goes on unchanged. There are plenty of other archaic anomalies which some agitated churchmen from time to time pronounce to be 'intolerable' but which the great majority appear to find quite tolerable. The generality of citizens looks upon the Church of England as a venerable, if curious, part of the English scene. They like to have it about, if only that they may criticize it or stay away from it. It agreeably adorns national and civic occasions with colourful pageantry and a measure of unction. A great many individuals resort to the church, if at no other times, at least when they want to be married or buried.

It would be folly to try to disguise the archaic aspect of the Church of England or to wax sentimental or romantic about it. But there is another side to the picture if we are considering the possible emergence of a church which will accept the axiom that religion is made for man, not man for religion. Perhaps after all this church is not so ill-fitted to be a seed-ground out of which such a church might grow. What at first sight look like its handicaps may prove to be its advantages. The very fact that no one in his senses can suppose the Church of England to be anything like the final embodiment of the kingdom of God or of the Christian movement in history should make it easier for its members to acknowledge the need for radical change than it is for the members of churches that have kept more up to date as efficient organizations and so can regard their present condition as defensible and worthy of preservation.

Again, the fact that the Church of England still has the framework of a national church, as distinguished from that of a gathered church, a sect or a religious denomination, is a constant reminder to its members and to the nation that it is inescapably involved with the whole of the society in which it is set. Even if, as Dr Barry, Bishop of Southwell, has lamented, 'what claims to be the Church of the English people has been becoming a "denomination", if not...a closed shop',[1] it does still ostensibly exist to serve the whole people, and not only those who hold a certain set of religious opinions or who are devotees of some particular brand of Christian belief and practice. As a matter of history, it has always aspired to be the church of the whole English people, 'whether they will hear or whether they will forbear'.

The Evangelical and Catholic revivals of the eighteenth and nineteenth centuries may have sought in effect to turn the church into a one-track religious denomination of an Evangelical or Catholic type, but they did not succeed in doing so, partly because the protagonists of each prevented the success of the other, but still more because, except among the more fanatical extremists, there has been a pervasive sense throughout the church that it is intended to be as comprehensive and all-embracing as possible and to provide a congenial home for many varieties of Christian experience. The attempt used to be made to maintain the comprehensiveness of the church by insistence on conformity to the moderate limits set by the Book of Common Prayer, but this attempt has been abandoned in practice, so that the church is now qualified to have room for whatever traditional forms of worship and spirituality still have life in them and also for new explorations and experiments.

It is an advantage to the Church of England that it has ill-defined or archaic standards of doctrine. It speaks with 'the stammering lips of ambiguous formularies'. As Mr R. C. Walls said in a letter to *The Times* newspaper (26 November 1953), 'The Church of England has many faults to repent of, but failure to define is not one of them. Her constitution, her sacraments, her liturgy, and her use of the Bible bear adequate witness to her faith.' The traditional and historical elements in the legacy of Christendom thus have the opportunity of proving how much they contain of enduring spiritual value. Traditional rites and ceremonies can still provide for many people what they cannot readily find elsewhere. In Bruce Marshall's

---

[1] Article in the *Church Times* (30 June 1961), p. 11.

novel *The World, the Flesh and Father Smith* the Scots bishop says:
'Whenever I look out on the hideousness and harshness of our
industrial cities, I thank Almighty God deep down in my heart for
having given His Church so many exquisite rites and ceremonies.
For it is not bread and circuses which people require, but poetry
and prayer.'

But it has been the happy manner of the Church of England to
allow to its members, and indeed to its ministers, great latitude in
the interpretation of its formularies and the adaptation of its customs,
when they have sought to come to terms with new knowledge, new
ways of thinking, and new social habits. That this is so was magnani-
mously acknowledged by a left-wing dissenter when he wrote:

It is easier to be heretical inside the English Church than outside it. So long as the
forms are observed, the thought may be free, but if the forms are given up the
thought is more strictly watched, more quickly suspected, and more severely con-
demned. It is as true now as it was in the times of Elizabeth or James that Anglican
thought may wander widely, while a Dissenter may not look over the hedge.[1]

It might be supposed that this doctrinal liberty would make for
vagueness or woolliness of belief and the prostitution of intellectual
integrity, and less friendly critics have often attributed these characteristics to the Church of England. I am far from asserting that they
have been non-existent, but freedom and liberality have been valued
within the church itself because they are favourable to intellectual
integrity, candour and honesty. At the same time, there have been
in the past, and are likely to be in the future, groups of ardent
precisionists or legalists who, while it would be disastrous if any
of them were ever in a majority, serve as minorities the useful
purpose of preventing other churchmen from getting away for long
with what is ill-considered or superficial.

It is also an advantage to the Church of England that it has an
indeterminate membership. The fact that all English citizens, who
are not committed to membership of another church, commonly
describe themselves as 'C. of E.' may from some points of view

[1] Henry Gow, *The Unitarians* (1928), pp. 26 f.

signify little or nothing or may even encourage hypocrisy and hum-
bug; but from our present point of view it means that the Church of
England is accustomed to providing a home, albeit often a distant
one, for all sorts and conditions of men. It certainly has communicant members though they are not usually registered as such, and
also it has its parochial electoral rolls which are not based on a
communicant franchise: in practice it is recognized that many people
who are neither communicants nor on electoral rolls are in varying
degrees members of the church. The church does not restrict its
ministrations to persons who satisfy any determinate tests, though
there are those within it who would like it to do so. Non-religious
Christians, semi-detached believers, and semi-attached agnostics, so
far from being excluded, are welcome in so far as they wish to be.
Any of them may be nearer to the kingdom of God than highly
religious conformists. It has been said that the distinctive role of
the Church of England is 'the Apostolate of the Indevout'.[1] Dr
Brunner has stated the theological ground for this refusal to draw
hard and fast lines:

Who can establish criteria to judge whether or not the Holy Ghost is really
active in a human heart to which God is only just beginning to reveal Himself?
Who would wish to propose criteria of membership which in certain circumstances would exclude precisely those whom God in secret has begun to draw
unto Himself? The boundaries of the Church face to face with the world must
therefore remain invisible to the eyes of men; a full dogmatic confession can
deceive just as much as the entire absence of any such a thing.[2]

No doubt this openness of membership can lead to acquiescence
in diluted or watered down kinds of Christian faith and practice.
On the other hand, it may give the Church of England an initial asset
in the coming time if we are right in supposing that Christians will
have in future to stand much more on their own feet in the strength
of the Spirit, exposed to all the currents of life in the world, altogether less docile to what is laid down or traditionally prescribed,

[1] See A. Fawkes, *Shall we Disestablish?* (1928), p. 37.
[2] Brunner, *op. cit.* p. 109.

discovering for themselves what really does hold good and make sense in this age of the world. In other words, the question is not prejudged in the Church of England how much 'religion' is going to be needed in future for loving God and serving men in union with Christ. A hundred years ago, F. J. A. Hort said that 'we may well be content to put up with comparative formlessness for I know not how many generations'.[1]

As regards the Church of England's relation to the state (the so-called 'establishment'), we have acknowledged its anomalous character, but it does not follow that it is just an archaic survival that ought forthwith to be liquidated. Sooner or later there will obviously have to be a new ecclesiastical settlement in England of some kind or other. For example, if a union between the Church of England and any or all of the Free Churches were achieved, a new ecclesiastical settlement would at once become necessary. Meanwhile we may well prefer to maintain the *status quo*, and to be satisfied with minor adjustments, until we are much clearer about what we want to put in its place. If the Church of England were simply disestablished—though in truth it would be anything but a simple operation—we might find that we had jettisoned the framework and the ethos of a national church and were landed in an episcopalian sect, a denomination that treated a theory about episcopacy as the *articulus aut stantis aut cadentis ecclesiae*. This sort of disestablishment would have the effect of turning the church in upon itself, and make it busy with reorganizing itself as a distinct denomination. The religious organizers, who of late have been employing themselves comparatively harmlessly in seeking to revise the canon law, would come into their own. The Church of England would be cleaned up and tidied up, so that everyone could tell just what it stood for. It is premature for any church to try to put itself in that position.

A further reason for desiring a continuation of the nexus between church and state is that it helps to keep the church aware of its

[1] See A. F. Hort, *Life and Letters of F. J. A. Hort* (1896), vol. II, p. 31.

obligation to serve the whole people in all areas of their need. It is also a safeguard against ecclesiastical inbreeding and the inroads of clericalism, since it brings an independent influence to bear upon the church, one that is directed to the interests of the nation and the laity. The nomination of bishops by the civil magistrate is an advantage that could hardly be retained if the church were disestablished. The civil magistrate—who according to the Bible is a minister of God and presumably no less susceptible to divine guidance than ecclesiastics —is more likely to make appointments that will keep the church open to the nation and directed to its service than would any purely ecclesiastical machinery. Since bishops have to be consecrated as well as nominated, the civil magistrate's office is limited.

The case for a nexus between church and state does not of course rest only, or chiefly, on the benefits that can accrue to the church from it. While we should not want in any circumstances to revive or return to the old pre-toleration type of church–state relationship, that is, one of exclusive privilege, there is still—in the tolerant, pluralist, democratic kind of society which we now have and want to maintain and strengthen—value and validity in the idea of a national church, recognized as such by the state.

A national church—that is, a church built into the constitution as a complement and counterpoise to the state and to civil government —is a standing witness to the fact that man, every man, is a twofold creature with a twofold allegiance, whether he realizes it or not. He is a citizen of an earthly temporal state, and as such has duties to perform and needs to be satisfied. But he is more than that. He has a mysterious origin and destiny and spiritual capacities for freedom and fullness of life which are not within the power or control of civil government. A man is not only a political creature, but also a spiritual being who belongs to a realm of eternal values which lifts him above all the realms of this world even while he is immersed in them. A national church, recognized as such by the state, is a constant, public and impressive reminder of this fact.

Then again, the constitutional conjunction of church and state is a sign that the authority of the state is neither final nor absolute. By recognizing a national church, a state acknowledges that there is a body in its midst that stands for man's belonging to a spiritual order, the kingdom of God, which is superior to itself. A national church, built into the constitution, expresses and secures the right of all citizens to say, 'We must obey God rather than men' or words to that effect. This can of course be said without an established church, but an established church, aware of its responsibility for the whole people, affords a stronger basis for the exercise of this right than voluntary religious societies can do. It was a perception of this fact after the onset of totalitarianism that weaned many Free Churchmen from their previous advocacy of a separation of church and state.

Once more, the constitutional recognition of a national church, whose ministry and services are available throughout the country, is a practical acknowledgment that human beings need more than the state can ever do for them, more than the provision of law and order, more than economic security, more than technical education. They do need all these things, but they also have spiritual, moral, social and psychological needs which the state as such is not competent to meet or satisfy. Men need not only the discipline of law, but also the spontaneity of love. They need to be treated not only with justice, but also with compassion and with generosity. They need not only administrators who will see to the framework of their lives, but pastors who will be concerned with them as persons. A national church should never in future claim that it alone is qualified to serve these needs or has a monopoly of these gifts. Rather, its task is to represent, to stimulate and to defend all those agencies—however little ecclesiastical or religious they may be—that minister to the freedom and fullness of man's spiritual life.

For the Church of England the great question is whether it can be transformed into such a church or is doomed to sink into the position of a religious denomination.

INDEX

INDEX

Lack, D., 23
Lampe, G. W. H., 163
Lao-tze, 107
Lawton, J. S., 155
legalism, 91 f., 176–81, 185, 247–51, 253, 256, 259
Leibholz, G., 244
Lewis, H. D., 30
Liberalism, 129 f., 139 f., 150
Linton, O., 158
liturgy, 144, 224, 236 f., 250, 256
Loisy, A., xi
lust, 88 f., 92
Luther, M., 185
Lux Mundi, x

MacIntyre, A., 10
Maclagan, W. G., 201
Macleod, G., 27
man's coming of age, 245 f., 253 f.
Manson, T. W., 164
Marcion, 126
Marshall, B., 258 f.
Marxism, 121
Mary Magdalene, 169
Mascall, E. L., 23 f., 152
mathematics, 27, 32–8, 41, 53
Matthews, W. R., 157, 162 f., 165, 170 f.
Maurice, F. D., 241–4, 250–3
Medawar, P. B., 29
Mersch, E., 73
Miles, T. R., 23
Mind, 29
miracles, 46, 128, 133 f., 140, 231 f.
Moberly, R. C., 155
Moore, G. F., 158
Mosley, Sir O., 14
Mozart, W. A., 121
Muhammad, 114, 117
mystery, 27, 60, 109, 125, 149, 151, 156
mysticism, 46 f., 113 f., 116, 132 f., 221 f., 227
mythology, 115, 117, 129, 181, 229, 254

Naboth's vineyard, 86 f.
natural law, 202 f., 231
natural theology, 3–19, 46 f.
naturalism, 48
Nazism, 244, 247
Newman, J. H., 99, 144, 251
Nicholls, D. G., 241

Niebuhr, R., 14
nirvana, 111 ff., 115 f.

Oman, J., 210, 231
Origen, 16, 144, 223 f., 225
original sin, 83, 101, 181, 188
Our Lady, 98–101, 185

Paley, W., 201
Paul, St, 79, 83, 94, 97 f., 114, 125 ff., 129, 134–7, 177 ff., 186, 223 f., 228, 235, 250 f.
Perry, M. C., 170
personal relations, 155, 159, 168, 182, 229
personality in God, 64, 111–16, 166, 227
Pharisees, 91 f., 127, 134, 177, 179, 248
physics, 27, 33 ff., 37, 39 f.
Picasso, P. R., 121
Pittenger, W. N., 172
Plato and Platonism, 4, 121, 132, 155 f.
Polanyi, M., 30
prayer, 25, 71, 221–37, 248, 253
Prestige, G. L., 156
presuppositions, 110 f., 117 ff., 129, 140, 200
pride, 84 f.
principles, 214 f.
Prism, 241
Prodigal son, 90, 181, 190
progress, 118
prophets, 132 ff., 222, 236
Prout, W., 31 f.
Providence, 12, 76, 78, 225
Psalter, 235 f.
psychic research, 154
psychoanalysis, 71, 78
psychology, 27 f., 33 f., 39, 41, 69–101, 130, 155, 161 f., 203 f.
psychotherapy, 34, 204, 245
punishment, 187 ff.
purpose, 26, 29, 36

Ramage, H. P., 32
Ramsey, A. M., 155
Rationalism, 128 f.
Raven, C. E., 70
redemption, 164, 183
Reformation, 127, 185 f.
religionless Christianity, 246 f., 253
Relton, H. M., 150
repentance, 90

267